I TALK TOO MUCH

I Talk Too Much

My Autobiography

Francis Rossi with Mick Wall

CONSTABLE

CONSTABLE

First published in Great Britain in 2019 by Constable

3 5 7 9 10 8 6 4 2

Copyright © Francis Rossi, 2019

The moral right of the author has been asserted.

A CIP catalogue record for this book
is available from the British Library.

ISBN: 978-1-47213-020-4 (hardback)
ISBN: 978-1-47213-019-8 (trade paperback)

Typeset in Bembo by SX Composing DTP, Rayleigh, Essex
Printed and bound in Great Britain by Clays Ltd, Elcograf S.p.A.

Papers used by Constable are from well-managed forests
and other responsible sources.

MIX
Paper from
responsible sources
FSC
www.fsc.org   FSC® C104740

Constable
An imprint of
Little, Brown Book Group
Carmelite House
50 Victoria Embankment
London EC4Y 0DZ

An Hachette UK Company
www.hachette.co.uk

www.littlebrown.co.uk

Contents

Prologue

For some people the past is a distant planet. Somewhere they used to live long ago that they can barely even remember now. Somewhere that doesn't really matter any more, in fact. Not me. For me, the past is always there. A story I can never really stop messing around with, trying to figure out how it all happened. Why it all happened. The past comes back to me any time it wants. Often when I least expect it.

Sometimes, I will be sitting around and something I thought I'd forgotten about, sometimes just the littlest thing, snaps back into my mind and I think, 'Ah, yeah! Now I get it! So that's what that was all about . . .' Sometimes it's bigger things, stuff that I just can't let go, no matter how hard I try, because it still bugs me. Still gets under my skin and makes me want to have a go. Hit back. Put it in its place.

My wife Eileen says it's because I never stop analysing things. That I go too far sometimes and won't stop fiddling with something in my brain until I feel like I've finally worked out what's going on. Only to come back to it again days, sometimes weeks, sometimes years later, and start analysing it all over again.

So if there are things in this book that seem contrary to you, that's fine. There are things in this book that definitely seem contrary to me too. Things I didn't really know about myself until I started putting down my thoughts. Things that I'm still thinking about, analysing, working out what really went on. Things I'll probably still be thinking about until the day I die.

Like my relationship with Rick Parfitt: I'm fully aware that now he's gone, everyone wants to get me to open up and tell them everything about that. But I can't. Not absolutely everything, once and for all, as if the story's over. Because it isn't. Rick was such a huge part of my life for so long – over fifty years – I'm still analysing what really went on there between us. I know what his family thinks. I know what the Status Quo fans think. But what I think about it is something I have to deal with every day, even though he's not around any more – *especially* now he's not around any more – and it changes from moment to moment.

I loved Ricky and I still do. He sent me bonkers a lot of the time and somehow he still manages to do that too. He was everything that I wasn't and used to wish I could be: flash, good-looking, talented, the glamorous blond – a real rock star, in the truest sense. Someone who lived for today and to hell with tomorrow, love 'em and leave 'em, no encores. Mr Showbiz.

While I was the opposite: an insecure show-off, always over-compensating, thinking about tomorrow. The dark-haired balding one; talented, perhaps, lucky, definitely. But the guy who always made damn sure he looked every gift horse in the mouth and counted every one of its teeth. Then made a note of it. Then counted them again.

They say opposites attract. That when opposites attract and things go well, they go spectacularly well. But that when

opposites attract and things don't go so well they go catastroph-
ically badly. Well, that was certainly the case with Rick and me.
When things were good, they were very, very good. But when
things were bad . . .

Anyway, we'll get to that. The first thing to make clear
though is that this is not just a book about my relationship with
Rick Parfitt, though obviously a large part of that comes into
it. Nor is this especially a book about Status Quo, the group I
have fronted for almost all of my life. Though, again, obviously
they play a big part in my story too.

This is a book, for better or worse, about me: Francis
Dominic Nicholas Michael Rossi. Though Rick always used
to call me Frame – because I was so wiry, with chicken arms
and legs. There were other names he called me too – when he
thought I wasn't listening. Then there's the lovely names my
wife and kids call me sometimes – to my face!

And then there are the names I call myself, sometimes when
I'm alone and brooding – analysing – retracing the steps of a life
that, by the time you read this, will be almost seventy years old.

A good time to stop, you might say.

Or an even better time to keep going, I say. Right now,
anyway.

Tomorrow might be different.

Mightn't it?

We'll see.

Chapter One

You Talk Funny!

The helicopter took off straight from the backstage area of Milton Keynes Bowl and within seconds the 60,000 crowd below looked like ants.

Actually, they had looked like ants to me even when I was onstage. By the time we did the encores, I was so coked I could barely see the guitar in my hands and I'd fallen over several times. I had to be carried offstage at the end by a roadie, who slung me over his shoulder.

All I knew for sure was that I'd never have to do this again. Stand up onstage with Status Quo and pretend to be enjoying myself. It was over. The end of the road.

Bloody hell, what had I done?

That was the question everyone was asking in 1984. Everyone, that is, except me. Like the coke-addled, tequila-guzzling, Mandrax-scoffing, dope-smoking smartarse I was, I was absolutely sure I knew what I was doing. Breaking up the band I had spent over twenty years building into one of the biggest in the world – why not? It was their fault. I was sick of the band, always making demands. How would I manage on my own though? Silly question. I would manage just fine.

I would have a successful solo career after leaving the band just like Rod Stewart had done when he left the Faces, wouldn't I? Or like Ozzy Osbourne had done after he left – got booted out of – Black Sabbath. Wouldn't I?

Um, well . . .

Anyway, that was all something I could deal with later. Much later. After I'd finished doing the Quo farewell tour. We billed it as the End of the Road tour, and all the publicity around it was about it being the last time anyone would get to see the band play live. They were almost all big venues, and where they were normal-sized we would double and triple up, doing multiple nights. Shows across Europe followed by forty-two shows in Britain, including a week at the Hammersmith Odeon in London, for which all 28,000 tickets were sold within four hours of going on sale. The finale was to have been a big outdoor show before 25,000 fans at Crystal Palace's football ground, Selhurst Park, in July. But again, ticket demand was so great we ended up adding one last big blowout show before 60,000 fans at the National Bowl in Milton Keynes.

I had been told by the record company that the end of Quo was probably going to be the end of my career. I just laughed and had another line of coke. I'd show them! I'd show them all! Ha ha ha!

I was thirty-five but the punk music press had been calling me a has-been since I was in my twenties. I didn't care. Fuck 'em all! That's what I told myself when I woke up on the floor each day.

The only one I felt sorry for was Rick. Poor Ricky Parfitt. Drummer Pete Kircher and keyboardist Andy Bown were pragmatic about the band ending. They were session guys who hadn't been there at the beginning and they would find another gig. Alan Lancaster may have still seen the band as his creation, and I might have thought of myself as the more bankable frontman. But no one loved being in Status Quo more than Rick Parfitt. No one relied on being in Status Quo as much as Rick Parfitt. His whole worldview was tied up in being the brilliant rhythm guitarist, successful hit-writer and good-looking blond singer in Status Quo. And, of course, all his fragile finances were tied up with Status Quo staying together.

I think he thought it was just another jolly PR wheeze, all this announcing the band's farewell. It wasn't until the helicopter took off after that final show and he looked out the window that it finally sank in. When he looked over at me, he saw that I really wasn't kidding. That I was done in, had it, gone.

The truth is, we were both scared. I was too scared to carry on. Rick was too scared to stop. I felt like I had gone as far as I could with Status Quo, with fame and money and expectation and criticism – three-chords-heads-down-blah-blah-blah. Yeah, funny, ha. Rick felt like he still had a long way to go, with fame and money and . . . what else was there? Bring on the dancing girls!

That had always been the difference between Rick and me. We were like night and day. I only ever saw the darkness. He only ever saw the light. He as Mr Show. Me as Mr Business. Neither one of us had it right though. Not then anyway. Not ever, I realise, now I look back.

Anyway, it was too late to turn back now. The band had been together in one form or another for longer even than the Beatles. Almost as long as the Rolling Stones. I'd had enough. And now it was over. Thank fuck for that.

Until Bob Geldof phoned up one day not long after and asked me and Rick to sing on his Band Aid record. Do what? Never! Status Quo was finished. Never to be seen again.

Typical Bob, he just yelled back at me. 'I don't give a fuck about that! Just get back together for the day.'

All right then, Bob, we said. But only for one day . . .

I was born in Forest Hill, south London, into a large house full of Italians. There was my dad and all his brothers and their wives, then all the grandparents and children. It was all one big family. My dad put an ice-cream van right in front of this lovely house and it pissed off all the neighbours. As soon as we moved in, the area went down. As soon as we moved out, it went back up again.

My mother, Anne, was born in a small coastal town called Crosby, on Liverpool's Merseyside. Her father was an Irishman named Paddy. According to her family, Liverpool was the capital of Ireland. All her friends called her Nancy. Mum was a Catholic so she was the same religion, but she was always a bit of an outsider to the Italian side of the family, as one of the first of the English wives, although she was always desperate to be thought of as Italian. My father, Dominic Rossi, was born in London but was about as Italian as it is possible to be. His mother – who everyone called Nonna whether they were related or not, including all the van drivers – came from a small Italian town called Atina, famed for its olive oil, red wine and beans. Not a bad combo. We all called our grandpa Pop. His brother was known as Uncle – to save confusion. Don't ask…

Names were always a funny thing in my family. I was given my dad's name, Dominic, as my second name and my younger brother has it as his first. I don't know why. I suppose they must have really liked the name. Before me, though, there had been a daughter, Arselia, who died because of a heart defect. My mother, being Catholic, took a vow that her next child would be named Francis – after St Francis of Assisi – and a few other saints, which is why I have the longest name in the family: Francis Dominic Nicholas Michael Rossi. None of this meant much to me at the time. It was only when I got to school that the name 'Francis' presented a problem as the other kids taunted me for having a girl's name. I tried to fix that by telling everyone my name was really Mike – or just Ross. Frankly, they could – and did – call me anything they liked as long as they left me alone.

Names and relationships were all very tangled in my family. In truth, I never quite figured out what relationship everyone was to each other. Nonna – my grandmother – was a Coppola, which I've been told is very good Italian stock. What's funny though is that when I looked the name up on one of those ancestry websites the following information popped up: In 1881, the most common Coppola occupation in the UK was Ice Cream Dealer. 100% of Coppolas were Ice Cream Dealers.

Guess what my dad's family all did for a living – that's right, selling ice cream! Apart from the ice-cream vans, they owned a shop on Catford Broadway called Rossi's Ice Cream. He was always trying to think of ways to bring in extra money. In the evenings, instead of ice cream, my dad would go out in the van and sell fish and chips. The last time I checked, the family still owned the shop and were now renting it out as a betting shop. I was born on a Sunday – on 29 May 1949. According to the modern version of the old nursery rhyme, Sunday's child is 'happy and wise'. Yes, well, they got that wrong. On the other hand, according to the original text from *The Oxford Dictionary of Nursery Rhymes*, 'And the child that is born on the Sabbath day/Is bonny and blithe, and good and gay.' Which doesn't sound right to me either.

At the time I came along we all lived in my grandma's large house in Mayow Road, Forest Hill, because my parents couldn't afford their own place. Pop – my grandfather, do try and keep up! – left all the ice-cream business to Nonna. By trade, he was a parquet-floor layer. As a teenager, my dad had been his apprentice. Then he nearly lost his hand in an accident at work. He'd told his younger brother Chas to drive the car to a job up north. Fine except for the fact that Chas hadn't actually passed his driving test. Which explained how he managed to drive across the street and straight into a bus.

My dad flew straight through the window and hit the road just in time for the bus to drive over his hand. They were still picking up bits of his hand when the ambulance arrived. Poor sod ended up having more than forty operations to try and save the hand. When my mum took me to visit him in the hospital I nearly fainted – they had sewn his hand inside his stomach to help it heal. That's what they told my mum anyway. He ended up with a deformed sort of claw for a hand. I didn't mind. Kids take things in their stride. He used to wave it at us kids and pretend to be a monster. We'd all run off laughing. It wasn't until many years later it dawned on me that he was very self-conscious about it. He didn't like it if people noticed it and wouldn't let his grandchildren see it at all.

When we moved from there a few years later to this sweetshop a few miles away in Balham, my dad still kept the ice-cream van going. When one of my uncles died, I heard my dad and all the other men talking at the funeral about how they were going to have to divvy up the remaining ice-cream routes. Business and family was one and the same thing to them. I was too young to know other families – English families – did things differently. By the time I'd figured it out it was too late and I was like that too. Work and family, that's all I've ever known. Evenings for me as a kid mainly revolved around sitting with my dad and his brothers listening to them tell stories about their day. How many cones they had sold. Who had had a good day out there in the vans and who hadn't.

These days, people talk about having a 'strong work ethic', and you could say I have one. But I just didn't know any different. Apart from going to church on Sundays – and even then it was straight back to work for my father on the ice-cream vans – we didn't really have what you would call 'days off'. Working evenings and weekends was just normal to me. I think this must have affected my attitude later when I became involved in trying to make it in a band. Strange hours, working on those days and nights when so-called normal people were relaxing, never worrying about things like holidays, putting every spare penny back into the running of the business, or in my case keeping the show on the road, none of this was a sacrifice to me. It was just the way I'd been brought up. People talk about rock musicians being like kids in a sweetshop: well, I was that kid in a sweetshop, and it never meant anything to me. The sweets were always there for selling. Sure, I would enjoy the fruits of my labour, but I still got out of bed the next day ready to work. I see now that this all came from my childhood.

As a result of this mixed bag of Italian-Irish-northern-cockney influences, I grew up with a very mangled accent. It was the same for my brother and our two cousins. Not that I noticed I had an accent, or at least not until people like Quo's Alan Lancaster pointed it out. From my mother came this mainly northern accent. You can hear it on 'Paper Plane' and some of the earlier Quo tracks. Dig out 'I (Who Have Nothing)' on YouTube from when we were still the Spectres and I sound completely Lancastrian! Plus, we were all listening to the Beatles and that's how they sounded when they sang.

From my dad I had this Italian-cockney thing going on. Because we spoke a lot of Italian at home but outside the home they wanted to be English, we spoke-a-like-a-this-a. And like-a-that-a. There was always a vowel on the end of every sentence. I spoke Italian most of the time until I was about seven but it got less and less as I grew older. I can remember going on holiday with my family to Italy when I was about five or six, playing with my cousins and speaking to them. In my memory we are speaking English because we understand each other perfectly. But in reality, I realise now, it was because we were all speaking Italian.

Going to school was what finally killed it off. For a while I would speak-a-like-a-this-a at school and proper Italian when I got home. But that quickly turned into what it is now. It had to in order for me to survive in south London in the fifties. Looking back now, though, I really regret that I can't speak Italian any more. Travelling the world as much as I have done all my life, and discovering that almost everybody speaks English, it makes me feel slightly ashamed that I can only speak that and nothing else.

As a kid, though, it was all about fitting in. And it wasn't just my accent I had to worry about. I was what used to be called 'sickly' as a child. Always coming down with something. Skinny, runny nose, always getting into scrapes. Tripping over my own shadow. My mother used to say to me, 'You had such a big head when you were a kid.' It's true. I used to fall down the stairs sometimes because my head was too big. I hadn't grown into it properly yet. Some people say I still haven't.

I was always falling over and hurting myself. My brother and I – just in shorts, no shirts – ran round this corner one summer's day and I fell smack on my face. I looked up and there was

Mother Agatha – one of the nuns from the Catholic school that we went to, Our Lady & St Philip Neri in Forest Hill. I quite liked her but she stood there staring at me with this look on her face. When we got back to school the next day she did this whole thing about wicked young men running around half-naked. It must have had quite an effect on me, remembering it now.

Something that left an even bigger impression also involved getting hurt in the street. Where we lived on Perry Rise in Forest Hill, when I was about five years old, I walked to school. I used to skip along, quite a happy little chappy. Then one day I was walking to school and saw this kid coming down the street towards me. As we passed each other he hit me around the face with his plimsoll. He hit me so hard with it he nearly took my head off! After that I was scared to go out on my own. They used to send my cousin with me because I was frightened to walk to school. I realise now that this affected me for years after. I didn't like going out, I was always frightened of people and getting hurt. That said, the fights I have had, I didn't feel anything. That's probably down to the sheer adrenalin – the fear. Either way, I don't like fighting. I don't like the fire it unleashes in people.

It took me years to analyse what had happened to me though. I was probably all the way into my forties before it finally dawned on me – that my fear of people all began with being attacked on the street by that kid when I was still at school. I decided that I had probably 'looked at him funny' on a previous day going to school. Not intentionally, just in that wide-eyed way you do when you're five or six years old. And that I'd probably frightened *him*. So he went home that day and told his dad there was this kid down the street who had frightened him, and his dad's done that dreadful thing dads do sometimes, where he's told his son:

'Just go up to him next time, son, hit him as hard as you can – and run!' Because it later occurred to me that was what he did after hitting me – he ran. He was frightened shitless! So the result was that two kids went away traumatised by that incident – in my case, for the rest of my life. I'm still frightened about most things because of that one moment from my childhood.

It's odd because I know when people see me on telly or on stage they think of me as super confident, a bit of a know-all, perhaps. But it's all a disguise. I'm actually always in fear of things becoming out of control. I'm in fear of people. It's hidden away in some of my best-known lyrics and it's probably one of the reasons why I got so lost in drugs for so many years. And it's there now in my insistence on a strict daily routine. Some people call it over-thinking things. Others say it's about being a control freak. No, it's just simple fear of the unknown – or rather, the sudden and unexpected. I always expect – and fear – the unexpected. That's why whenever I'm presented with a new idea, my first reaction is almost always: no. Then, later, much to everyone's annoyance, including my own, I might be coaxed into changing my mind. You'll see that happens a lot as you go further in the book.

My wife Eileen isn't so sure this is all down to one kid hitting me. Status Quo PA and my good friend Lyane Ngan argues with me about it. But I know I'm right. I mean, I hate it when people say, 'I know I'm right.' But in this case, I know I'm right. (Smartarse.) That doesn't mean I'm never wrong. It's only when you discover just how wrong you've been about things sometimes that you learn anything valuable about yourself and the world. And what's wrong one day might be right the next. We live in the realm of relativity. So you can never be absolute about anything, really, can you? But about this kid hitting me I'm absolutely certain.

Once on the tour bus, Rick, Quo keyboardist Andrew Bown, Dave Salt, our old tour manager, and I were reminiscing about school. Andy was saying how all he ever wanted to do back then was draw. I was saying how I'd love to go back in time and learn more, because I missed so much of it at the time through always being ill. And Rick said, 'Fuck all that. I know all I need to know.' Such a sweeping statement! *I know all I need to know.* How do you know that? And if it's true, how dull must the rest of your life be? You know all you need to know so you never want to learn anything new ever again? But Rick was like that. Full steam ahead, no looking back. You might as well throw the towel in then and give up. I'm trying to learn all the time. Yes, many things once you learn about them, you've cracked it. But there's always something or someone else ready to come along and teach you something more, something different.

This might also have something to do with the fact that I did most of my learning on the hoof, through experience. Because I missed so much of school I was never going to be an educated kid. These days the school would have held me back. 'The silly sod hasn't learned anything. He hasn't been here!' But back then because I grew up in retail, it was less of an issue. Everyone just assumed I was destined to go out and sell. I was talking to my brother Dominic about this recently. We were both the same. We grew up knowing we would have to go out into the world and make money through selling, either in a shop, or off a van like my mum and dad, or some other way.

Kids that went to university back then, they were a type of person. I'm not knocking them. They were thirsting for knowledge. Subsequently, it's become a badge that people wear. My kids have got it. But when the youngest one, who is studying psychology, said to us, 'I'm not quite sure about this,' I thought, 'Good lad!' My attitude is, no matter how well or badly you were educated, you should never stop learning. Going to university doesn't guarantee that, though. I've met a lot of very stupid people that went and a lot of very smart people that didn't. And vice versa. The rule is there are no rules. These days, my wife's friends are like the League of Nations. There are Australians, Americans, Kiwis, Thais, Japanese, a couple of Indians, Irish and an Iranian. I have said to some of them in the past, 'Why are you so keen for your kids to go to university?' They say, 'To get a good job.' I say, 'Not just to be happy?' By 'good job', of course, they mean money. Meaning a nice car, a nice house and all that stuff. Yet that was all frowned on when I was a teenager, under the banner of materialism.

I just wish I'd known all this when I was a kid. Instead, for much of it, I felt like an outsider, an oddball. I'm sure a lot of people felt like that at school. For me, it was partly to do with my 'strange' accent, slightly northern, slightly Italian, slightly cockney. I lost count of the number of times I got told as a kid I had a 'poncey' accent. How they worked that out, I don't know. But then a lot of other kids thought we were rich, or at least very well off. So did the guys in the band, in fact, when we first started playing together as teenagers. Somehow people always just assumed that I had money. But we didn't live in a mansion. We lived in a nice house. My mum and dad aspired to own their own property because that's what retailers did, but we weren't rich. Other kids from school would come to the sweetshop we had in Balham and go, 'Wow! All them free sweets!' I'd go, 'Where?' I didn't know what they meant. For us kids there weren't any free sweets. They were shop sweets that my mum and dad sold to customers for our bread and butter.

Even the Catholic Church thought my dad was the bloke to go to for handouts. He ended up supplying free ice cream for the church summer fete, so they could keep the money for their good works. But we were brought up Catholics so we did the whole thing. Holy Communion, confirmation, confession . . . once you're indoctrinated with that at two or three years old it's almost impossible not to go to church for the rest of your life. Though in later life, I've succeeded. But it's been back and forth all my life. You see so many people that went through the same thing, managed to get away from it then have it all kick in again once they have got children. Boys and girls always had their first Holy Communion separately, but I had tonsillitis – again; I had it a lot as a kid – and missed my first Communion date so I had mine with the girls from a convent school. Freud would probably say that was when Catholicism and fun with girls first became intertwined in my mind. And Freud would be right.

For anybody who is religious, let me just say: I have no problem believing in an all-knowing, all-seeing, all-loving, all-powerful supreme being. I say 'supreme being' because I don't want to pick one out that alienates everyone else. I'd be happy with 'a higher reality', or 'the universe', or 'energy', 'life itself' – all fine by me. You can find the truth anywhere. Even Catholicism has good points – the importance of family, the dignity of work, taking responsibility for your actions, just basic good vs evil stuff. But what's the rest of the shit for, Catholic or otherwise? 'Don't you touch that! You're a dirty boy!' You know what, you're wrong. Touching yourself is lovely. We lie to kids straight from the off, telling them these things are bad or wrong and go against God. But deep down inside they know you're wrong. So when you go out of the room they're going to play anyway. Only now they feel guilty about it afterwards.

My mum was very religious, being a good Catholic girl, and therefore extremely adept at making the rest of us feel guilty if we didn't go to church. She actually believed I was an immaculate conception and told me so forcefully many times. Hence being named after St Francis of Assisi. As I got older and found the courage, I would challenge her and say, 'If I'm an immaculate conception, what is my brother then, the dirty one? And how did my dad feel about that anyway?' She hated that. Blasphemy! Most of the time, though, she was a lovely, fairly normal sort of mum. It all changed when I was nineteen and she underwent this sudden massive religious conversion-cum-breakdown. At which point she informed my brother and me: 'I'm not your mum. I'm Annie.' I took it all in my stride at the time, but grew very upset about it as time went on, as I realised I'd suddenly lost my mum. But that's all for later.

My dad was a lovely man. Born in London but very much still an Italian. Or Italian-cockney. He used to go around saying, 'Arseholes!' when things didn't go right. But in that lovely Anglo-Italian voice, 'Arsssols! Bluddy arsssols!' I used to love being with him. He was always going off to work, that was the trouble. So I didn't get to spend as much time with him as I would have liked. It was great when it snowed or rained because then he would have to stay home. I was very like that with my first three kids, because I was still in my twenties and like my dad always having to go out on the road for work – only in my case I didn't come home at all for weeks and months at a time. It's the same for everyone in show business. I didn't mind at the time, but looking back I see the pattern. Any excuse to get out of the house and away from all the domestics. Later, as a much older dad, with more time spent at home, it was different. I loved being with my kids. It wasn't until I was already middle-aged and my mum and dad had divorced that I got to know my own dad a little better. He was a lovely man, loved music, very proud of me. I remember playing him that Shania Twain record, 'You're Still The One', and he practically got his willy out, he'd be in ecstasy. I'm the same whenever I really love a piece of music. Bluddy arsssols!

Because of my mum, I used to go to church every Sunday as a child. Then stopped when Quo took off when I was in my early twenties. Then started again a few years later. Then stopped, then started again. You could say writing and making music is an act of creation and tie it in with God. I wouldn't necessarily put it that way, though. I don't create religious music. But I do go into a kind of ecstasy when I'm listening to really great music sometimes. I can cry.

In my forties I found myself going to Sunday mass at my local church, John the Baptist, in Purley. I even had my own kids confirmed into the Church, that's how confused I still was by the whole thing. I ended up in church one Sunday with Eileen when it finally hit me that I just didn't believe in it any more. I looked around and thought: if there were anything really genuine going on here the kids would be riveted. Kids have those antennae. They can't help it. Anything going on, they know about it even if they don't know exactly what it is, they just know something interesting is happening. But they weren't interested at all. The opposite. You could see by their faces. They were thinking: can we go yet?

One really lovely thing my childhood did leave me with was my love of winter. I love it when it's grey and cold, because whenever the weather was bad my dad wouldn't go out in the ice-cream van. My dad was the king of just being. You know, they don't call us human doings: it's human beings. And my dad could just *be*. He was never bored by having nothing to do. For him it was a luxury. He could just *be*. He was brilliant at it. So as a kid I loved having him around the house. If I looked out the window and it was snowing I'd be so happy because I knew my dad would be in the house all day just hanging around being happy. He'd still be going round the house doing odd jobs but at least he'd be home. I used to dread the summer because I'd never see him. He'd be out all day and night in the van, working. So even now I dread the summer coming – plus it gets too hot and I just don't like it. I prefer to be indoors, rain lashing against the window, drawbridge up.

I told my dad all this before he died and he amazed me by saying, 'I hated going out, too, son. I loved being at home with your mum.' He used to get up and drive to my grandmother's place in Catford early, 6.30 every morning. Go and load up, get in the ice-cream van and come back home for about 9.30 a.m. Have a wash and brush up. Then he'd come downstairs and have something to eat with my mum. Then be ready to go on his rounds. Do the schools. The playgrounds: all the streets where kids might be out playing. He said that my mum would often try to stop him going, standing there in her baby-doll nightie. He told me: 'She was a good girl. She knew how to get her own way.' I was listening to this, not quite knowing how to react. I said, 'Really?' He beamed and said, 'Yeah!'

But that was my dad, full of life. People used to think he'd been on the booze because he was always so up. But the truth is he never touched a drop. It sounds simplistic to say but my talent for showing off on a stage must have come from my dad. That delight in making other people happy. My mother was different. She had a lot of friends, people that loved her. But there was definitely a streak of Irish melancholy there too.

A weird uptightness that came to the fore as she got older – and more religious. She would break down. These days they'd have offered her all kinds of different medicines and therapies. But this seemed to be just part of who she was. Maybe that's where I get my own propensity for gloom from: I'm the most positive person in the world one minute – then the world's biggest worrier the next. Either that or the drugs. Maybe both . . .

The truth is, when I look back on myself now as a youngster, I think: oh, what a dickhead! I was trying to follow things, people, trying to fit in. That's when I met Alan Lancaster. We were the same age and at Sedgehill Comprehensive School in Beckenham. Sedgehill was tough. All the kids from the local council estates went there and it was all about how hard you were. Anyone seen to actually be enjoying lessons was looked down on and treated accordingly. There were kids getting their heads kicked in every day. I liked learning but I did not want to have my head kicked in. So I developed a hard-nut exterior, and being mates with Alan really helped with this as he was the genuine article.

Mainly, I was obsessed with pop music, especially the Everly Brothers. I loved the sound, the songs, and I loved the look of the guitars. Alan was more into Del Shannon, the Shadows and Nat King Cole. Most of the other boys at school were into sport, mainly football. I didn't like football, which Italians traditionally are really good at. Our sports master at school was a nutcase, yelling at us to 'Get stuck in!' and 'Hack him down, boy!' What a turn-off. To this day, whenever the rest of the band start going on about football I completely lose interest. (So does Andrew Bown.) I tried rugby and it was a complete non-starter. The pitch was frozen and so was I, and I ended up getting knocked all over the place. Horrible.

I later discovered that there are a lot of musicians like that. They weren't sporty so they retreated to their bedrooms and sat there practising guitar. People like Pete Townshend and Jimmy Page, Eric Clapton and David Bowie. In my case, it wasn't just that I didn't like sport. Outside of music, and watching a few films and reading a few comics, I really didn't have anything else to connect to. We used to have one of those big old beige Bush wirelesses with the handy handle and lit-up dial. Tuned into Radio Luxembourg. There was something very modern about that radio, almost futuristic too. I would sit there nodding along to whatever pop song it was playing.

There were hardly any songs on the wireless I didn't like in those days but the ones that really stuck out were things like 'Red River Rock' by Johnny and the Hurricanes and 'The Young Ones' by Cliff Richard. Cliff's record had the same eerie effect on me that something like 'Stairway To Heaven' would have on a generation of Led Zeppelin fans years later. It felt profound, wise beyond its years, especially the pay-off: 'Cos we may not/Be the young ones/Very long . . .' Even as a twelve-year-old schoolboy, that one would have me almost weeping with nostalgia.

Another instrumental that always sent me into a deep swoon was Acker Bilk's 'Stranger on the Shore'. Sweet Jesus, as my dad would say . . . that sultry quivering clarinet, those seashore strings. If that came on the radio on a Sunday morning as we sat there having sausages and bacon, we would fall into a collective blush, our emotions all spooned-out and stirred slowly in front of us on the table. None of us would speak, just all plugged into the same good feeling.

Then came the Beatles and everything – everything – changed overnight. Not just music, but literally everything. Unless you lived through it you simply cannot comprehend what a big change to the world it was when the Beatles came along. It was the start of the sixties, the start of a whole new post-war world. They were on the side of the angels yet they had better tunes even than the devil. No musician alive before or after the Beatles hasn't been enormously affected by them.

In terms of learning to play an instrument, I'd messed around on a harmonica when I was about four years old. Then I had a little Hohner Mignon accordion, those Italian ones you see with what looks like a piano keyboard down one side. But you had to have lessons to learn that and I didn't have the patience at that age. I wanted to be out in the garden playing with my brother and my cousins. The TV was pretty rubbish back then – only two channels, which no one in our house watched anyway because they were so busy working all the time.

All this somehow went into my thinking about music too. I desperately wanted to learn the guitar but from the word go the only real way I ever had of measuring success would be in how popular what I did was. I wanted to get good but it wouldn't mean anything if nobody liked it. All performers are like this if they are honest. The minute you put yourself on a stage and try and sell tickets for people to come and watch you, that's how you really measure success – by how many people actually pay to see you. I always wanted to know how many people were coming to a show. How many records a certain song had sold. And how did that compare to other songs? Other crowds? My dad and his family always talked about 'turnover' and that's exactly how I've always measured success. By how many tickets we've sold, how many records. How many 'pieces'.

I imagine some people reading that and thinking I only got into music for the money. Well, that was not the only reason.

But I definitely saw it as a means to an end. I was either going to make it as a musician or start driving an ice-cream van. It would have been easier to simply become part of the family business. But I chose the hard way. Learn to play an instrument, try and find a band. Then play every shithole that will have you until something big happens – or doesn't. As is the case for most people that are crazy enough to decide to try and do something in music.

The thing that's harder to explain is where my musical influences came from. It was the Everly Brothers that got me dreaming of playing guitar and making music with my own brother. Dominic was a couple of years younger than me and therefore completely under my command in those first tender years. Or so I liked to think. In fact, my dear brother was already his own man; he was just much nicer than me and therefore quite happy for me to make grand plans for us both, knowing full well he wasn't going to pay the slightest bit of attention when the time actually came for action.

For example, I'd convinced myself that Dominic and I could be like the English answer to the Everly Brothers, and so we both agreed to ask for guitars for Christmas when I was nine. I pictured us sitting there trying to sing and strum along together. But Dominic got cold feet at the last moment and asked for a train set instead. Which actually worked out fine in the end – he became an accountant. My accountant. Cheers, Dom! That is, until he decided he didn't like the way the music business works. In fact, Dominic was very much the opposite of me in some ways. I was high-strung and nervous and always looking for the angle. He was quieter, calmer, more trusting and giving in many ways. Like I say, he was simply nicer. It didn't always work to his advantage, like when Dom and I were adults and my mum went completely bonkers religious. I was married and the band was starting to work all the time, so I couldn't have been there as much even if I'd wanted to. Dominic would stick with her, give in to her mad choices, hold her hand and tell her reassuring things. I wasn't having any of it. I was off, out the door, again, too busy following my own nutty dreams to want to be held back by her. Dom, he hung on in there, bless him.

Whoever we were, or thought we were, or would one day be, my parents let us boys get on with it. They didn't fall over themselves to push us in any particular direction, but they were quite supportive in a quiet sort of way. That helped me much more than I realised at the time. It gave me the impetus to keep going. Otherwise I might have abandoned the guitar completely. But even when Dominic decided his train set was more fun, I find it interesting that years later in Status Quo I would develop this guitar-singing 'brother' relationship with Rick Parfitt. That was absolutely not a conscious thing for me, but I look back now and I see it all too clearly. I also see the influence of Everly hits like 'Wake Up Little Susie' and 'Bye Bye Love'. Those big strumming chords are right there in Quo hits like 'Caroline' and 'Down Down'. The way the vocals blend for me and Rick until they sound almost like one voice is also pure Everly Brothers.

What's far less obvious though are the other, much deeper musical influences that I now realise were at play. For example, an old Italian novelty song called 'Poppa Piccolino'. This was done by loads of different singers, from Petula Clark to Diana Decker and even the Billy Cotton Orchestra. The first time I heard it was when my mum played it for me to cheer me up after I'd fallen down the stairs again. I always used to say I loved that song so much not just because it was so jolly and catchy but because of the fuss my mother was making over me at the time. I used to joke that I enjoyed the attention so much I threw myself down the stairs again the next day. Only she figured out my game and threatened to throw me down the stairs herself if I didn't stop pestering her.

The record stayed with me though – and for far longer than I imagined. Until one day I realised how much the Quo sound had to do with that Italian shuffle beat that 'Poppa Piccolino' had. That very kind of singsong ta-da-de-dah beat. If you listen it's in nearly all the biggest Quo hits. I had assumed it came from my fascination for blues-influenced British sixties bands that used that brush-and-pan shuffle too. It was at the heart of my love of American country music as well – which, if you want to get really deep here, is derived from traditional Irish music. Hello Mum!

Whatever the origins – and like most music, I suspect it can be found around the world – the fact was I fell in love with that shuffle rhythm. You could say it's in my blood.

When I was eleven, I joined the school orchestra. Not as a guitarist but as a trumpet player. That was when I first met Alan Lancaster, who I would go on to form Status Quo with, and another kid named Alan Key, a laidback boy who played the trumpet like I did. Lancaster played the trombone.

Alan Lancaster was a short-arse, but he was the guvnor. He made that clear from the off. Always had plenty to say for himself. A born leader, you might say. I quickly became a follower. I was strong on the outside, but Alan was the real deal. He probably saw the group as his group, and no one was about to argue with him. He was known to be handy with his fists, put it that way. Eventually, as my confidence grew, I would challenge him. Remind him that no one was the leader of the group; that we were all in it together. But Alan wasn't the kind of bloke to back down in an argument and we ended up having a lot of rows about it. It didn't change a thing. Alan never backed down about anything. That said, democracy in a group never works. You have to have leaders or the whole thing just never goes anywhere.

Early on, though, that suited me because I was not your typical alpha male. Having Alan as your schoolmate meant you were safe from all the other hooligans, the ones who told me I had a girl's name in Francis and that I spoke funny. Even Alan, when I first met him, told me: 'You talk fucking poncey like, doncha?' But I started hanging out more and more at his house. I loved his mum and dad. That expression: salt of the earth? Alan Lancaster's mum and dad really were.

Alan's mum, May, was an absolutely lovely and decent woman. I always assumed she had Spanish blood because she was dark and passionate. She used to make a big fuss of me. His dad, Harry, was really nice to me too. He was an ex-boxer. One of those blokes who used to come home from work every evening, take his shirt off and have a wash at the kitchen sink in his string vest and a shave for the evening. He wouldn't have a shave for work.

I was there one day waiting for Alan to get ready. His dad said: 'You'll wait forever for that boy, you will.' So we're watching the telly and there's some bloke on there who's reasonably well spoken and Harry calls out: 'Here, May! Look, it's like Ross on the telly!' Ross was what he used to call me. She came in the room, had a look and went, 'Naw. He's one of us now.' I was so proud to think I'd become more like them, more like that working-class south London Jack the Lad. The kind that would frighten the shit out of people. 'Don't you fucking try it with me, boy! I'll fucking have ya!' I knew I couldn't really be that, I was far too wimpy to frighten anybody. It just felt so good to be accepted.

Even when I'd got the other kids at school to stop making fun of my name – now Mike or Ross – and my accent – now cor blimey guvnor – they still found ways to pick on me. They said Italians always stank of garlic and ate worms – spaghetti. So I would put on this tough kid façade. I learned to swear a lot and pretend to be this macho Jack-the-Lad funny guy. Like Alan Lancaster: except he didn't need to be funny. He was genuinely tough. I had to be funny because that was my best defence, always. But I never felt like I was being myself. I knew it was all just an act. My eldest son, Simon, was somewhat similar when he was growing up, though under different circumstances. Just being hypersensitive. Simon now works in musical theatre and opera – he's an incredible singer – and he told me that when he finally got into that world he really felt happy, that he had found his true element in which to thrive. What I've got, I've had to fight for every step of the way. Putting up a front, while secretly peeking out from behind the mask waiting for it to be safe to come out and play – as myself and no one else.

Where we lived in Balham, it was a world apart from Forest Hill, where we'd lived with Nonna. It was rough. Prostitutes didn't wait for night: they just stood on street corners asking passing motorists if they wanted 'any business' in the middle of the afternoon. More than once my mother went outside to try and break up some fight the working girls would be having in our shop doorway. I knew they were 'bad girls' but even if you'd explained to me precisely what they did I wouldn't have really paid much attention. I was eleven when we moved to Balham and though I'd been fiddling around under the blankets for a while, the world of sex was not something I had given a lot of thought to. I didn't equate playing with myself with having sex with a member of the opposite sex. When some of the older kids in the neighbourhood told me and my mates about some barber in the high street who would give boys a fiver if they let him give them a wank under the barber's sheet, we all talked about it for a few days.. A wank was just a wank. But being given a fiver – that was a fortune to us back then. We soon came to our senses though. Our brains were catching up with our bodies and going down the barber's didn't seem like such a good idea.

Meanwhile, as a teenager I did more or less become part of Alan's family. For better or worse. The Lancasters were an archetypal hard-as-nails old south London family from Peckham. They had a black cat called Nigger. But they were an amazingly close loving family, and I was so happy to be considered part of it during those years. It made me feel for the first time as if I belonged somewhere other than at home. It made me feel safe. But I look back now and see it as a failing of mine. A real weakness of character that I could be so easily led as a kid, that I was so desperate not to stick out from the crowd. They were good people but they weren't my people. I was just happy to be allowed to be with them. Not a good foundation for any healthy relationship.

There are lots of areas of my younger life I look back on now and cringe. I'm sure a lot of people do. I think that's a good thing, because it shows you're learning as you go, through your mistakes. It's often the ones that look back on their childhoods and see no mistakes at all that are the ones to watch out for. Rick Parfitt was like that. But Rick was an only child and a lot of only children are like that, in my experience.

Even though Alan was the leader when we were kids and could be very intimidating, he used to like the idea of us being pals and being so different. I was tall and he was short. Years later when we were still trying to get Quo off the ground, Alan showed me a picture of Simon and Garfunkel. He said, 'Look, that's you and me, that is.' One tall blond one; one short dark one. I was like, you're right! But inside I was thinking: that's not how I see us at all. But Alan was happy and that's all I really cared about when I was young, keeping other people happy, so that they wouldn't take against me. And I could fit in. Didn't matter into what. Just so long as I wasn't left outside in the cold.

Chapter Two

Happy Campers

I learned to play guitar by listening to records and trying to play along. First just pop records that I happened to like, then anything and everything. Guy Mitchell, who was my mother's favourite, I remember trying to play along to. Connie Francis and 'Everybody's Somebody's Fool' was another one I seemed to pick up easily. Mind you, I had a thing for Connie Francis as a kid and imagined meeting her and bowling her over with my uncanny ability to play her hits. I loved her voice: that catch in it that made it incredibly sexy to a pre-pubescent boy – plus, she was Italian. It was only much later when I looked back I realised I was listening to a sort of pop version of American country. I've loved country music ever since.

I was never going to be a virtuoso guitarist. I only ever went for one proper guitar lesson and that was from some dodgy geezer at Len Stiles Music on Lewisham High Street. This was a record shop that also sold musical instruments including electric guitars. Len Stiles was the place where you hung around smoking your Nelson cigarettes and yacking about music. This guy gave lessons there and I thought this must be the place to learn. But when I asked to be shown some Everly Brothers tunes this old fellow looked at me with scorn. 'We don't do any of that rubbish here, laddie!' Calling me 'laddie' also put me right off. It sounded so old-fashioned. I walked out never to return. It was two lessons in one: my first and my last!

After that, there was this feeling that even trying to learn an instrument was somehow out-of-date. It didn't help that all the teachers usually offered were old dance tunes or ballads. I wanted to play the Everlys' '(Till) I Kissed You', not some old waltz. It seemed like you had to learn on your own if you wanted to learn how to play the modern sounds you heard on the radio. There was a real disconnect in those days between the older and younger generation, particularly when it came to music. The music teachers objected to showing younger players like me how to play such 'rubbish' as the Everlys or the Beatles, who I'd also fallen for, just like everyone else in 1962. They were like the Everlys in that they played guitars, had really catchy songs, and this brilliant vocal harmony thing going on, where the voices all sounded like one.

Now there are some smartarses out there who will be sniggering at this info and thinking how this explains the, in their eyes, 'limited scope' of Status Quo's music – the old heads-down-three-chords-no-nonsense-boogie label. And I will concede they might have good reason – up to a point. But while I was never going to be able to play guitar to the same jaw-dropping level as an Eric Clapton or Jeff Beck, I was determined I was going to become a bloody good songwriter. Besides, if you listen properly you'll discover that whether it's me playing something relatively straightforward like 'What You're Proposing', which was a huge hit for us in 1980, or Clapton on fire in Cream, we are both playing the same bunch of chords. It's not about how many – or how few – notes you can play or how fast, it's all about whether the music touches your soul – or your groin.

There are only so many notes and chords you can play on a guitar and it's all about the *way* you play them. Which means it's all about *who* you are, not what you are. There's a story I like about the great American guitar player Chet Atkins. Chet could play anything from country to pop and all points between. He was known as Mr Guitar. Well, this story about him might be apocryphal but it says it all really. He was sitting in a chair playing one day, just for fun, in some guitar shop or somewhere. And one of the customers stopped to listen and said to him: 'My-oh-my, Mr Atkins, that guitar sure does sound pretty.' Chet looked him over and said, 'Yeah?' Then got up, put the guitar back on its stand, and said: 'How does it sound now?'

The moral being, anyone can pick up and play a guitar. But only you will ever sound like you. And that's what you aim for. Making the guitar do something that is real to you. Of course, it took me a long time to work that out for myself. But whenever people make jokes about Quo only being a three- or four-chord band, it says more to me about the people saying that than it does about what Quo have achieved as a band.

Anyway, practising the guitar or trying to learn stuff I didn't actually need to know at the time went right out the window for me the moment I mastered the basic chords. I'm not saying that's good. These days I practise every single day. But as a kid it probably made me even more single-minded about starting my own band and simply going out there and playing anywhere that would have us.

By the time I met Alan Lancaster I was into the 'heavy' stuff. That is, all the American rock and rollers like Jerry Lee Lewis, who used to frighten the hell out of me, and all the other wild and crazy singers like Little Richard, Eddie Cochran, Gene Vincent, Chuck Berry . . . I'd also discovered Buddy Holly by then, who was similar to the Everly Brothers, except even more exceptional in that he had this really exciting take. The hiccupping voice, that great band he had behind him. Those songs, the best of which he wrote himself . . . And he wore glasses and was not the typical good-looking pop star. Like a lot of other aspiring young British musicians of the time, I thought, if he can do it then there's a chance for all of us.

Alan and I were still in the school orchestra playing our brass instruments when he and the other Alan – Key – started talking about having a little beat group outside school. Alan Key's older brother was in Rolf Harris's backing group, who'd had big hits with 'Tie Me Kangaroo Down, Sport' and 'Sun Arise', which was a really big deal at the time. He would let Alan Key use his spare Fender Stratocaster, which I was very envious of. We had another mate from school, Jess Jaworski, playing keyboards, and Alan Lancaster on bass. He had somehow managed to get his parents to fork out for a blond Höfner bass. I was amazed – and impressed. It was a beautiful-looking instrument, but he couldn't afford a guitar case so he used to carry it around in an old plastic shopping bag.

Our drummer was a lad called Barry. I can only remember his first name, which he will hate me for, but he probably already hates me anyway – I'll explain in a moment. That left me on guitar, which was fine while we were just mucking around playing Shadows instrumentals like 'Apache' and 'Kon-Tiki'. Not that I could manage to play like Hank Marvin. I was far too lazy to learn that – most of the lead instrumental work was done by Jess on the keyboards. But then the rest of the band wanted a singer – and decided that it would have to be me. This was not something I had bargained for. It was one thing to know all the words to 'Wake Up Little Susie' or 'Love

Me Do', quite another to get up on a stage and sing them for an audience. But it was made pretty clear that if I didn't do it they would look for someone else who would. So I held my breath and jumped in at the deep end. And . . . it seemed to work. I think I sang 'Michael (Row The Boat Ashore)'. Well, we made such a noise you couldn't really hear the vocals that well, so I was safe for the moment. That's how I looked at it.

The singing malarkey had begun when we were playing in the school orchestra. We were basically modelling ourselves on Kenny Ball and His Jazzmen, a modern trad band from Essex who had quite a few hits in the early sixties, led by trumpeter Kenny Ball, who would set aside the trumpet here and there to warble a few vocals. We would do one of Kenny's big hits, 'When the Saints Go Marching In'.

But it was all just school stuff, we knew that. Singing while playing guitar in a group, that was another level, but I smile about that now because the fact is I'm pretty sure we never actually got around to playing any gigs. We would just rehearse in Jess's bedroom. The group was named the Scorpions. But then Alan Key, who ironically was the one who really pushed for the group to happen, decided to leave. He announced that he planned to marry his girlfriend – who was, literally, the girl next-door to where he lived – as soon they reached sixteen, and that he thought it best if he stepped down from the group now to allow us time to get someone new in. Alan was lovely like that, always nice and thoughtful. Far too nice, you might say, to be a working musician.

Stepping down was a very noble thing for a fourteen-year-old to do, and very generous and forward thinking. As I discovered later, most young guys in groups sooner or later faced the choice of settling down with someone or giving everything up to try and make it as a musician. Most of them leave it too late to decide, though, and this either lumbers the group they are in or completely messes up their relationship. In my case, it would be the latter. Alan Key, however, somehow foresaw this and did the right thing. His reward is that he's still with the girl of his teenage dreams all these years later – and I'm still in the group. But then it never felt to me like I went from some safe sort of home environment where a so-called normal life was mapped out for me. School, job, wife, kids, death. For the Rossi family, school was what we learned at home; jobs was what we did at home; wives were meant to fit in with that or not at all; kids were for wives; and death was something that was never going to happen to me, thank you very much!

This is when John Coghlan came into the story. Not to replace Alan Key, but to take over from Barry. It was a bit complicated but the short version is that Barry's dad had wangled us a proper place to rehearse, which was this old garage in Lordship Lane, Dulwich. It was next-door to the south London headquarters of the Air Training Corps (ATC). All the air cadets went there, which is how we met John, who was one of the cadets. We had only been in the place a few weeks when we discovered that the air cadets had their own group that also used to rehearse there. They were called – wait for it – the Cadets. One night we walked over to check them out. They were all a little bit older than us and although they hadn't done many gigs either, it was obvious they were streets ahead of us at that stage – especially the drummer.

That got us plotting. Barry was a good bloke but a pretty average drummer. Hardly surprising: he was only a kid, like us. But John was on another level as a drummer. The difference was really noticeable. You can fake it a fair amount if you're not that good at guitar or bass, but drums are so important in a group and you've either really got it or you don't. I have to confess, though, there was another reason why not having Barry around any more suited me. I was 'seeing' his girlfriend. How I remember it, she was the one that instigated it. She was bigger than me and used to getting what she wanted. I'm not saying she held a gun to my head, but the first time she went to give me a blowjob I couldn't understand why she kept moving her head down there. The truth is I didn't know what she was trying to do – put my knob in her mouth? Bloody hell! Whatever will they think of next?

When the whole thing came up about stealing John for our group, I didn't say anything to the others but it's fair to say I was relieved. That's a group for you: selfish to the bone. I was going to say 'young groups', but actually it's groups of any age. You always want to get better at the music – and get your willy seen to. Sorry, Barry. But you'd have probably done the same.

So we brought John in and he was amazing – his playing really took us into another league musically. We were now the Spectres and John joining on drums was the moment where we started to take things seriously. He had already left school; he'd been at another comprehensive called Kingsdale, which was in Dulwich. He was also three years older than the rest of us, and an air cadet, which also lent him an air of authority. Though not to Alan Lancaster, of course, who would take on anybody, no matter how old – and win, usually. Most importantly, John Coghlan was already what you would call a 'proper' drummer. He'd taken lessons from someone called Lloyd Ryan, who really was a 'proper' drummer, having played with people like Matt Monro and Gene Vincent. Ryan was an amazing character who would go on to play with all sorts of sixties stars like

P. J. Proby, the New Seekers, Tony Christie . . . He also, rather wonderfully if a little bizarrely, went on to become the manager and chief spokesman for the masked wrestler, Kendo Nagasaki.

We knew we'd moved up a gear the day John arrived for his rehearsal with us. He turned up in a minicab. Minicabs were still a new concept in 1962 and we all thought he'd been chauffeured! Later, John levelled with us, saying his dad had told him: 'Make it look good, son.'

Thankfully, John used to be the most un-flash sort of guy you could hope to meet. For a drummer – they are mostly mad – John was quite quiet. Except for those times when he wasn't. Times when he got the hump about something and literally just exploded. John wasn't much of a joiner-in, let's put it that way. He kept himself to himself, didn't feel obliged to pretend to be anything he wasn't, and just got on with his drums. The main thing was, John was a good drummer – and he knew he was a good drummer. The rest of us were still hoping to be good one day. This is where Alan Lancaster's sheer bloody-mindedness came in handy.

It was this line-up – me, Alan Lancaster, John Coghlan on drums and Jess Jaworski on keyboards – that began working properly as the Spectres. Alan's dad had arranged for us to play a regular weekly show at the Samuel Jones Sports Club. My dad would pack our equipment in the back of his ice-cream van and drive us. There wasn't much of a turnout, just family, really, and a few mates. But I would not allow the group to start playing until Alan's mum got there. Her approval meant so much to me. Once we started, we would do a few covers – instrumentals and chart stuff – then do a runner after about half an hour. It forced us to become professional – or semi-professional. It was hard for a bunch of school kids, and also for

John, who had left school behind when he was fifteen and was throwing in his lot with us. It would have been easy just to let the whole thing fizzle out.

This went on until one night this bloke came up to us after we'd finished and uttered the immortal words: 'I want to manage you.' To us, this sounded like 'I want to make you stars.' Because we didn't know what a 'manager' actually did. We thought he would just give us money and get us on the telly. Or something. We didn't know what he would do. We just said, 'You'll have to ask Alan's mum.' So May gave him the once-over, decided he'd probably be all right and suddenly the Spectres had a manager. Whoopee!

Our new manager's name was Pat Barlow and as it happened he had zero experience of the music business. He was a gas fitter who had done all right for himself, to the point where he now ran his own gas showroom. He wasn't a big cheese with millions at his disposal, but he was 'flush', as we would say. He'd made some money and now fancied, as he put it, 'getting into this pop music game'. Why not? The Beatles were enjoying their first hit singles. The Rolling Stones hadn't released a record yet, neither had the Kinks or the Who, yet there was this feeling suddenly, especially in London, where you could just make something happen simply because you were young and 'with it'. Or maybe all teenagers feel like that when they are making their first steps beyond school.

Either way, Pat Barlow fancied having a go at turning the Spectres into the next Shadows, maybe even the Beatles. Or at the very least, turning a profit. The important thing is Pat began beavering away for us and the gigs began rolling in. He may not have known anything about the music business but he had the gift of the blarney and he never gave up. He would get on the phone and not get off again until he'd dug up something for his 'boys'. Now we were playing places like the El Partido club in Lewisham, which became a well-known mod club. Pat also got us a Monday-night residency at the Café des Artistes in Chelsea. Even though most of us were still at school, we'd be playing there until the early hours of the morning. Our parents all knew Pat would be there to look after us, though, and drive us all home afterwards, so they were fine with it. Pat was like another parent to us. One time when my hair had gotten quite long – well, long for those days, which meant it had grown past my shirt collar – Pat grabbed me by the neck and cut off about six inches of hair from the back with a pair of scissors. I put up with it though because I was still a schoolboy and he was a grown-up. In those days, neighbours were allowed to give you a clip round the ear if they thought you were being unruly and your parents wouldn't say a thing.

We trusted him and so did our families – especially when some money started coming in. My mum and dad might not have fully understood the sort of music we were into but they totally got what was going on when they saw it bringing in money.

Overnight, our equipment got better. I was able to buy a new Guild semi-acoustic guitar. Alan splashed out on a smart new Burns bass guitar. And we started getting into clothes – clobber. At first, that meant wanting to look like the Beatles, all in the same blue suits. It was just the way all the pop groups dressed in the early to mid-sixties. There was this fella down in Lambeth who would tailor-make them for us at £12 a go. Alan decided he needed a more special kind of suit – he still saw himself as the leader and he felt he needed something to mark him out as such – and so he paid £25 for his. Watching us onstage, you couldn't tell the difference – they were all the same shade of blue. But in Alan's mind his suit was just a little bit better and that kept him happy.

In our own way, we were all becoming a little bit cockier, I suppose. The next logical step was to get a record out but none of us had the faintest idea how to go about making that miracle work. Even Pat couldn't sweet talk any record company people into delving into the deep south of London to come and see us play. This went on for months and months until Pat had the bright idea of trying to get us onto the bill with one of the groups that the record company crowd would definitely turn up for. But again, easier said than done.

Then, sometime towards the end of 1964, Pat saw an advert for the Hollies, who were playing at the Orpington Civic Hall in Kent, and decided to try and blag us onto the bill as an opening act. How he managed I don't know but somehow Pat pulled it off and, sure enough, by the time we took the stage in Orpington, sometime early in 1965, we were convinced that this was our big break. That the place was packed with leading music-biz impresarios just dying to sign this hot new group they had heard so much about.

We were dreaming, of course. I have no idea if there was anyone at all from the biz there that night but by the end of it I was praying there wasn't. We were awful. We were so crippled by nerves we could hardly stand up straight, let alone play and sing. The whole thing felt like a giant setback. I thought: that's it, we've blown it now. But I was fifteen. I hadn't come even halfway to blowing it yet. That was something I'd be much more successful at later, once we were famous.

Our real big break, not that we saw it quite that way at the time, was when Pat excelled himself and got us an audition for a summer season booking at Butlin's Holiday Camp in Minehead, Somerset. Now this was genuinely exciting stuff. Half a century later Butlin's is still a good affordable holiday spot for families with young kids, or older relatives. Back in 1965, though, it was like Britain's answer to Las Vegas. Until Butlin's came along, a typical working-class family holiday was a week at a bed-and-breakfast by the sea, the sort of places that were usually a few spare rooms in someone's house, which you were locked out of all day. Butlin's came along and suddenly Britain had actual 'resorts'. Places where the kids could play at the fair all day and the adults could grab a drink and put their feet up at night. For teenagers, Butlin's also offered the previously unknown pleasures of living away from home for months at a time, getting all your meals provided and chasing as many pretty girls as you could find. And you didn't have to look very hard, obviously.

The first few nights we played there as the Spectres I thought I'd died and gone to heaven. The Butlin's holiday camp in Minehead had only just opened a couple of years before and was the newest and most 'glamorous' of the various camps around the country. The day we arrived was genuinely momentous for me. It was my sixteenth birthday, and who happened to be at the check-in centre at the very same moment we arrived but the guy who was to become my lifelong musical partner, Rick Parfitt, and my future wife, Jean Smith! Not that I knew any of that yet, obviously.

Being part of the 'nightly entertainment' meant we got a lot of attention. It was my first summer after leaving school, too, so the whole thing was like a rite of passage for me. That might sound pretentious but I can't overstate what a big step up the Butlin's gig was for us.

In fact, once we had left school, Jess Jaworski decided he'd had enough of late nights and an uncertain income, and decided to stay on at school and take his A levels. This is another make-or-break moment for any aspiring young musician. You can only survive on dreams for so long. If you haven't made it after a certain time, it seems only sensible to throw in the towel and get a regular job like everybody else. But this Butlin's booking definitely represented a turning point for the group and Jess rightly recognised that. For Jess, it was time to be thinking about things like apprenticeships or college and solid offers of paid employment. For some aspiring musos the big decision to pack it in comes at thirty or thirty-five. Some never give up the dream and find jobs that allow them to keep playing at weekends and what have you. Jess saved himself – and us – a lot of unnecessary grief by making his decision early and good on him for doing it.

The guy Pat managed to find to replace Jess on keyboards was Roy Lynes. Roy was even more laidback than Alan Key and even older than John Coghlan. Alan Lancaster and I were both sixteen when Roy joined and he was about twenty-two: a pretty big gap at that age but what a lovely fella – and a great keyboardist too. Until then he'd been a full-time inspector at a car-parts factory. But he had his own equipment, could really play and slotted right in, in time for Butlin's. We used to joke that it was Roy's organ playing that covered up all the mistakes Alan and I made on the guitars.

The novelty of playing at Butlin's soon wore off, once we realised what a treadmill we were on. We had an afternoon slot, in which we were expected to keep the punters entertained for up to three hours. Then a repeat set the same evening, at the end of which we barely had enough energy to crawl into bed, let alone spend the rest of the night chasing dolly birds, as they were charmingly known. We found ourselves playing over fifty songs a set – twice a day, six days and nights a week. By the third week we had turned into zombies, virtually playing in our sleep. I was practically eating packets of throat sweets for breakfast, my voice was so raw. But that was when we became hardened pros. With that sort of workload, you either gave up quite quickly and went home or you dug down and sucked it up. Well, we weren't going home, no way. In the end, it made us strong as individuals and really tight as a musical unit. By the time we returned to London at the end of the summer season we were completely transformed. No gig would ever be too daunting again. We were still boys but we were now boys that could look after themselves. We were pros. Lived it, breathed it. Hardened, roughed up, no longer virgins. In any sense . . .

I also learned how to communicate with audiences, whether they were friendly or hostile, and at Butlin's they could sometimes be both at the same time. We were booked to play at this venue on the camp called the Pig & Whistle, which was exactly as it sounds – a pub. Albeit a bloody big one. You could get twelve hundred in there easy, but they would all be seated at tables and chairs. There was a little space on the floor down the front of the stage where people could dance. But mainly they sat at their tables and drank – and drank and drank. That is, when they bothered to turn up.

There was another venue on site called the Rock and Roll Ballroom, and we couldn't understand why they didn't put us on there. In the end, they did get us to play at the Rock and Roll Ballroom, and we thought that was a decent break until we had our first performance and realised that no one bothered going there towards the end of the night. They were all at the Pig & Whistle getting plastered. For some of our sets we would play to about twenty people. Then there would be a huge rush of people coming in for the last half an hour, when the Pig & Whistle had closed.

We did start to build up the crowd in the ballroom eventually, though. We also soon learned not to overreach with the music. We'd arrived with the notion that we were this exciting new band, very hip with our own ideas, playing some original material mixed in with covers. But we wouldn't play anything too obvious or that was currently in the charts. Boy, did that change quickly! The first few shows we came out and treated the crowds to a very cool selection of hits from the Everly Brothers, Chuck Berry, some early Elvis, plus a couple of our efforts – and died a death. People either started calling out for requests or simply wandered off.

The clue to what we needed to do to keep the punters happy came each night when Roy took the lead vocal on this really drippy version we did of 'I Can't Help Falling In Love With You', which he sang like a pub singer doing Elvis. It went down an absolute storm, people standing and cheering at the end. That was when we learned another important lesson: ultimately, it didn't matter what songs we liked particularly, it only mattered which songs the audience liked best. This was a rule that would apply, we discovered, even after we'd started making records and having hits. You could follow whatever 'artistic vision' you had on the albums, but God forbid if you didn't play the hit songs live.

Never does that rule apply more than when you are playing live before a paying audience. They are in charge, not you. We learned the bare bones of that fact at Butlin's, and we never forgot it. You could see how all the other acts there adapted what they did to keep the crowds happy. One band, the Olympic

Five, would grind through their set until they came to this one number they did called 'The Hucklebuck', this Chubby Checker tune that had been the follow-up to his most famous hit, 'The Twist', but had never been released in Britain. This band had got hold of the song and really went to town. The drunker the crowd got, the more they absolutely loved it. As soon as the band went into 'The Hucklebuck' the whole place went mad!

We would see this and think, all right, we get it. We knew what we had to do. We just didn't have the right songs yet. What we did have though, after our experience at Butlin's, was a much more dynamic live band and a much greater professionalism. We also had – although we didn't know it yet – a new member of the band. His name was Ricky Harrison and the first time I saw him I was convinced he was gay – although that wasn't the word we would have used back then. He was all blond hair and tight trousers and a big toothy grin. Over-friendly. Which made me suspicious, because I wasn't used to other blokes being so nice. I was used to geezers and hard men. This Ricky Harrison, he wasn't like that at all.

Turned out he was in another of the acts at Butlin's that year – this little cabaret trio called the Highlights, which was Ricky and two girls, twins, called Jean and Gloria Harrison. The girls were dark-haired and Ricky was blond, that was their image. They would start their show with 'Whole Lotta Shakin' Going On' and a couple more crowd-pleasers, then the girls would disappear for a costume change and Ricky would sing 'Baby Face'. Cheesy as hell but the crowds loved it.

They were on at the Gaiety Theatre, which was much more grans and kiddies than the room we were in. The idea was Ricky was the girls' brother – which we believed until he explained that it was all part of the act. That his real name was Richard

Parfitt, but that he'd never liked the Parfitt name anyhow, and was happier as Harrison. It was the girls that had named him Ricky. And, needless to say, far from being their brother he had managed to have affairs of some sort with both of them at different times. This sort of complicated behaviour was, we were soon to discover, very much the way things would carry on for Rick, as I came to know him, for the rest of his life.

Rick had come up and introduced himself to us while we were playing one afternoon. It became obvious pretty quickly that he saw what we did – being in a pop group – as more along the lines of what he wanted to do than singing with the girls. He was a big Cliff Richard fan and he definitely fancied himself in that early Cliff mould as naughty-but-nice rock 'n' roll singer. I liked him straight away, even though I assumed he was a 'poof', which *was* the word we used back then. I admired him for being so camp. When he told me he wasn't a poof I almost didn't believe him.

Rick very quickly became friends with me and Alan. With Roy being that much older and John being a dark horse, as they say, having a new pal my own age to run around with was great fun. Rick had been born seven months before me, making him a Libra – one of the signs that a Gemini like me is meant to get along with. He came from Woking, Surrey, which is effectively deep into the south-west of London – close enough to where Alan and I came from to make him one of us – almost.

Rick was just really nice, easy going and great fun to have around. Unlike me, he didn't seem torn up inside with anxiety and being self-conscious. Things just seemed to come more easily to him. Or that's how it seemed anyway. Rick was an only child and like most only children he'd grown up showered in love and affection. Not spoilt so much as simply feeling he was unbeatable. Always looking on the bright side. Never say die – 'What me, worry?' One of those guys that walks around with a kind of glow, the kind you want to like you. It was partly this and partly because he was so unlike me, more how I wished I could be, that we became such good friends so quickly. It was only much later I discovered how much Rick actually wanted to be more like me, but we'll come to that.

Rick really proved himself to me when I got thrown out of the digs we were staying in at Butlin's, after I was caught sleeping with a girl there. The girl I would marry soon after, in fact. She was named Jean Smith and she was working at Butlin's with her sister, Pat, and I know it sounds corny but the first time I laid eyes on her I told myself: 'I'm gonna marry her.' I just knew.

I'll never forget the morning I got kicked out of my digs because that was the day Jean and I first had sex. She was a virgin – which all 'good' girls were before marriage in those days – ha, bloody, ha – and I had actually had trouble trying to get my willy into her. We tried for two or three nights running before I finally managed to do the deed. It was more relief than anything – for both of us – when we managed at last. I doubt either of us really enjoyed it. We were both just getting going again one morning soon after when the landlady – this feisty Scotswoman – came in and virtually dragged me off Jean.

First she threw Jean out – 'Ya wee tart!' – and then me. I was looking at sleeping on the beach on my own until Rick came to my rescue – by letting Jean have his room, and offering to kip out on the beach with me. We spent the next few nights sleeping under some old deckchairs we made into a kind of makeshift hut. Other nights we curled up in phone boxes or in the stalls of the public toilets.

That was when we first became close. My friendship with Alan was very up and down by this point. We were always falling out. Rick would be very perturbed when he saw us having a fight. One day, we'd just come offstage and the two of us just lit into one another. I've always hated violence. I'd start crying afterwards. But I think Rick was more upset by it than Alan or me. The next thing, Alan got off with one of the twins. I can't remember exactly which one he slept with. They were so alike. But I know Rick was beside himself. He was madly in love with Jean (from his group, not my Jean) – and even though I think it was probably Gloria that Alan got off with, the whole thing did Rick's head in. That said, Rick and Alan got on really well. Again, they were the same age, had similar interests, Alan with his flash suits, Rick with his tight trousers.

When the season came to a close and we all prepared to return home, back to our separate lives, you could tell how sad Rick was. He'd already become part of our gang. It wasn't until later though that he told me he wanted to become part of the group. I just assumed he'd go on to become the next Des O'Connor or something. But we did manage to stay in touch, mainly through Alan. Rick would pop up from time to time, staying the night over at Alan's parents' place. Now and again he would turn up at one of our shows.

It was around this time we finally got to make a record. Pat Barlow had somehow managed to wangle us a deal with Piccadilly Records, a subsidiary of Pye, whose best-known act was Joe Brown and the Bruvvers.

We had recorded a few numbers – just playing them live in a small studio in Soho we rented for the afternoon – and Pat had posted out copies of the tape to various record labels and publishing companies. Absolutely no response until a chap named Ronnie Scott – the head of a songwriting publishing company called Valley Music and not to be confused with the famous British jazz player who later opened his own eponymous club in Soho – phoned Pat out of the blue to say he'd heard the demo, thought it showed 'promise' and would we like to come in and discuss a deal. The result was an invitation to go in and record with the in-house producer at Pye, John Schroeder.

John was an old head on young shoulders. He was only twenty-six when he won an Ivor Novello Award for co-writing 'Walkin' Back to Happiness', a number for Helen Shapiro. He had the John Schroeder Orchestra, which had some easy-listening hits and did things like the theme tunes to TV shows like *The Fugitive*. He was a lovely man, always very encouraging. He would tell Pat: 'The Spectres are *that* much away from greatness!' And snap his fingers. We loved him.

However, our first single with John was a cover of 'I (Who Have Nothing)' – no laughing at the back there! – which had been a big hit in 1963 for Shirley Bassey. Apart from the fact it was based on an Italian song called 'Uno Dei Tanti', I had absolutely no affinity for the song whatsoever. But the people at Piccadilly thought it was a great idea and who were we to argue with a proven hit-maker like John? Also, Alan really liked the song. In fact he actually suggested it, I seem to recall. So like the good boys we were, we did it. You can listen to it today on YouTube but I would consider it a personal favour if you didn't. In the end, everyone from Joe Cocker and Petula Clark to Liza Minnelli, Katherine Jenkins and Donny Osmond did covers of that song and I can assure you our version is still the worst. Let us never speak of it again.

Rick, though, thought this was the most amazing thing that had ever happened. He started trembling when he first held the record in his hands. By then the Highlights had split up and we all knew he was looking for something new. He was working as the driver of a bread van and I really sympathised, knowing how close I had been to driving an ice-cream van. In fact, we all did various part-time jobs to help bring some money in. Alan did a bit of window cleaning sometimes and I worked for a while for the London County Council as a gardener and for a time at the local opticians' shop.

Then Pat Barlow came up with another of his brainstorms. Why didn't we get Rick in the group with us? Some bright spark at Piccadilly had put the idea in Pat's head: that we needed another voice in the group and another guitarist. In fact, he was looking to replace me as the frontman, though that only became clear to me a little later. He was after someone with a better voice. A 'proper' singer. As usual back then, we just went along with it. Plus, Rick was a real friend by then. If it had meant auditioning strangers we probably wouldn't have gone for it. But it was Rick – and he was blond and had those tight trousers. And he could sing. The others also thought it was a good idea. Even Alan, which really surprised me, because he would question every decision, big or small. Later I realised that Pat had rather shrewdly spoken to Alan about it first before mentioning it to the rest of us.

So we told Pat to phone him up and ask him. I think Rick said yes before Pat had even finished getting the question out his mouth. The very next day Rick turned up at the place where we now rehearsed, in this basement in Lambeth Walk below Pat's gas showroom. He set up, plugged in his guitar – and out came this horrendous noise. We hadn't realised until that moment that Rick wasn't particularly good on the guitar. That we'd only ever really seen him play 'Baby Face'.

After he left, the others wanted to get rid of him. But I insisted he stayed. I could see he had something, and of course he could sing, and I thought, well, he could only get better on guitar. The others grumblingly went along with it. Though we did secretly keep his guitar unplugged from the amp for his first gig with us. It was the only time we had to do that though. Rick really saw joining the group as his big opportunity. He was determined to learn fast.

And that's exactly what he did.

Chapter Three

Matchstick Men

Having Rick Parfitt – as he was now properly known – in the group didn't quite work out the way Pat Barlow and the others had imagined. I think they thought they were getting a new frontman who could sing and play guitar. Instead, Rick and I developed almost immediately into the kind of two-man harmony line-up I had always envisaged back in the days when I wanted my brother to join me in an Everly Brothers-style group. By the time Rick joined, the Beatles were the biggest thing going and they had a similar set-up with John Lennon and Paul McCartney. It was the same with Mike Pender and Tony Jackson in the Searchers and lots of other groups of the era like the Merseybeats.

There was also another aspect to Rick joining that really made the group better, at least from my point of view. That was, I liked him! Roy was too old for me to really relate to on a one-to-one level. John was too quiet – until suddenly he wasn't and he erupted. And Alan was too domineering for me to relax around.

Rick was the same age as me, and very easy going. He was just nice. A gentle soul really, with a great sense of humour.

He could also be very sensitive. That was definitely something I hadn't experienced from the rest of the group. As a teenager, if I got fed up or pissed off I would often cry. Alan would be apoplectic. 'Stop crying! You're embarrassing me!' But Rick would actually come up and give me a hug and try and comfort me. He was always a hugger.

The very first gig he did with us I lent him some of my clothes because he didn't have any trendy stage gear of his own – or so he kept saying. He actually had some nice gear but he wanted to make sure whatever he wore fitted in with the rest of us. We really were like brothers. On the early tours, we would sometimes share a bed. Not in a Bowie or Elton sort of way, I should add. More like Morecambe and Wise in those sketches where they would lie in bed together bickering and making fun of each other. Young men often did share beds in those days. Or if it was twin beds we would push them together. This was fine until one of us would pull a bird. On many occasions, Rick would be in one bed with some girl and I would be in the bed next to them, having to listen to what was going on. He had a row with one girl and she got up and said, 'I need a piss,' and went to the toilet. I remember thinking: classy. Then when she came back she said, 'I feel like knifing someone.' I didn't sleep another wink that night. Neither did Rick.

Because everyone always just assumed Rick was gay in those days – he and I would ham it up on occasion, holding hands in public. That would send Alan and John – the macho guys – completely insane. Especially Alan, who I think, genuinely, had his doubts about us. To put it in context and help understand such prejudices, it's only fair to point out that homosexuality was illegal in Britain until 1967. Being openly 'queer' could get you in all sorts of trouble, starting with the law – and ending, if you weren't careful, with Alan yelling at you.

The live music scene had changed while we'd been away all summer and the sort of beat-group, sub freak-out stuff we'd been doing in the Spectres was out of date. We had also released a second single – 'Hurdy Gurdy Man'. No, not the superb Donovan hit from a year later but a little ditty that Alan had come up with. It was very bouncy and poppy and a complete flop. There was a third single, called '(We Ain't Got) Nothing Yet', a cover of a song that had been a hit in America earlier that year for the Blues Magoos. I thought we might stand a chance with that one as we pretty much copied the original note for note and it was very catchy. But no, that died a death too.

It was the beginning of the mod era and new London outfits like the Small Faces, the Kinks and the Who. Suddenly Pat was finding it nearly impossible to book the Spectres, so we changed our name to The Traffic – until it was announced a few months later that Steve Winwood of the Spencer Davis Group had left to form a new band – called Traffic. It didn't seem fair that he could do that as we'd been there first, as it were. But he was Steve Winwood, who'd had number 1 records with 'Keep On Running' and 'Gimme Some Lovin'', and I was still mowing lawns. So we changed our name to Traffic Jam – take that, gobshite! We also ditched the straight suits and skinny ties and 'experimented' with open-necked shirts with patterns on them. Crazy, man!

Pat, bless him, did everything he could to keep the show on the road. As Traffic Jam we got more gigs and even landed a spot on Radio 1's *Saturday Club*, a popular Saturday morning show hosted by Brian Matthew. We also picked up some paying gigs providing support for some American acts, most notably

P. J. Proby, who was more famous by then for splitting the crotch of his trousers onstage than he was for his hits. We also worked with a female vocal group called the Dixie Cups, who'd had hits like 'Chapel of Love' and 'Iko Iko'. They were great girls. What I remember most of that job though was getting to know their guitarist, this very cool black guy who was the first person to really make me aware of what a big role marijuana and amphetamines played in so many musicians' lives.

Up till then we had steered well clear of anything like that. We knew about 'uppers', as they were called. And we'd heard about 'dope smokers'. But like most teenagers in the mid-sixties that was the sum total of our knowledge, other than drugs were 'bad' and might make you think you could walk off the top of a building. It would be another couple of years before we really got stuck in. Touring with the Small Faces was the turning point for all that. They smoked joints as often as they smoked cigarettes, took speed every day, and were heavy into psychedelics, although the whole LSD thing was something I never personally enjoyed and steered well clear of. Instead, Stevie Marriott, the brilliant singer and guitarist of the Small Faces, became the guy who got Rick and me into sharing a half-bottle of brandy before we went onstage each night, and a joint afterwards. Until then John Coghlan was the only one who ever had a few beers. The rest of us were still drinking Tizer.

I really enjoyed touring with those guys. Stevie and the boys and I shared a lot of the same tastes in clothes. Because of the image of Quo that would emerge in the seventies of the double-denim and long hair, people don't realise what a clotheshorse I've always been. Back in the sixties when we were making our first records, I was mad about clothes. The right shoes, the right shirts and jackets. You would be in some boutique in Carnaby Street and you would bump into Rod Stewart or Stevie Marriott and it would be a competition to see who could get their hands on the best clobber first. To this day, I always like to dress smartly, even if I'm only at home relaxing. I'm not a gym-pants and trainers guy at all. I like proper shirts with the top button done up and I like my shoes to be polished. I don't really like slovenliness in other people either. Call me superficial if you like but I am a great believer in 'clothes maketh the man'.

The other big change in my life in 1967 came when I married my Butlin's sweetheart Jean Smith. She was now a mod, too, and I'd been obsessed with the girl from the moment I met her but it had been an on-off kind of thing between us and I look back now and see how that also added to the allure. When you can't have the thing you think you want most in the world, it drives you to want it even more, especially when it involves matters of the heart.

To begin with, Jean had scarpered after the time we got caught in bed together and my landlady threw me out. While I was roughing it on the beach with Rick, Jean had quit her job and run off with a pal to find another job at some other seaside holiday camp. When I found out I was devastated. No mobile phones in those days, no way of instantly staying in touch, so I didn't hear another word from her for three weeks. I just assumed she'd run off and left me. Then suddenly she was back. I was overjoyed, thinking my worries were over. Instead it was just the start of Jean running off and leaving me whenever things got rough, then coming back and me being pathetically grateful. Teenage love. Thank God I never have to go through that again.

Then the ultimate bombshell: Jean was pregnant with our baby. I was just seventeen when she found out. That would be big news today. Back in 1967 that was the clincher. There was absolutely no question of not having the baby. Abortion wasn't even legal in Britain at the time. Then, as a Catholic, that was never going to be an option anyway. Plus, and this was the real reason, I was madly in love with her. That left just one option: getting married. Which is what we did in June 1967 – the so-called summer of love. Because Jean was seven months pregnant at the time, a proper Catholic wedding was not allowed so we simply had one of those I-do-you-do quickie jobs at the local register office.

The only other people there were my mum and dad, Jean's mum and her sister. My mum wasn't going to come at all. She was so aghast at us not being able to get married in a Catholic church she wanted nothing to do with it. Then she acquiesced on the day. I had turned eighteen just a couple of weeks before and did my best to treat the whole affair as a sort of very with-it, Swinging London type deal. No suit. Instead I wore my Carnaby Street stage clothes, which at the time meant a yellow-and-green striped blazer, pink shirt and white trousers. Jean, whose tummy was huge, wore a flowery pale green smock. She looked amazing, actually.

There was no honeymoon. I don't think it even crossed our minds. It was all about making sure the baby wasn't born out of wedlock. The day after the wedding we moved into the spare room at Jean's mother's house in Dulwich. Her husband had died a few years before so she had plenty of room. Two months later our son, Simon, was born. Married couples having kids at such a young age was much more common then. In my case, it was no big deal as I'd always had a big extended family around me and all the kids were brought up equally among the various relatives. Nevertheless, it was never going to be easy under the circumstances — teenage parents trying to bring up a baby while one of them was working away a lot — but the whole set-up conspired against us making a proper go of it. Jean's mother wasn't much help. Jean had always kept me from meeting her mum before we were married. Now I found out why. The woman could be very difficult. It was as though she had leapt straight from the pages of a Les Dawson joke about mothers-in-law. She would sit slumped in the armchair, chain-smoking, with her old-fashioned dress pulled up around her hips so that you could see her big old-lady knickers and she would do the most evil-smelling farts. Much to her poor daughter's annoyance and embarrassment.

She also didn't really understand or care about whatever it was I thought I was doing poncing around in a pop group instead of getting a proper job. My own family probably felt much the same but didn't show it so much. The way they looked at it, I suppose, was that if and when the music thing didn't work out for me, I had a job waiting for me on the ice-cream vans. All Jean's mum knew, though, was that I wasn't around much at night and that I was around too much during the day. She was in Jean's ear about it too. And so it started. 'We've got a baby now. It's time you stopped messing around wasting your time in the group and settled down and started bringing in money for the family.' It got to the point where Jean gave me an ultimatum: 'It's either me or the group!' Again, it's one of those things that happen to almost all aspiring young musicians at some point. So much so it becomes another rite of passage where you have to choose which road you're on. In my case, I simply said: 'You knew about the group before we got married, you knew that's the way it was. If you want to change your mind now then fine, but I'm sticking to what I said I was gonna do.'

She accused me of being cold, unfeeling, uncaring. But I had been crazy about this girl. I loved my son. And I knew that if something good didn't happen for the group soon I probably would have to get that 'proper job' after all. Apart from the grief about giving up the group, I loved being married and being a young father. I took the whole business of having children extremely seriously. But even this became something Jean and I couldn't see eye-to-eye on. I believed in being strict, in having rules, boundaries, teaching your children right from wrong. Jean was more sixties about the whole thing. She used to tell people: 'My children will be able to do anything they want.' I would say, 'No, they bloody won't!' and another argument would kick off.

In the end, I took to locking myself in the toilet. It was the only place in the house where I could guarantee myself five minutes' peace. It was pretty horrible, this freezing toilet with a cold, hard wooden seat. It was more like a cupboard than a room. But I began spending longer and longer in there. I even started bringing my guitar in there with me. It was so small I had to hold the guitar up vertically. But I'd be in there for hours, my feet up against the wall, toying with the guitar and singing to myself.

At the urging of John Schroeder I had begun writing my own songs. We were all having a go. The fact that the Beatles and the Rolling Stones and the Who and the Kinks all wrote their own material meant we had to try and emulate those feats if we wanted to be seen in the same bracket. Otherwise you did what groups like The Hollies and Manfred Mann did and went around to all the music publishers in Denmark Street. My first attempt became our one and only single as Traffic Jam. It was called 'Almost But Not Quite There', and as a song that described it perfectly. For some reason I can no longer remember the song is credited to Pat Barlow and me. The lyrics were definitely mine though and concern the age-old problem of leaving your sexual partner 'almost but not quite there'. Clever, I thought at the time. Until the BBC decided the words were 'too suggestive' and promptly banned the record.

Having just gotten married I did start to think that maybe Jean and her mother were right and I should think seriously about trying my hand at something else. I'd spoken to my dad about working for him on one of the ice-cream vans. Word had got back to us that the people at the record company were also having serious doubts too. The only one who wanted to give it one more go was John Schroeder. This probably had more to do with John thinking about his own reputation in the business than any greater concern with our career – he had enjoyed a lot of success, and he didn't want to have to chalk us up as a failure.

It was decided we would go into the studio with John one final time and see what could be done. It was make or break time. We were all painfully aware of that, none more so than me as I'd taken it upon myself to be the one to try and come up with a song that had real hit potential. I was desperate not to be forced into quitting the group and – dreaded phrase – settling down. Which is how I found myself with my guitar locked in the toilet at home again one day. Until then I'd deliberately been trying to ape the sounds of other groups in the charts, picking up little phrases here and there, imitating choruses.

Now I fell back on something much more fundamental to my musical upbringing. For some reason, I had 'Poppa Piccolino' in my head, the song I used to love as a kid. In particular that jolly little melody that pulls at your sleeve. I started messing around with it on the guitar, slowing it down and making it more sort of freaky 1967 style. I also had the Jimi Hendrix version of 'Hey Joe' in my head. I loved his version and in particular that ultra-groovy gunslinger guitar. So I started messing around with that too. Next thing, more out of idle curiosity than serious intent, I kind of put the two together – the itchy intro to 'Poppa Piccolino' and the lazy guitar strut of 'Hey Joe' – and I had this whole new thing that actually sounded really good.

By now, Jean and her mother had gone out with the baby so I let myself out of the toilet and set myself up again on the couch. I started improvising these sort of spacey lyrics – until I had a title and a song called 'Pictures of Matchstick Men'. People always assume because of the title that I took inspiration from the famous L. S. Lowry pictures of the industrial north. In fact, that had nothing to do with it. Really it was me just trying to imagine what it was like to take LSD.

I sat there on the couch playing the new song over and over. One minute I thought it was the best thing I'd done. The next I thought it was a bit of a joke, just a novelty song I'd patched together. I couldn't get it out of my head though. Then I played it to the group and they all liked it too. The real test though came when we went into the studio to make what we knew might be our last record with John Schroeder. John listened, liked it well enough, and said it would make a good B-side for the next single. He meant it as a compliment but I was knocked back. The song John had planned for us to record as the A-side was this really rather mediocre song called 'Gentleman Jim's Sidewalk Café'. It was exactly the kind of cod sixties crap that we'd already failed with.

Once we'd recorded both tracks, though, John's innate talent for spotting a hit came through and he suggested flipping the tracks, so that 'Pictures of Matchstick Men' was now the A-side. The only change to the track he suggested was to the vocal. I had originally sung it falsetto. John said to try it in my natural singing voice, which I did and – bang! – suddenly we had something. We all knew it the minute we sat back to listen to the finished track. Then John added some final touches to make it really stand out on the little two-inch speakers of a transistor radio – the way most people listened to music back then on the radio: that lovely wah-wah guitar that shimmers between the verses and that phasing audio effect that the Small Faces had used on their 'Itchycoo Park' single, which was in the charts at the time.

We recorded the track in October 1967 and it was scheduled for release the first week of January 1968. Before that we had another small detail to attend to: yet another change of name. The palaver at the BBC over the 'Almost But Not Quite There' single had left a stink over the name Traffic Jam. Plus, Steve Winwood's Traffic had already enjoyed no fewer than three massive hit singles since then. Pat got his thinking cap on again and came up with what he thought would be a great new name for us – the Crow Bars. We were in the middle of rehearsing in his basement when he came down the stairs and suggested that one. We sent him straight back up the stairs again with a boot up his arse.

The next one he came up with was even worse: The Muhammad Alis. Pat thought this was particularly good as we could then use the slogan: 'They're the Greatest!' As a group, we did consider this one, which just shows you how desperate we were to keep the group going. Fortunately for us, Pat couldn't get the necessary legal permission to use Ali's name so we were back to square one.

Pat's next idea, though, was a good one. We'd told him we needed something that sounded really up-to-date, like Pink Floyd or Amen Corner. Pat excelled himself this time and came up with Quo Vadis, which was the name on the label inside his shoes. We agreed it definitely had a certain ring to it. The shoe thing was a bit off-putting though. Then someone — almost certainly Pat — suggested 'The Status Quo' and we knew straight away that that was the one. It was one of those phrases that was just around at the time — young people were always talking about challenging the status quo. It was 1967, the Beatles had changed the world from black and white to colour with the *Sgt. Pepper's Lonely Hearts Club Band* album. Young men were burning their draft-cards in Central Park, New York. In Britain we now had Radio 1, the *International Times* and Mick Jagger being sent to prison for dope. Pat pointed out that people would be mentioning the band without even realising it. Heavy, man! I wasn't so sure about that. All I knew is that I really liked the name — the Status Quo. Like the Rolling Stones, the Pink Floyd and the Small Faces.

Then 'Pictures of Matchstick Men' came out in the New Year — and nothing happened. That was it for me. I had passed my driving test in December 1967, then spoken to my dad again about driving one of his vans. He had actually ordered a new ice-cream van, which I was at home waiting to take possession of when the phone rang and it was Pat. He said, 'The bloody single has only gone in the top 30!'

You what? You what? You fucking what? It was what they call a slow-burner. Radio Caroline had played the record a couple of times, so then some London stations picked up on it. Then Radio 1 got hold of it and spun it a couple of times. The next thing we're in the top 30 and it's on the radio all the time. The following week it had gone up to number 11 and the week after number 7. And then we were invited onto *Top of the Pops*! Look, Mum, we're on the telly!

Even people old enough to remember what a weekly institution *Top of the Pops* was for most of its forty-year existence probably need reminding what a huge deal it was to be on there back in 1968. With only two national TV stations in the UK at the time (yes, there was BBC2, but you needed a special aerial to receive it so only a small percentage of people had it), to be invited on to perform your latest single on *Top of the Pops* was to guarantee you a massive-selling hit. So it proved with 'Pictures of Matchstick Men'. Although it only got to number 7 in the British charts, it went gold for us, for sales over one million. It also went on to become probably our biggest hit single around the rest of the world, reaching the top 10 in dozens of different countries. It also became our only big hit in America, where it reached number 12. It became such a big hit for us that we didn't realise how successful it was until years later. No social media or internet to keep a check on things like that back then; you relied solely on what the record companies told you and they weren't in a hurry to tell you much in case you started asking tricky questions like, 'Where are all my royalties then?' Particularly the ones in America.

We were so skint at the time we did *Top of the Pops* that we were on tour working as the backing group for the beautiful black American singer Madeline Bell, who would become really famous a couple of years later in the group Blue Mink. She had her first solo album out, *Bell's a Poppin'*, and she was a great singer and an amazing performer. We would end the show each night doing a duet together on 'It Takes Two', which had been a hit a couple of years before for Marvin Gaye and Kim Weston. It was the last number of the night and at the end we would kiss. Just on the lips. The first time we did it spontaneously and we started doing it every night. Then one night in Manchester, some arsehole in the audience yelled: 'Fuckin' hell, lads! Didja see that? Fuckin' nigger kissed him!'

It was a horrible, excruciating moment and I felt so ashamed – for being white, for being male, for coming from the same country as whoever this wanker was. Madeline, who'd been putting up with crap like that her whole life, just shrugged it off. But it was a real lesson to me. I'd put up with racist slurs when I was a kid but I'd assumed I'd left all that behind me. Wrong again. In fact, you only had to pick up on TV shows like *Till Death Us Do Part*, and the ravings about 'sambos' and 'coons' of the hugely popular Alf Garnett, to gauge how far behind the times we still were in Britain. It was satire but the vast majority of people didn't get that. They just loved Alf for being 'outspoken'. We lived in a world where we still talked of 'coloured people' and gollywogs.

Life was full of hard-won lessons suddenly. After the tour ended, when I did get around to asking about where the money was from all the sales of 'Pictures' I discovered, the same as almost everybody else did back then – and to this day, I have no doubt – that our deal with Pye entitled us to exactly half a per cent of the wholesale price of the record. A single in 1967 retailed for about seven shillings, or 35p in today's money. Wholesale price would have been approximately half that. Which meant we received approximately 0.087 pence per copy sold. My arithmetic might be off there but let's just call it bollocks. We had a slightly better deal with Valley Music in terms of songwriting royalties, but even that was heavily watered-down after they'd licensed the song innumerable times to various labels around the world, hardly any of which ever reported back sales or royalties – at least not to us. That's before you get into all the tricky little clauses in the contracts that cover such things as the recording of the material, everybody's wages and 'breakages' – which related back to the old shellac disc days when records broke very easily, but had little to do with the new wobbly vinyl we were releasing our music on – all of which gets deducted from your income.

None of which, I have to be honest and admit, overly concerned me when I received my first royalty cheque for 'Pictures' – £1,200. Roughly speaking, around £20,000 in today's money, though you also have to factor in that the purchasing power was huge in 1968 compared to now. For £1,200 in 1968 you could get a mortgage on a decent-sized house in south London, or a flash new car like a Ford Capri (whey-hey!) for about £800. So I nearly fell over when I opened the letter containing the cheque. I thought, it must be a mistake. I won't tell anybody in case they ask for it back. Then I showed Rick and he started to hyperventilate. But he was pleased for me. He also vowed to try writing some more songs. None of us ever expected to make that much money out of the group. Suddenly everyone wanted to come up with a song for our next single. This could be a pain in the arse. Not because I wanted to hog the limelight but because the others would come up with some daft ideas. Alan decided we should be making music like Pink Floyd and wrote a song called 'Sunny Cellophane Skies', which he also sang. It wasn't at all bad, but it wasn't 'Interstellar Overdrive'. Rick and I also had our first real goes at trying to write together, coming up with 'When My Mind Is Not Live', this time with Rick singing lead vocal. It was very much a song of its time, to put it politely. Meaning: about as cheesy and self-consciously 'sixties' as our stage clothes were at the time.

The biggest culprit in trying too hard to come up with an obvious follow-up to 'Pictures', though, was me when I wrote the song that did become our next single, the cringe-inducing

'Black Veils of Melancholy'. Apart from the horrid title, it was essentially 'Pictures' all over again, only not as good. Right down to the – cover your ears! – 'Poppa Piccolino' guitar tickle at the intro. That said, no one was more surprised than me when it spectacularly failed to follow the success of 'Pictures'. I thought I'd cracked it, reinvented the wheel: done the classic follow-up, same as the original but just a bit different to keep you interested. That was just supposed to be the way things worked back then. Wrong. I'd come up with a dud. Oh dear . . .

By then I'd spent the money I'd made from 'Pictures' on a deposit for a place of our own for me, Jean and Simon. I'd managed to get us out of Jean's mum's house by then, thank God, but only as far as a room in my parents' house. Now, with the royalties I received, I was able to afford to rent us a flat in Lordship Lane, Dulwich. Bob Young and his wife had rented a flat in the same building. It was probably Bob who told me about the empty flat. Our place was directly above theirs, and both flats were above the local Co-op supermarket on the side of the building where they had their own morgue. I believe you can still get very reasonably priced funerals from the Co-op. Bob and I would joke about ghosts but neither Jean nor I gave a shit. It was just great to finally have a place of our own.

What was left of my royalty money went back into keeping the band afloat. When 'Black Veils' was a flop I really did think I'd dropped a bollock. For all I knew, we were destined to only have one hit. Thankfully, things didn't go that way. In fact, over the years, 'Pictures of Matchstick Men' has turned up in all sorts of unexpected places, from the soundtracks to movies like *Men in Black III* and computer games like *Mafia 3*, to cover versions by Camper Van Beethoven and even Ozzy Osbourne.

The thing most people in Britain recall most about the single, though, is of course the clip of us miming to it on *Top of the Pops* in all our 'swinging' Carnaby Street clobber, which seems to turn up on every documentary ever made about the 1960s.

We certainly had a look. We couldn't take any credit for that though. It was this young gun named Tim Boyle who turned us on to all that. Tim worked as an agent at the Arthur Howe agency and booked all our gigs. It was Tim who first took us to places like Take 6, Lord John and the Carnaby Cavern in Carnaby Street. We got to know the main guy, Colin, who was also one of the usual dancers in the audience at *Top of the Pops*. Colin was ultra cool and would tip us off as to which other groups had been in that week and bought clothes. You'd pull a jacket out and Colin would go, 'No, don't pick that, Stevie Marriott was here yesterday and he bought one the same.'

Rick and I had our trousers specially made for us at a place in Soho called Bona Clouts – real crotch-grabbers with massive 22-inch bell bottoms. We'd have our hair styled in the same places all the other groups did too. It was a real scene. One of the major worries when 'Black Veils' was a flop was that we wouldn't be able to afford to go to any of these places again. Not long before that, Pat had sat us all down at rehearsal one day and told us: 'OK, boys. You can now all give up your day jobs. From now on I want you to only concentrate on this.' By then we had our own tour manager, which felt very big time, and we were out on one of those multi-act package tours you got back then, doing twenty-minute sets alongside Gene Pitney and Love Affair. Suddenly it looked like we might be applying for our old jobs back. We were living on our nerves, in that respect. Even when things went well, as with 'Matchstick Men', none of us ever thought we would last as a group more than five years, tops, if we were lucky. That's very much the way things were back then. And if we weren't lucky – well, the charts were littered with acts that were one-hit wonders. You'd be in despair when a record didn't do well, which at that stage was most of the time, and over the moon when one did, like 'Matchstick Men', but only for a couple of days before you started worrying again about whether you would be able to follow it up.

Fortunately, this time we were saved by the songwriting team of Marty Wilde and Ronnie Scott, who gifted us a really catchy little ditty called 'Ice in the Sun'. Marty had made his name as a singer in his own right in the late fifties with successful covers of American hits like 'A Teenager in Love' and 'Sea of Love'. Ronnie was an original pop impresario, promoter, manager and hit songwriter. Both of them were old-school hit-makers and, frankly, we were lucky to have them on our side. Ronnie worked for Valley Music and Marty had already recorded his own version of the song, which I thought was really good. It was backed with a full orchestra but what we did with it was much more 'psychedelic pop' – which Marty had overseen himself in the studio. The masterstroke was when, on an inspired whim, he ran a coin over some piano strings – making that little zing sound you hear on the chorus. It was like adding tinsel to a Christmas present, the finishing touch that set the rest of it off nicely.

It certainly did the trick for us, giving us our second top 10 hit that year. God, I was pleased. Though mainly just relieved. We lived to fight another day, and spend even more money in some expensive Carnaby Street boutique. On a practical level it meant we could now go out and headline some shows on our own, at which we even started to get screaming teenage girls. Well, usually about fifty of them a night. But who's counting? All right, we were. Especially Rick, who would get very jealous when girls would write their names and phone numbers in lipstick on the side of our van. I used to get the most. 'I love you Mike xxx' — as I still was then. Not because of my looks — Rick was always going to be the winner in the group in that department — just because I was the singer. I understood that. Rick, though, didn't like that at all. He even took to writing his own name in lipstick on the van when he thought we weren't looking. 'I love you Ricky xxx'. He used to consider himself the master-forger but we all knew it was Rick using his own lipstick.

Did we ever take advantage of the situation, though? Of course we did. We were teenage boys living high on the hog at the height of the free-love sixties. It would have been weird not to make the most of it. It didn't mean I didn't love Jean and my baby son. It just meant I was a normal, hot-blooded, stupid teenage boy. Not just that but one that had been on the telly and now had screaming girl fans throwing themselves at him. The fact that we would be away on the road, staying in a different hotel every night, only added to the temptation. The next morning though I would always be filled with remorse, thinking: what have I done? I'm not going to lie and say we all felt like that. None of the others were married or had kids yet. They were entitled to do whatever they pleased. For me, it was a big deal, though. Even later on, when we became properly famous around the world and the temptation and opportunities were even greater, I always used to get my mind in a tangle about it. I would find myself in my room after a show with some drop-dead gorgeous girl and I'd be in the bathroom pretending to have a piss, already changing my mind, wondering how best to get rid of her. Then when I came out she'd already be in the bed. Well, what was a poor lapsed Catholic boy to do?

I wouldn't say we were getting too big for our boots but we were starting to get used to being on the telly and radio. Walking into the dressing room, we'd sing, 'Hi ho, hi ho/We are the Status Quo/With a number one we'll have some fun/Hi ho, hi ho . . .' It was Alan that came up with that one.

The other really big thrill was putting out our first album, which we did in September 1968. In another in-no-way-intended-to-cash-in-on-our-biggest-success move, the album was titled *Picturesque Matchstickable Messages from the Status Quo*. The title was another Alan suggestion and, to be fair, we thought it was very clever. You could see what we were going for. It was a bloody silly title, though, which of course proved to be too much of a mouthful for people to ask for in record shops. Nevertheless, it did sneak into the UK top 10 for a couple of weeks and went top 10 in West Germany and number 12 in France. Considering we hadn't even played yet in those countries it was pretty mind-boggling to be told that.

The other reason I was pleasantly surprised, shall we say, is that, to be honest, I didn't think it was very good. Albums – LPs, as they were known – were still second thoughts to most record companies back then, unless you were the Beatles, and we were definitely not in that category. As a result, the twelve tracks on the LP included eight tracks that had been singles or B-sides already, shored up with covers of things like 'Spicks and Specks', an old Bee Gees hit from 1966, 'Sheila', another old hit, this time from Tommy Roe, and 'Green Tambourine', which had been a big hit for the Lemon Pipers not long before.

It also contained what was supposed to have been our next single, a fairly dreadful bit of pop plod called 'Technicolour Dreams', which had been written by a mate of John Schroeder's named Anthony King. It was kind of like 'Pictures' all over again but without any of its redeeming features, like a memorable chorus and verse and intro and . . . oh, forget it. As long as it was a hit we weren't worried. Only we never got a chance to find out. Pye scrapped it when the LP dropped out of the charts. It meant we ended 1968, our big breakthrough year, on a bit of a low.

Determined to take the bit between our teeth and really make sure we came up with a sure-fire hit this time, Rick and I sat down together and wrote a song called 'Make Me Stay a Bit Longer'. Listening back to it now, it might just be the first thing we ever did as a group that contained musical signs of the band we would become in the seventies. It didn't have that insistent shuffle that we would perfect on our biggest seventies hits, but it certainly had a more straight-ahead rock feel than any of the singles we had put out as the Status Quo before then. Rick and I were fairly chuffed with it. It was released in January 1969, just as we were about to go on tour in West Germany with the Small Faces. Both 'Pictures' and 'Ice in the Sun' had hit the charts there so we were really looking forward to it. We were bolstered by the fact that as we left 'Make Me Stay a Bit Longer' was picking up rave reviews in music papers like *Disc* and *Melody Maker*. We kept phoning home to find out where it was in the charts – only to be told it hadn't even got into the top 100.

When we got back from the tour we were so disillusioned that Rick and I started talking about leaving and forming our own group. At one point Rick and I had managed to persuade Pat to sack Alan. But then we had some gigs coming up so we agreed to take him back on a three-month trial – that lasted for the next twenty years. By now, though, it was clear to me that Rick was the only real friend I had in the group. Alan still thought of himself as the leader and was just harder to get along with than Rick, while John and Roy were older and less relatable to us at that age. Plus, Rick and I thought we'd written a pretty good song together. The music critics seemed to agree. But for some reason it had flopped as a Quo single. I don't know if a touch of it's-not-us-it's-them crept into our thinking, or whether we were just fed up of being in a band with Alan, who still treated us like we were lucky to be in his group, or John, who could fly off the handle and be very off sometimes. It was probably to do with all of those things. We were just looking for excuses probably. Also, we had just had a really enjoyable few weeks on the road with the Small Faces, who Rick and I just felt we had more in common with at that stage. They were cheeky chappies. We were cheeky chappies. They had come back to London knowing that Stevie Marriott was about to leave the group and that it was probably the end for them. At which point, me, Rick and Small Faces drummer Kenney Jones came up with the great idea of forming a band together.

Our bright idea was we were going to form a power trio. You have to remember, power trios were all the rage at that point. There was Jimi Hendrix with his band the Experience; Taste with Rory Gallagher; Blue Cheer, who were a huge American band. Biggest and best of all was Cream, with Eric Clapton, Ginger Baker and Jack Bruce. The fact that Cream had just broken up and Jimi Hendrix had now gone beyond the idea of a power trio, bringing in all sorts of extra musicians, had left a gap in the market, we felt.

It just seemed to be the way music was going in 1969. The flower-power era was over and bands were getting 'heavy', to use the then latest phrase. Stevie Marriott had left the Small Faces with the ambition of starting a much heavier-sounding group, which he did with Humble Pie. Even the Beatles had abandoned the whole *Sgt. Pepper's* thing and released a hard-rocking single with 'Get Back'.

So there we were, me on lead guitar (though how I ever hoped to be thought of in the same bracket as Hendrix or Clapton I don't know) and Rick switching from rhythm guitar to bass, and Kenney on drums, jamming for all we were worth in secret in this rehearsal room in west London and . . . it just wasn't happening. Expecting Rick to switch to bass wasn't even the half of it. We would probably have gotten a dedicated bassist in anyway and let Rick get back to rhythm guitar, which he was getting really good at, if things had developed. It was Kenney, bless his heart. He was brilliant at improvising on the drums but he just couldn't stop playing. It was like he'd been let off the leash and just went wild, all crazy rhythms and percussive beats. It was great – except it didn't leave any room for me and Rick to come in, or not for long anyway. After the first day Rick and I looked at each other and went, 'Er, it's not working, is it?' The next day we were back rehearsing with Quo. We never told them. They found out eventually, of course, but by then it was much later and things had changed again.

Chapter Four

Three Grand Deutsche Car

We came home to more doom and gloom when our next single, released in April 1969, barely scraped into the top 50 – another song by John Schroeder's mate Anthony King, a horrible, soppy ballad that Rick sang lead vocal on this time called 'Are You Growing Tired of My Love'. It didn't help that Rick was being told to sing it like a Bee Gees song. It was all very hit and miss, with an even gloomier B-side written – and sung – by Alan called 'So Ends Another Life'. We had only been the Status Quo for barely a year and we were now officially has-beens. Still, we'd managed to come back before – we would again, right?

Maybe.

Looking back now you can see the seeds that were sown for the rewards we would reap a couple of years later, but at the time 1969 felt like one big downer. Even the songs we were recording sound flat and uninspired now. At the same time, we were all starting to write more – including the first co-writes with our road manager, Bob Young, who I would later go on to write some of the band's biggest hits with. We met Bob in 1968 when he was working as tour manager for Amen Corner. We were on one of those package bills together with Gene Pitney as the headliner. Bob had been offered another job with Jethro Tull, who were big news at the time. They had offered him £10 a week. We offered him £15. Bob came with us.

He was a great road manager, which is what we needed, but more than that he was just a thoroughly good bloke, a few years older than us, enough for us to respect his greater experience but not enough to make him an outsider. So we pinched him. Prior to becoming a roadie, Bob had been in a group called the Attack and he could sing and play. In Basingstoke, where he came from, he'd run a blues and folk club where he also performed. It was one of those places where people got up and recited poetry. Bob was one of them. It meant he was also good at lyrics – an art I hadn't quite mastered yet. Some people might say I still haven't quite mastered it and when I'm feeling particularly down I might even agree with them. The reality is, though, that with Bob as my new songwriting partner I was about to come up with some of the biggest hits of the 1970s. Practice makes perfect is what they say and it's as true of songwriting as it is anything else. Also, once you've written one hit, you've overcome that obstacle in your mind. You know you can do it again. It's just a question of hanging on in there long enough to get the chance. Then, once you've had two, three, four . . . you don't even question it any more. You just expect the goods to come to you every time you sit down with a guitar. They don't, of course, but that's another lesson you learn as you go through your career. Thankfully I hadn't gotten to that hurdle yet.

Quite soon, we had him up onstage with us playing harmonica. Next thing, he's jamming with us while we are messing around trying to write songs. Him and Roy Lynes got on well. They were about the same age and Bob was good at putting words to some of the melodies Roy came up with on his keyboards. Alan Lancaster then jumped in. Between them they helped come up with four of the twelve tracks that would make up our second album, *Spare Parts*. Rick and I were also writing together but only three of our songs made it onto the album – which was fair enough as Alan and Bob were coming up with better stuff than us at that stage.

The only thing none of us were able to come up with was another hit single. This led to us recording what was meant to be a sure-fire hit: a cover of a Goffin–King song called 'You're Just What I Was Looking for Today'. The Jerry Goffin–Carole King songwriting partnership had come up with some of the biggest hits of the sixties. The Everly Brothers had done a demo of the song a couple of years before but not released it for some reason and it was really up and catchy. Loving the Everlys as I did, I thought we were definitely onto a winner. But the version we did of it was so slow and painful it sounded like a funeral march – or a funeral crawl, to be more precise. We managed to turn a great soulful song into a dirge. Pye refused to release it as a single.

Instead, we ended up recording a cover of a song the Everly Brothers had actually written, which had been a huge hit for them in 1965, called 'The Price of Love'. Another version of the song by Bryan Ferry would also be a top 10 hit in 1976. Our version, though, was even more turgid than the Goffin–King monstrosity – and was decidedly not a hit. At which point, Pye went into full panic mode and, in an effort to try and make back some of the money they had spent on us since our last hit eighteen months before, stuck out a 'greatest hits' album called *Status Quo-tations*. This was basically some of the tracks from our two albums thrown together with our only two hit singles. It came out in time for Christmas as we slogged away on the road playing every ballroom, college, club and youth centre in Britain – and was also not a hit.

The only bright spots were when we played some more shows in West Germany. Our records were still doing reasonably well there – even 'Are You Growing Tired of My Love' had reached the top 30. So we were able to get on the telly there and headline a few shows every other month. The rest of the time, though, it was sheer drudgery. For our first year as the Status Quo, following the success of 'Pictures of Matchstick Men', we had been treated as pop stars. We had been dressed, our hair styled, our singles picked for us, our whole career mapped out for us by the record company. All we had to do was show up and smile. Now all that went out the window. We weren't getting any new clothes and the Carnaby Street clobber was now out of date. Our hair was getting longer and nobody cared. It felt like maybe even John Schroeder and Pat Barlow were losing interest.

It was during this very low time for us, though, that we slowly began to figure out our own path. Rick and I had gotten to know Colin Johnson, one of the main bookers for the NEMS agency, who was closer to our age, and always full of energy and knowhow. He had a charisma we liked. Nothing seemed to faze him, unlike poor Pat Barlow, who was struggling to know what to do with us now that our music and image was changing. It was nothing we had planned particularly but our evolution from pop group to rock band was now underway. Pat had been like a father to us but he would probably admit he had now taken us as far as he could, with his limited dealings in the music business back then. Colin was also very paternal in his attitude toward us but he had that confidence that comes from having worked with a lot of different bands in the business. He also made us laugh. We felt by going with Colin we would be in safe hands again. Colin just seemed to have his finger on the pulse of where music was going at the start of the seventies. I hated having to tell Pat, though. He'd driven us around when we were still kids at school. He'd fought for us to get our record deal. He'd been there when we had our first big hit. But he'd also been there while we were having our many misses.

I felt terrible, we all did, and in the end we sat down and wrote him a letter. Bob Young actually helped us compose it. We rationalised it by saying if we wrote him a letter then we could put down our thoughts in black and white. Which was true. Except the real reason was we didn't have the bottle to tell him to his face. So we wrote this letter and posted it. In the years to come, we would see more people come and go. I grew very philosophical about it. You can't make people's decisions for them, you can't live their lives for them. It could have just as easily been me getting my marching orders in the early days, if I hadn't kept up my end. When they brought Rick in that was my wake-up call. You just have to keep going.

In the end, it turned out to be the right decision for the band. It wasn't just Pat. We felt all the people in power we'd been dealing with up till then, including Arthur Howe's booking agency, were now losing interest in us. Colin, meanwhile, was moving on to start his own company, Exclusive Artists, which looked after a load of chart bands like Manfred Mann, Middle of the Road and Edison Lighthouse. We decided that if Colin was interested we could do a lot worse than have him as our manager. In the end, Pat was probably glad to get shot of us. Even John Schroeder had to admit what we were doing wasn't working and was open to new ideas.

None of which would have made a blind bit of difference in the larger scheme of things if we hadn't also begun to change as a band, musically. We were so sick by then of chasing a hit, of trying to look and sound like whatever the latest trend was, we'd even stopped playing 'Pictures' and 'Ice in the Sun' some nights. The audiences had changed too. Playing a college or ballroom in 1970, we were now confronted with full-on, dope-smoking hippies. We also noticed that the audiences often sat on the floor at gigs now. They would sit there with their heads bowed, listening intently, not watching or dancing. This meant they could also pass each other joints. When we really got going, though, they would bow their heads, their hair falling over their faces, and start nodding in time to the music. Rick was the first to pick up on it. Next thing, he's also bowing his head down, wagging it, his hair covering his face. Then Alan and I started doing it and it became our thing. But all we were really doing was mirroring the audience. I don't think I went to the hairdressers again for another ten years. Not having to live up to a fashionable image completely liberated us as a group and as people. That was when I knew I never wanted to be trendy again. The trouble with trends is they come and go so quickly. Somehow, without even trying, we had found a way to never go out of style – by never being in it in the first place. Freedom!

At the same time, it just seemed to be the way all the bands were now thinking. Hit singles were no longer a big deal, or at least they were no longer the only things that mattered. Groups like Led Zeppelin didn't even bother releasing singles. It was all about being 'real'. Not manufactured. Which was fine by us, as we'd given all that up anyway. Rick and I were much more interested in album-oriented groups of the period like Chicken Shack, Fleetwood Mac, Steamhammer, Canned Heat . . . harder-edged rock bands with a strong blues influence. Touring Britain in early 1970 we just decided to do our own thing without overthinking it. In all honesty, the others cottoned on to it before I did, especially Alan, who always preferred the heavier end of things. Then in Germany one night Rick and I were listening to 'Roadhouse Blues' by the Doors blaring insanely loudly out of the speakers and it just blew the cobwebs away. Suddenly I could see clearly what we needed to be doing.

It was with this new attitude in mind that we chose for our next single a song by another young Valley Music singer-songwriter named Carl Groszman, who'd been brought to our attention by Ronnie Scott. Carl had come up with this simple blues shuffle called 'Down the Dustpipe'. It suited what we were now doing at our gigs perfectly. Simple but tight and upbeat with a heavy blues element. Bob Young would get up with us to play it, wailing away on his harmonica, and that also became a feature of the new Quo.

What I loved about 'Down the Dustpipe', which I had only just cottoned on to, was that it incorporated that fabulous Italian shuffle, only amped up and given a bit more whizz-bang. It just came so naturally to me – that perfect marriage of pop and blues – and to the rest of the band. At the time, there was a question mark over whether Pye would pay for us to make another album, but they were happy for us to record 'Down the Dustpipe' as a one-off single. I'm guessing the thinking was probably, well, if this isn't a hit we'll just drop the band from the label. There was certainly no over-egging the pudding in the studio. We just went in and played it as we would live, more or less, with John Schroeder pushing the buttons.

It could have been the end of us. Instead, it became a hit. It took about six months to do it, mind you, very slowly creeping up the charts. But that in itself gave us six months more of life while the record company waited to see how high it would eventually get to. At first Radio 1 ignored it. In a telling comment that prefigured the sort of cheap comments the band would start to get in the seventies, Tony Blackburn, the Radio 1 breakfast show host, said something on air like: 'I don't know about "Down the Dustpipe", I think that one should go down the dustbin.' Charming. Nevertheless, eventually 'Down the Dustpipe' climbed to number 12 in the UK charts. I don't think we even did *Top of the Pops*, though we did do a live session playing the song on a Granada TV show called *Doing Their Thing*. That was the first time we went on in our new sort of look. In fact, if you have a peek at the video on YouTube what you will see is the band in transition, halfway between the flower-power look and the double-denim look we were about to become famous for. Alan is wearing a waistcoat – as are Bob and I. But Alan is still in a flowery shirt, I'm in what appear to be green trousers and Rick is in T-shirt and jeans – with his head bowed, face hidden beneath curtains of long blond hair. John is in what look like brown trousers and a long-sleeved T-shirt. It's pretty obvious no one has been 'advising' us on our clothes and that we must have got dressed in the dark. But it's definitely more us than those cheesy old clips of us miming to 'Pictures' from two years before. (I remember we also performed the song on a show called *The Golden Shot*, which was presented by Bob Monkhouse and was enormously popular at the time. We were told to stand around a JCB Digger. 'Dustpipe' – digger? If you say so, mate.)

How you dressed onstage in the seventies became quite an issue, in fact. With Bowie came glam, which meant every would-be star band in the land adopting something from David's wardrobe, from Slade and the Sweet to Rod Stewart and Elton John. Then came punk and then the New Romantics and then whatever next after that. How you dressed defined your place in the pantheon, at least in Britain. Staying outside that bubble, Quo became impervious to fashion. It's not much different these days. If anything, it appears the business has gone backward, in that even the coolest groups have been 'helped' with their wardrobe by a team of stylists and make-up experts, even if it's only to dress down. I say: wear what you like. Have whatever haircut you like. As long as the music is good. That's all that people really remember.

With 'Dustpipe' giving us our third hit, Pye let us make another album, which we called *Ma Kelly's Greasy Spoon*, a reference to the types of places we found ourselves eating in while we were on the road, which we were constantly in those days. Those places all seemed to be run by the same stone-faced middle-aged woman with a cigarette butt dangling from her lips, hence the 'greasy' sepia picture on the front of the album sleeve. I'm not sure if we meant this, but looking at the picture now it's also quite a good metaphor for the music evolution we were undergoing – from pop dandies to down-and-dirty blues-rockers. (This only really works though if you pretend not to notice the fact that her cigarette isn't actually alight.)

The success of 'Down the Dustpipe' really put the wind back in our sails. Immediately we all set about writing our own songs in that vein. Bob and I also started writing together for the first time, coming up with our own take on the 'Dustpipe' shuffle-blues-boogie with songs like 'Spinning Wheel Blues'. By now Bob was more than just a tour manager, he was a friend. Rick and I would often even travel with Bob in the equipment van rather than with the others. It gave us a breather from Alan laying down the law or John throwing a wobbler.

Alan also weighed in with his own take on our new direction, especially a nine-minute piece he'd worked up based on two songs played back-to-back, 'Is It Really Me'/'Gotta Go Home'. This, along with our version of 'Junior's Wailing', which was a Steamhammer original, with Alan doing lead vocals, began to dominate our live sets. When people trot out the old heads-down-no-nonsense boogie shtick, it's material like this that comes to my mind. We would perfect it and come up with our own original material, especially later things like 'Forty Five Hundred Times', which could go on forever when we played it live. But it all started back in 1970 when we threw all our preconceived ideas out the window and just went for it, for good or ill. Plus the audience smoked so much dope at concerts back then they were happy to sit in a smoky fog all night listening to the same boogie beat.

The truth is, we had no more clear idea of what we were doing in 1970 than we had before. The big difference was we were playing stuff we enjoyed and just hoping for the best, rather than have a definite plan in mind. Where we missed a trick was in not including 'Down the Dustpipe' on the album. Putting singles on albums was frowned on at the time. The Beatles didn't do it. The Rolling Stones didn't do it. So we didn't do it. But the result of that was that – huge sigh of relief – *Ma Kelly's Greasy Spoon* actually got us back into the UK albums chart.

The upshot was that Pye allowed us to go in and record a new single, after the album had come out, which we did, taking our lives in our hands and recording a new song Bob and I had come up with called 'In My Chair'. Again, very much styled on the same narcotic shuffle beat of 'Down the Dustpipe', only much slower and moodier, and very much the template for all the future hits Bob and I would write for Status Quo. (As part of our ongoing reinvention we had dropped the 'The' from our name.)

'In My Chair' took even longer to catch on than 'Down the Dustpipe' had but eventually – one step at a time – it insinuated itself into the charts, reaching a towering peak of, um, number 21. (Worth pointing out here, perhaps, for younger readers, that we actually sold about three times as many copies of that single than the average number 1 song sells now.) We didn't care. We felt completely vindicated. It was just a case now of building up our audience. That meant staying on the road. And I mean: Staying. On. The. Bloody. Road. I get weak at the knees now when I look back on the tour dates list from those years. Between 1968 and 1971 we basically didn't stop – except for recording dates here and there. In fact, the only space I can see is a couple of weeks in March 1971 – when I'm fairly sure we were recording more songs. After which we went back on the road and stayed there until about 1979. I am only slightly exaggerating when I say that.

We were also starting to make some money again. At the time 'Matchstick Men' was a hit, as well as the equipment van, the band had a big American Pontiac Parisienne – this huge beautiful deluxe car with a long-legged bonnet and big smiley-face grille. We would travel to gigs in this thing, making out we were big stars. No money but a nice flash set of wheels. Once we started having chart records again in the early seventies though, I would come home from some runs of shows with about a thousand pounds in cash in my bag. We all did. Most of my money would go to the family, paying the mortgage and bills for Jean and Simon. It was a similar story for Alan, who had recently gotten married to his long-term girlfriend, Patricia. John still lived at home with his parents.

Rick, who wasn't married yet and was always the most flash among us, bought this huge maroon Bentley. Followed by a black and silver Bentley. Followed by a Merc. That's if I remember correctly. Rick was always getting a new car. I think he just used whatever money he had in the bank at that moment and splashed out on it. This was to be something Rick would do throughout his career – right up to the end. A flash car was always more important to Rick than having money. Who's to say he wasn't right? He certainly enjoyed himself. There was a certain member of Deep Purple, who were one of the biggest groups in the world at the time, who always used to walk around with a huge wad of cash tucked into the belt of his jeans, so that it flopped down over the belt. He would stand at the bar, flicking through this bundle on his belt, going, 'Who wants a drink?' Everyone in the pub would be thinking: flash git! Well, Rick wasn't quite that bad but he was from the same school, shall we say. Rick believed a rock star should look and behave like a rock star. Fair enough, but have a day off now and again, surely? Not Rick. Rolls-Royces, Porsches, Bentleys, Jags, Jeeps . . . you name it. And a long list of very attractive blonde girls to sit next to him in them. I wasn't built that way. I still remember with a smile how he tried to persuade me to buy a Bentley as well. He had this thing in his head where it would be great if we both turned up for engagements driving a Bentley each. He couldn't understand why I pulled such a face when he suggested it. I'm not saying I wasn't quite envious at times. But I was always more the dope smoker, curled up in his smoky den with his books and records, passing judgement on the world through his window. Well, most of the time anyway. I could also be a rock star arsehole when I wanted to be, particularly when alcohol came into my life in a big way as the seventies really took off for us. I just wasn't quite as unashamed about it as Rick. He lived for the attention, thrived on it. Needed it.

It was also around this time that Rick met the girl he would eventually marry. It was while we were on the road in Germany again. Her name was Marietta and she was a teenager who had just started at college. Marietta was very much Rick's type in every way except one: she wasn't blonde. No problem, he just got her to dye her hair blonde. This was something Rick would do with all the women he married. He did it later with his second wife, Patty, and then again with his third wife Lyndsay. He simply loved the idea of walking into a place with a beautiful blonde on his arm, so that it would be two blondes walking into a place together. A bit like his idea that he and I should turn up in the same sorts of cars, he had it all figured out. Anyway, Rick and Marietta had a whirl-wind romance. One night she was a girl in a club in Hanover. The next she was on her way over to England to meet Rick's parents. Although Marietta was younger than Rick she was very sophis-ticated by comparison – her family was very well off. She used to smoke a cigarette through a long holder like Marlene Dietrich. When Rick asked her to marry him her father was outraged. According to Rick, he actually offered to pay him to stop see-ing her. Rick's reaction was classic – and typically impulsive: he whisked her off to the local register office in Woking and married her there. Then took her back to his parents' council house on the Shearwater Estate, where they lived in one of the rooms.

While this is all going on, the band is still gigging endlessly. It was easier for me and Jean because she had the family around her and she wasn't a kid living in a foreign country. Rick would be away for days at a time with us, leaving Marietta alone at his parents' place. They loved her and treated her well but it wasn't easy for a young girl to be alone in a strange country with no husband and no friends around. It didn't help either that when she told her father what she'd done he hit the roof.

In the end, though, he calmed down enough to invite her and Rick back to Germany, where the family put on a proper German wedding for them. Then they came back to Woking, moved in together and did their best to work things out from there. I know she wanted to go to university but somehow that didn't happen. Then she went to be a teacher, teaching German at this school in Horsham. But that didn't work out. Rick said it was because of the mini-skirts she wore to the school each day. She wasn't much older than the boys she was supposed to be teaching and so she left there. It was very chaotic and typical Rick. Act first; think later. But they did seem happy together. Certainly, I'd never seen Rick so happy and settled. Blonde wife, maroon Bentley, nice guitar – he was made up.

Roy Lynes, on the other hand, was not having a good time of it. We were on our way to a gig in Aberdeen when he jumped ship somewhere around Stoke-on-Trent. He'd met a girl and fallen in love, and that was it for Roy. I can't say I blame him, though we were a bit put out at the time having to continue the tour without him. Roy was in his mid-twenties, he'd given this pop star lark a damn good go and now he was tired of travelling up and down the country. Then he met the love of his life and he made up his mind. It was obviously the right decision for him too. Many years later, during a tour of Australia, where Roy was now living, he came to one of our shows – and brought the girl with him, who he'd been married to ever since. He seemed really happy, too.

I look back on those days in the early seventies now and see it as a wonderful time for us all. Yes, we had fears and insecurities. But there was a great innocence to everything we were doing. We knew it could all end tomorrow. It already had 'ended tomorrow' for us a few times. But somehow we had managed to keep going. Now, with Colin in our management corner, a new direction to our music that felt good and proper for the first time and a look – if you could call it that – that required zero maintenance, there really wasn't too much to worry about. Or if there was, I had become very good at ignoring it and just keeping my head down concentrating on the guitar. (Though not that much, obviously, or I would have been a hell of a lot better.)

One of the reasons for this newfound calm, I now realise, was the fact that I had become much more of a dope smoker by this point. Ever since Stevie Marriott first turned us on to the pleasures of being blissed out on good Lebanese Red, or Moroccan, or Afghani Black, or the number of other brands of cannabis resin that were on offer in those days (this was long before the current hyper-strength strands of homegrown hydroponics that are available now in the UK), I had begun to much prefer smoking a joint to having a drink. For one thing, it offered a whole new perspective on things. Music sounded better. Jokes sounded funnier. Bad news didn't travel so fast. Even sex was better, or certainly more fun.

The other thing I found smoking dope was useful for was writing songs. In terms of inspiration, it really seemed to work. Of course, if you weren't careful you would come up with quite a lot of nonsense as well. But in the main it seemed to unlock the creative juices and I began writing a lot of the songs that became the foundation of the Status Quo catalogue. A good example of that would be 'Mean Girl'. If you listen to 'Mean Girl' you can hear the building blocks of all the hits we would have over the next decade, especially in 'Down Down', with its revved-up boogie beat that stops and starts. (According to my co-writer here, Mick Wall, that is. Personally, I'm not sure.)

Bob and I wrote that one. I still get asked why Bob and I wrote so many songs together, as opposed to Rick and me, or Rick, Alan and me. The answer is obvious really: I came up with better songs with Bob. Rick and I did try to write more songs together, and carried on trying right up until the end. But we never really came up with much that stood out. The problem was that as soon as Rick would come up with something that sounded good, I'd ask him to stop and go back so we could work on it, build it into something. But Rick was always convinced he could do better – always. I'd be going, 'No, Rick, stop! Go back. That was great, that little riff or melody.' He'd be like, 'No, I can do that much better, come back to it later.' Then he'd either forget what he'd done or go back and ruin it by trying too hard to make it better and better. Rick was like that in all areas of his life. He'd buy a car – the best car in the world, according to him. Then get rid of it two weeks later. Naw, never really liked it. Same with women in a lot of cases. He always thought he could do better.

Writing a song with someone else is very much about chemistry. Rick and I had a lot of personal chemistry in the early days. We were best mates. But in order to write a song you need more than that. The relationship needs a driver and a carrier, and maybe we were too similar. In the best songs each of us wrote, Rick and I were always the drivers. We both still needed someone else there to bounce off. But for me that always worked best with people other than Rick. And for Rick it was the same. In fact, he also began writing more with Bob. Anyway, it was all about who had the best song, not who wrote it.

There was also less tension when I wrote with Bob, because he wasn't in the band. There was no agenda. Bob was just Bob – even after we started having really big hits, he never changed one bit. He wasn't interested in the spotlight, didn't care about recognition. Just got on with his job, which was all about maintaining good relationships. The band could be bastards sometimes – all bands can when they are frazzled from weeks of one-nighters – and Bob would be our shield. We called him Bob Young: Friend of the People. He's still like that today, bless him.

Another song I wrote with Bob around this time would also become one of our most famous hits, though it would be another three years before it evolved into the rocking version we finally released. This was 'Caroline'. We were idling away an afternoon on holiday with our wives and children at this hotel in Perranporth, Cornwall, in the summer of 1970. I've always loved country music and 'Caroline' began life as a sort of country tune, slow blues with a bit of a lilt to it. We liked it so much we made a demo of it. It was only much later when we were scrabbling around for material that it became transformed with its police-siren riff and jet-propelled rhythm.

Instead, our next single in 1971 was a song Bob and I had written, again very much in the shuffle boogie mode we were now pushing ahead with, called 'Tune to the Music'. We were convinced we were onto a winner – only to see it completely flop. Again! Argh! It came out in March 1971 and the radio utterly ignored it. It probably didn't help that we were having a rare few weeks off the road at the time, trying to make another album. We did a show at the Marquee club in London with Thin Lizzy supporting us and it was one of the best gigs we'd done. Lizzy were amazing. We were no slouches. And the crowd loved it. Packed the place out. Played the new single. Then went home to write some more songs and wonder why having a hit was so bloody hard.

The album we released later that year, *Dog of Two Head* (that's right, no 's' on the end), is these days regarded by hardcore Quo fans as one of our early classics. I always wonder if it was so bloody good why it was such a commercial flop. Yes, it managed to get a foothold in the top 30, but only for a couple of weeks before disappearing down the ladder again. It's true it contained some of the best new songs Bob and I had written like 'Mean Girl' and 'Gerdundula' (the latter a wonderfully catchy little ditty, written by us under the pseudonyms Manston and James, and named after some pals of ours we'd met on the road in Germany named Gerd and Ula – geddit?). They would later become chart hits for us after we had become properly famous and the record company decided to cash in on some of our old material. Some people blamed the title of the album, saying it didn't make sense. But we named it after a saying our roadie Paul Lodge – Slug, we called him – used all the time. We thought it was funny, ha, yeah. Maybe not so funny as an album title, though.

When the album wasn't the big success we had hoped, our relationship with Pye really suffered. I honestly can't remember if we were dropped by the label – probably – or whether Colin Johnson stepped in and called a halt to proceedings. But we began 1972 with no record label. It was a case of In Colin We Trust. Stay out on the road and leave him to work on the small print. That was my attitude anyway. The irony was that even though we didn't have a record deal our fan-base was growing. Colin made sure of that by keeping us working continually on the road. Still, he had an uphill task trying to get us signed to one of the other big London-based labels. To some of them we were damaged goods – four albums already out, none of them more than modest hits. A handful of successful singles spread over a four-year period. Once again, there was talk round the campfire of maybe splitting the band up and starting again with a new line-up – and yet another new name.

This was not an idea I was prepared to consider for longer than the time it took me to roll another joint. I had recently become a father again, to another beautiful baby boy, who we named Nicholas. For me there was no choice but to soldier on with the band. Luckily, the crowds were coming to the shows and Colin was able to use that to attract the newer, longer-haired generation of record company executives down to see us.

It was a strategy that paid off in spades when he persuaded a relatively new label called Vertigo to sign the band. They were part of the Philips/Phonogram Record Company, which was huge and very commercially mainstream based. Vertigo was designed to cash in on the new young 'progressive' rock artists that had come along. 'Progressive rock' didn't mean then exactly what it means now. Long musical epics full of widdly-widdly keyboards were not a prerequisite. It was just a term really to differentiate singles acts from album-oriented bands. So they had signed new bands like Black Sabbath, Gentle Giant, Nazareth and Uriah Heep, gambling that with a bit of nurturing these sorts of acts would deliver handsome sales in the long term through the success of their albums.

Colin had somehow managed to make them see Status Quo as being in that mould. Told them to forget about the poncey flower-power hits of the sixties and see us for what we were now – denim-clad, long-haired (back when long hair still meant something), above all, *serious*. And that serious album-buying rock fans saw us that way too. The clincher was when we appeared halfway down the bill on the Sunday night of that year's Reading Festival. Everyone in the business who mattered was there ligging backstage.

There were about twelve bands on, including us, on the Sunday and it would have been easy to get lost in the pack. But John Peel, the ultra-hip Radio 1 DJ, who was DJing at the festival that year, had decided to champion us. It's well known now that Peel loved to champion the underdogs and that's what we very much were at the time. He introduced us onto the Reading stage that year, calling us something like 'one of the finest rock 'n' roll bands in the world'. That's what it sounded like to me anyway. Whatever he said it got the most enormous cheer and we ran on feeling ready to take on the world. It became one of the best shows we did all year – and at the end of it Vertigo couldn't wait to sign us.

There was some fiddly nonsense with Pye, whereby they got a cut from our first few records with Vertigo – which was charming considering the tiny royalty we had been on with them but if that was the cost of our being given a second chance at a new label we didn't care. Within a couple of weeks we were in IBC Studios in Portland Place in London making what would be the album that changed all our lives forever – *Piledriver*.

From the moment we started work on it, everything about *Piledriver* was perfect. Even the name, which Colin Johnson came up with – a piledriver being a wrestling term, not the over-the-top American-style WWE wrestling you get now, but the original two-falls, one-submission variety you got on British television on a Saturday afternoon back in the sixties and seventies, when guys like Mick McManus and Jackie Pallo were the big stars. A piledriver is when one wrestler grabs his opponent, turns him upside-down and drops to his knees, driving the opponent headfirst into the mat of the wrestling ring. It was a term – and an image – that perfectly suited the music Status Quo now stood for. Hard, direct, undeniable – and actually quite humorous, if you shared that sort of bloke-ish knockabout humour. How that explains the picture of a gorilla holding a rocket on the back of the album sleeve I don't know, though. Perhaps the album art people weren't wrestling fans, who knows?

The other thing that was great was that for the first time in our careers we got what can only be described as 'artistic freedom'. The freedom to make exactly the kind of music we wanted to without having to worry about what other people thought or whether we had a chance of getting on the radio. We didn't even have a proper producer for the album. It was just the four of us setting up our gear as we would at a gig, then playing the songs pretty much exactly as we would live – very, very loud. The only luxury was that if we weren't happy with a take we could do another. And another. And another, if we wanted, though we were on such a hot streak we hardly did more than two or three takes of anything.

We were also fortunate that the A & R (artists and repertoire) guy who had signed us to Vertigo, Brian Shepherd, was a real music-first person. He'd been a roadie for Magna Carta, a progressive folk-rock group who were also signed to Vertigo, and really believed in the 'vision thing'. What we didn't find out until later was that Brian had been keeping an eye on us for several months. Brian, who would later become managing director of Phonogram, was a hugely experienced record man who had first joined Philips Records in 1963 before going into producing. He had returned to take over the running of the Vertigo label just before we were signed. Brian was to become a hugely influential figure in our career. Come what may, Brian was always there to lend an ear and offer wise counsel. He became our champion at the label.

It was Brian that encouraged us to do our own thing, that we didn't need anyone else to show us how to be true to ourselves musically. I wasn't sure yet if that was strictly true but Brian proved himself a true friend of the Quo time and again over the next ten years.

Things like 'sound levels' didn't even enter our heads. We just went at it like kids in a sweetshop. The end result was an album that more than lived up to its name. We had really started to come into our own as songwriters, too. Bob and I wrote three of the eight songs – the opening track, 'Don't Waste My Time', which became a major highlight of the live show forevermore; 'Paper Plane', the track that was chosen as the single; and a now-for-something-completely-different ballad, 'Unspoken Words', which was a beautiful slow blues where I got to be Eric Clapton for five minutes and Rick, who sang the lead vocals, got to be George Harrison.

Rick and I wrote two songs together: 'Oh Baby', which was a right little raver, almost rockabilly, which we sang in unison Everlys style, and 'Big Fat Mama', which Rick sang and which was destined to become another really big song for Quo fans. Alan also had a hand in two songs: a lovely ballad called 'A Year', which I sang and Alan co-wrote with Bernie Frost, a lovely man who will come back into our story later; and a co-write with Rick, which Rick sang, called 'All the Reasons'. I love it that Alan, the hard man of the band, co-wrote two of the loveliest songs we ever recorded. Then to finish off the album Alan sang lead on our (very) long version of 'Roadhouse Blues', the toasty blues shuffle by the Doors, which helped cement our decision to go in a similar direction.

As if to mark the corner we had turned, in terms of becoming masters of our own fate, musically, at least, *Piledriver* became the first Quo album where I was listed as 'Francis' Rossi. Up to then, I had still been listed as 'Mike'. My hair was now longer than a girl's but the blurring of sexual identity, at least in music, was in full sway by 1972. If you could have 'Alice' Cooper you could certainly have 'Francis' Rossi. Besides, as I kept telling people, unlike Alice or Elton or Bowie, it's my real bloody name!

I even loved the cover of the *Piledriver* album, which was the three-man frontline of Quo – me, Rick and Alan – all pictured together with our heads down, hair falling over our guitars. John may have been miffed not to get his picture on the cover but that wasn't really the point. Drummers are like goalkeepers, it's always their lot to be considered last. None of us got our faces on there, though. It was just this brilliant image that completely summed up what Status Quo had become and what the music on that album signified. You can call it heads-down-no-nonsense-mindless-boogie but that is to wilfully misinterpret what that image really said, not just about us as a band, but our fans as a people – that we were all united as one, in service to this music that really moved us all. You know something is really good when it takes on a life of its own and from the moment we finished making *Piledriver*, that's what happened to Status Quo. The whole thing just took off – and we're still waiting nearly half a century later for it to come down again.

It was as simple as that. 'Paper Plane' came out as a single in November 1972 – our first release of any kind for over eighteen months – and immediately became a hit, reaching number 8 in the charts that Christmas. It's still one of our fans' favourites. It began life as one of Bob's poems, which we turned into the lyrics of the song. (That 'three grand Deutsche car' it famously mentions in the verses refers to the very real Mercedes 600 the band was now travelling in, thanks to our advance from the Vertigo deal — one of those luxurious German limos with forwards- and backwards-facing seats and drapes for the enormous rear window; massive front grille; power divider down the middle. Looked like a Rolls-Royce, only better!) You turn up for a gig in one of those, you feel like genuine rock royalty.

'Paper Plane' also became a hit in several countries in Europe — and New Zealand, which was nice as I'd never been there. When the *Piledriver* album was released ten days before Christmas, it flew into the UK charts and went to number 5. It would stay in the UK album charts for the next eight months, a phenomenal amount of time. The album was also a hit around Europe but not New Zealand. It did get into the Australian charts though. I'd never been there either. That Christmas I was as happy as a dog with two dicks, as we used to say back then. We all were, especially Rick, who was now able to live out his fantasies in full.

We ended the year with a New Year's Eve show at the Greyhound, which was like our hometown gig, in Croydon. I can't remember anything more about it than that. The party had started when 'Paper Plane' and *Piledriver* were both in the top 10 at the same time and it had continued right through Christmas. The thing that does stick out for me all these years later is that a week later — six days, to be precise — we headlined our first show at the Rainbow Theatre, in Finsbury Park. The Rainbow was then the most prestigious rock venue in London. It held about three thousand people, and the fact that we were suddenly able to headline it said everything about the new status of Quo. (Shit joke, sorry, couldn't resist!) The Rainbow was where Eric Clapton would stage a famous show later that month, and where Rod and the Faces and Bowie would play. The Rainbow was where you played if you were a big rock band with a record in the charts. Suddenly, that meant us. Well, not suddenly.

It had taken ten years to achieve this 'sudden' success. But that's where we now were, top of the world, Ma! All we had to do now was come up with another hit album and single. Then another and another and another and . . .

Chapter Five

Get Down!

If the first ten years of being in the band, from the Spectres to Status Quo, had been about trying to make our dreams come true, the next ten years would be about living that dream, but somehow seeing it turn into a nightmare.

It all started so well. In 1973, Status Quo was suddenly hot property. Colin had merged his management company with Billy Gaff, Rod Stewart's manager, to form Gaff Management, and he made it known to us that we were his big priority that year.

We did our first shows in New Zealand and Australia at the end of January, headlining some and opening on other, bigger dates for Slade, which was mind-blowing. Not just the people, who were so friendly and so into the group, but the weather. It was all rain and snow when we flew out of London, but it was in the middle of summer over there. It sounds a cliché but the whole prawns-on-the-barbie, cold tinny and bikini-girls on the beach scene really brought home to us the feeling of having stepped into a dream. We went from there to touring these huge venues in West Germany with T. Rex, getting screamed at by Marc Bolan fans and being hounded by denim-clad German lads who wanted nothing more than to get very, very drunk while we played very, very loudly for them.

We came back from that and began a two-month headline tour of Britain topped off with another two sold-out shows at the Rainbow. Did it go to our heads? Of course it did. It is meant to, isn't it? For all the newfound success none of us had the faintest idea that it might last longer than a couple of years – if we played our cards right and got lucky. So we made the most of it. Apart from the money and the three grand Deutsche car, this was when we got more into dope smoking. All of us apart from John. Years later Rick would talk about how he was never that much into hash or marijuana and that he would feel alienated from me and Alan and Bob, who all liked a puff. But that's not how I remember it. In my memory, Rick was as into enjoying a joint after the show as anybody.

Rick probably liked his cigarettes and his speed and his booze more. But dope was definitely part of his thing too in those days. I was twenty-four, having the time of my life, and as far as I was concerned smoking a few joints was fuelling my creativity – man. It really was, though. Bob Young was the same. We didn't see dope smoking as drug taking. We felt it was certainly better than drinking to get high, which is something I had never enjoyed.

Another thing we were now getting more than our fair share of was groupies – not ardent girl fans looking for a bit more than just an autograph. I mean, real, proper groupies, as the term was understood in the early seventies. In the current MeToo climate this has become a tricky subject to try and explain. But the fact is that back in the late sixties and early seventies there were dedicated groups of girls that devoted most of their spare time to looking after bands. Not just having sex with them but actually taking care of them. Feeding them, showing them around places other than the hotels and venues, mending their clothes, shopping with them and having meals, listening to their boring stories, putting up with them, knowing they would only be together for a short time. In the days before email and mobile phones and texting and FaceTime and all the other ways we now have of staying permanently in touch with each other no matter where we are in the world, being away from home on the road for weeks and months at a time was a wearying, lonely existence. You'd get the high from doing a good show – and the lows you suffered when the show had been a disaster – but mostly you'd get that weird disconnected feeling of not knowing where you are, of not having anyone new to talk to, of being stuck in the same car/dressing room/ hotel with a lot of smelly men who you have gotten to know far too well. Being detached from reality, basically.

This is where the groupies came in. They weren't manic fans, jittery just to meet you. They were used to being around bands. They knew the scene. They would become your best friends – for a few hours or a few days – before you moved on to the next part of the tour and they moved in with the next band. There was even a magazine in the US specifically for groupies called *Star*. Groupies weren't one-night stands. They had their own role on the road. The novelty of having sex with strange girls every night had already worn off. As the singer, I had gotten used to getting the best-looking girl back to my room. But the whole thing would fill me with anxiety. It was the same for all of us. In the end we would often rather have a polish than full-on sex with a stranger – a 'polish' being what we used to call masturbation. We had all known each other since we were teenagers, so wanking was no big deal to us. A few sweaty knobs all swinging in the same room together was a fairly ordinary occurrence for us back then.

One night, in Munich or somewhere like that, the local promoter gave us this 8-mm porn film – or blue movie, as we used to call them. Again, you have to picture a world where video-recorders haven't been invented yet, let alone smartphones. So we would get these films and run them through an 8-mm cine camera. You would stick a white sheet up on one of the hotel room walls and we'd all sit there 'entertaining' ourselves.

On this particular occasion, for a laugh we got Bob to aim the projector out the window onto the side of the building opposite our hotel. Suddenly the people on the street were being treated to these 20-foot-high film images of people having sex. At the same time, we had a few of the regular groupies in the room with us. They were all game for a laugh, but they couldn't interest us. They were all gorgeous and shoving their tits in our faces going, 'You like fuck, Englishman?' I was like, 'Sorry, love. Not tonight. I'm having a polish, can't you see.'

We didn't really encounter the real dedicated groupie scene, though, until we got to America – which became the next place we went to play for the first time in 1973. Talk about a culture shock. Going to America back then was like going to the moon. We went from headlining the Sunderland Locarno, supported by the John Peel Disco, straight to playing a private showcase for our new American record company and assorted media people at the fabled Whisky A Go Go in Los Angeles, once the home of the Doors, Love and Frank Zappa. Vertigo didn't have an operation in the US so Colin had done a separate deal for us with A & M Records. This was the label formed in the early sixties by Herb Alpert of 'Spanish Flea' fame. It had mainly specialised in easy-listening acts like Burt Bacharach and the Carpenters. By the start of the seventies, though, it had branched out to include album-oriented rock acts like Joe Cocker, Procol Harum, Humble Pie, Free – and us.

At the time, the brand of hard blues-based rock we now specialised in was hugely popular in America. Rod and the Faces were already huge there and so were Zeppelin and Black Sabbath, Deep Purple and so on. It seemed like only a matter of time before the American audience took to us as well. Except, of course, things are never that simple.

It all began promisingly enough. We had a forty-five-date tour booked, mostly opening for bands like Slade, who we had already become good friends with, Savoy Brown, Dr Hook, Tim Buckley, Climax Blues Band, Manfred Mann's Earth Band, ELO . . . anyone that would have us, basically. There wasn't much emphasis on putting together bills that would suit just one particular audience. It was all about working hard each night to win over new audiences wherever you happened to have arrived on the map.

We also did a number of headline shows at various clubs, including three nights at the Whisky in LA and runs of shows at small but raucous places like the Draft House in Colorado, the brilliantly named Fat City in New Jersey and, right at the end of the tour, a week-long residency at K-K-K-Katy's in Boston. We still didn't have any records in the US charts when we returned home in July but we had left with a lot of goodwill in the bank, especially in Canada, where we had done a couple of shows and where the records were now starting to sell.

One other thing I still remember from that tour, which would have an unnervingly lasting echo through the years, was something that happened to Rick. I think we were in San Francisco and we were in the dressing room getting ready to go on when these girls sort of wandered in. Nothing particularly unusual for those days. But one of them was this extraordinarily beautiful woman who walked straight up to Rick, pointing at him, going 'You… You…!' I think we were all thinking, I wish it could be me… me… she was going for. But not after we saw Rick, the next day. He never really told us what happened, just that he'd spent a very strange and disturbing night with this girl, who he'd gone home with after the show. I don't know if she laced his drink with LSD or what happened but Rick came back completely freaked out. There was definitely something very witchy about this girl and whatever she did to get inside Rick's head, I don't think he ever really got over it. Years later – many years later, towards the end of his life – he would sometimes accost me, when he'd had a few drinks, perhaps, pointing his finger at me, going, 'You… you…!' before unloading whatever crazy stuff was on his mind. There was so much crazy stuff going on in the seventies to do with drugs and weird people that came to your shows in America that I quickly put it out of my mind. But, I swear, Rick never really got over it. Whatever 'it' actually was.

Coming home to London, top of our agenda was to record a new album – and though no one was spelling it out, a new hit single. Singles were still looked down on in the album-buying rock community. It was the reason we hadn't rushed to try and record an immediate follow-up to 'Paper Plane'. In 1973, according to the rules of the music press, which was becoming immensely powerful in the business back then, you could either be seen as Slade or Wizzard – one big hit single after another, but no one really paying much attention to your albums. Or you could be seen in the same bracket as bands like Free and the Faces – one single per album, maximum, with all attention being aimed towards your albums. Even David Bowie, who'd taken off massively the summer before, only released one single, 'Starman', from his *Ziggy Stardust* album. We very much saw ourselves in the latter category.

Of course, the so-called rules were broken all the time. Elton John seemed to have a new single out every other week. But mainly the serious new faces like Roxy Music, Bowie and Mott the Hoople were all about shunning the idea of being seen to rely on hit singles. Like us, Roxy would begin their career with stand-alone singles never intended for any of their albums. Bowie also followed up 'Starman' with two stand-alone singles. It gave them the huge profile a radio hit would do, but it kept their integrity intact as album-oriented artists. It was an idea that appeared to be backed up when our old label, Pye, released two singles back-to-back from the *Dog of Two Head* album – 'Mean Girl' and 'Gerdundula' – to try and cash in on our new success while we were away in America. 'Mean Girl' got into the top 20, but 'Gerdundula' barely made the top 40.

Lesson learned: fans – real album-buying fans who read *Melody Maker* and the *NME* each week – were not so easily taken in any more. Meanwhile, I was fretting quietly in the background, desperate for 'Paper Plane' not to turn into another one-off like 'Pictures of Matchstick Men', here today, gone later today. No one was pushing the point, but I knew in my bones that the thing that would really keep the show on the road was another hit single. There is a music business saying that began doing the rounds later in the seventies, when bands started to come to their senses about such things: art for art's sake; hit singles for fuck's sake. I wouldn't have said it out loud at the time but that is how I was feeling as we got ready to make our second album for Vertigo.

As a dad with two kids now I also felt the pressure to keep the money coming in. After the Vertigo deal was signed and we got some money I was able to lay down a deposit on a mortgage to buy a four-bedroom semi-detached house next door to where one of my Italian aunts lived in Forest Hill. The price of the house was £10,000, the equivalent today of about £128,000, though again you have to amplify the purchasing power of a pound in those days. You wouldn't be able to afford a one-room flat for that money these days. So we were lucky to be living in a time where such things were possible. But at the time, the responsibility for coming up with the monthly mortgage payment weighed heavy on my mind.

At the same time, there was a much greater feeling of confidence about the band in 1973. We knew we'd cracked it, that we just needed to keep our eyes on the road ahead and not get distracted. It was a great relief, though, I have to admit, when Bob and I remembered the country song we had written three years before called 'Caroline'. We were scrabbling for material to make up both sides of the album (anyone under the age of forty reading this, you'll have to Google what side one and side two meant in the old days of 12-inch vinyl). Like *Piledriver*, we were back in IBC Studios in London, blasting everything out as loud as the speakers would let us and recording to tape what we came up with. We only planned on having eight tracks, four each side, again the same as *Piledriver*. But we didn't have enough, so we included tracks like 'Softer Ride', which was another song Bob and I had written but which we agreed could be credited to Rick and Alan just to keep the peace as they were moaning that they didn't get enough of their songs on record. It was originally just the B-side of 'Paper Plane' but it was a good track and deserved its place on the new album. And 'Caroline', which might have been a disaster but we were short of material and, blow me down, it sounded fantastic speeded up and given the full Quo treatment. I knew it was a hit the moment Rick started blasting out the chords. I put a sort of finger-wagging riff over the top, then Alan and John came piling in and we were off to the races.

By now we knew what we were supposed to sound like, what our fans really liked most about us, and the rest of the album followed suit. We only had one slightly more plaintive song on there, 'And It's Better Now', which Bob and I co-wrote, and that earned its place fair and square. The melody and arrangement were so sweet you could eat them. The two most memorable tracks on the album, after 'Caroline', were of a different class though. The first, 'Roll Over Lay Down', which opened the album, was another song that Bob and I had come up with, but which again we agreed to have credited to the whole band. Colin Johnson had talked Bob and me into allowing that to happen, just to keep the others happy. They had seen how much money had been coming to us for writing 'In My Chair', 'Mean Girl' and 'Paper Plane', particularly after we had negotiated a much more equitable deal with Vertigo than the one we had with Pye. Colin could see Alan, in particular, getting more and more bent out of shape about it, to the point of starting to argue for more of his songs to be included on albums or chosen as a single, simply to try and keep up with the money I was now earning.

At first, Bob and I were like, 'But Colin, that's not fair! We wrote that song!' But we soon saw he was right. The choice came down to either finding a way to placate Alan and the others, or bowing down to the demands and starting to use more of their material. I didn't care who wrote what, but I did care whether we had another hit. So we went for the four-way credit on 'Roll Over Lay Down', and it worked, especially when a live version of the song was later released and became one of our biggest hits. It's still one of my favourites to play. It sounds like the theme tune to a Clint Eastwood movie, as some baddie rides his horse into town looking for trouble.

The real monster on the album was the final track though, 'Forty Five Hundred Times', which Rick and I came up with together. It is now regularly voted one of our best songs ever by diehard Quo fans. Rick came up with the gently noodling intro after he'd had a few drinks one night, and it was incredibly melodic and almost plaintive. We were sitting in the studio, in a circle, just improvising over the top. Then Rick just started riffing and the song took on a whole new aspect, becoming more epic as we ploughed on. The finished track was almost ten minutes long. When we played it live it could go for twice that length if we were really going for it. It became sort of like our 'Stairway to Heaven', at least to the Quo fans. The absolute highlight of every show, the pinnacle of total Quo-osity, if you like. We would end it – the three of us in a line – Rick, me and Alan – all heads down banging away on our guitars, hair dangling, the crowd going crazy. It was almost like a spiritual communion between me, Rick, the band and the fans.

What still baffles me is exactly when we recorded all the tracks. All I remember about 1973 is being on tour all over the world. We even did the Reading Festival again, this time as special guests for Rod and the Faces on the Saturday night. It felt big time. It was big time. When did we stop long enough to record some songs? No idea. That and the making of *Piledriver* always overlap in my mind. That said, a lot of things are now a blur from those days. But then a lot of things were rather a large blur even at the time they were happening.

Like *Piledriver*, we plumped for a one-word title for the album. In this case, a simple *Hello!* – another title Colin Johnson came up with, but with an exclamation mark this time. Even the cover had echoes of *Piledriver*, all four of us this time lined up. Not banging our heads but standing with arms aloft, pictured in triumphant silhouette. Quo's None More Black cover, as it became known after Spinal Tap came out.

Then we crossed our fingers and let Vertigo do the rest. Sure enough, and to huge relief and no little pride all round, 'Caroline' was released in August and went straight into the charts, getting as high as number 5 – the highest any of our singles had gone at that point. *Top of the Pops* here we come – again. In fact, we were starting to feel like veterans of the show. Kenny Everett was the presenter the first week we did 'Caroline'. He was the coolest daytime DJ on Radio 1 at the time. So cool he'd been sacked at least once for some perceived outrage. He'd only just gotten his job back when he did *Top of the Pops* with us. About a week later he left Radio 1 again to become one of the inaugural DJs at the newly launched Capital Radio. We were beginning to feel bulletproof. John Peel loved us. Kenny Everett approved and played our records too.

Then something happened that we had never really dreamed possible before – *Hello!* came out and four weeks later it went to number 1, knocking the new Slade album, *Sladest*, off the top spot. I sat there with a copy of *Music Week*, the big weekly industry magazine at the time, which had all the charts in it, just staring at the albums chart page. The same week *Hello!* went to number 1, the latest albums from the Rolling Stones, David Bowie, Genesis, Lou Reed and the Carpenters were all below us in the top 10. Then there were the real heavy-hitters like Perry Como (number 3) and Max Bygraves (number 10).

It didn't matter who they were, we were higher than them. I'm not the kind of bloke to tempt fate by gloating but I don't think that copy of *Music Week* left my hands that entire week. To say we were happy doesn't describe how we felt at all. We were doing a show in Helsinki when we got the phone call. It was that time of the year when Finland has twenty-four-hour sunshine and I don't think any of us went to bed for a week.

By the time we were finishing the year with some more British concerts, *Hello!* was already the biggest-selling album we'd ever had. It also gave us our first gold record for over 100,000 sales in the UK. It was our biggest around the rest of the world too. It just seemed to take off everywhere. Everywhere, that is, except America. Which in those days, like now, was still seen as the Holy Grail for British rock bands. The perception was you hadn't really made it big until you'd made it big there.

We weren't worried though. We had our own cunning plan to make it big in America. Well, not that cunning actually. We just decided to tour our arses off there as much as we could over the next year and see what happened. The same as every other hopeful British band had done since the Beatles. In the case of bands like Black Sabbath and Deep Purple, and solo acts like Elton John and David Bowie, this strategy had paid off in spades. Unlike those guys though we didn't have any hit records in the States to open the doors for us. Instead we quickly fell into the same commercial chasm as bands like Slade, Cockney Rebel and T. Rex: artists that were huge in Britain but couldn't get arrested in America.

It certainly wasn't for the lack of trying on our part. Between 1974 and 1976 we did five long tours of the United States, either opening for big acts like Sabbath, ZZ Top and Lynyrd Skynyrd or headlining our own club and ballroom shows. We went down really well with the American crowds too. Our brand of high-octane boogie rock was always well received. There were many nights when local promoters or radio people would tell us we were the best band they had seen come through town since the Stones or whoever. Big record sales were always just around the corner, we were told.

The crux of the matter, though, had nothing to do with how ordinary people felt about the band. It was all down to the bigwigs that ran the label in America. Not the men at the very top like Jerry Moss, who co-owned the label with Herb Alpert, but the guys that ran the A & R and promotions departments. Their jobs were to prioritise the various records they had coming out on the label. So, for example, Rick Wakeman's 1974 solo album, *Journey to the Centre of the Earth*, was given a huge push at the personal behest of Jerry Moss, and as a result it went to number 3 in the US that year. Now, I'm not picking on Rick, who as well as being one of the finest musicians this country has ever produced is also a lovely man. He deserved every minute of his success. And, yes, it's also true that because he had been a member of Yes, who were huge in America, he was already well known over there. But, without meaning to labour the point . . . *Journey to the Centre of the Earth* was a mainly instrumental progressive rock album with just two tracks on it – side one and side two. Hit singles it did not have. Yet A & M was able to make it one of the biggest American hits of the year. Our question was: if they can do that for Rick and his symphony, why can't they even get us in the top 100 with 'Caroline' or any of our other singles like 'Break the Rules', which became our next big hit in Britain, or 'Down Down', which was the hit after that and the biggest-selling single of our career everywhere else in the world?

Even after we switched labels in America to Capitol, which was the US wing of EMI, we didn't fare much better. Again, we were going down a storm with American audiences, yet you could never hear any of our records on the radio. The key as to why almost certainly lay in a conversation I was told Colin our manager had with one of the main men at an American company around this time. Pushing to know why no one seemed able to get any of our songs on the radio over there, he was presented with the following proposal: 'You pay off my mortgage and I'll get your record on the charts.'

We were so outraged when we were told this we asked Colin to tell them where to stick it. Sure enough, apart from some of the new 'progressive' FM stations that operated independently in the States at that time, where some longhair might decide to play the whole side of an album if the fancy took them or they'd smoked enough dope, Status Quo remained resolutely off the American radio airwaves.

Finally, after yet another twenty-four-date American tour, in April 1976, we said fuck that and never went back. Not for another twenty years anyway. We were finally persuaded to return to America in 1997, when we did precisely two shows: one at the House of Blues in LA and one at the Irving Plaza in New York. They both went very well but that was that and we didn't go again until 2003 when, off the back of some shows in Brazil and Mexico, we crossed the border and did half a dozen House of Blues-style shows across both coasts.

Our decision to forget about America wasn't entirely based on a fit of pique. From our point of view we had tried our best for three years – all to no avail. Meanwhile, these long tours were costing us a fortune. We always returned from America in debt. Meanwhile, our records in the mid-seventies were now selling millions all over the rest of the world. During the same period when we were flogging our guts out playing everywhere and anywhere they would have us in America, we were now doing major headline tours all over Europe, Japan, Australia and, of course, Britain, where we were now one of the biggest bands in the country. In the three years we spent trying to break America, we had another three number 1 albums in Britain, and another six top 10 hit singles, including our first number 1 with 'Down Down'. We had also seen what happened to Slade, whose singles were going straight into the charts at number 1 in Britain when they decided to spend the next two years concentrating on America – at the same time exactly as us, as it happened. But instead of throwing in the towel like we did, they doubled down and moved over there in 1975. But even that didn't work and by the time they came home again their career had stalled. We took that as a salutary lesson in how not to do things. At least, not while things were going so well for us everywhere else in the world.

Over the years there have been times, I confess, when I do wonder what might have been if we'd played the game with the powers that be in America, if we'd paid that guy's mortgage off, bought all the ounces of coke the radio people constantly demanded, and we'd been able to get a hit song on the radio. But then I think, what else would it have given us? More fame? I've been famous enough now for nearly all of my adult life, long enough not to need any more of that. In fact, I quite like the anonymity when I go to America these days with my wife Eileen to visit her family, or to see members of my own family that live out there. It's nice not to have to keep noticing people giving you funny looks when you walk into a shop or restaurant. The only big change had we made it in

America would have been money. And again, it's not as if I've been exactly poor. Being big in America might have added an extra zero to my personal wealth, but as one of our old accountants used to say, 'You can only wear one pair of shoes at a time.'

There was also, if I'm honest, the comfort-zone factor. By the mid-seventies everywhere we went we were now travelling first class. Not just on planes and in hotel suites but in our personal lives too. Next thing, we'd be roughing it again in America. Playing small venues, being treated like beggars. We hadn't worked so hard back home to go through all that again.

When *Hello!* went to number 1 in 1973, our earnings for headlining a concert hall in Britain went up astronomically. By the time we got to *Blue for You*, in 1976, we'd had another three chart-topping albums, a top 10 best-of compilation, six major hit singles, and we had just recorded a two-night stint at Glasgow Apollo that would comprise our first live album, simply called *Live!*, which would get to number 3.

During that time our fees for one of our shows had doubled then tripled, then gone up again. It was the same all over the world (except America). We were now touring major venues for weeks and months at a time in West Germany, where the venues were all arena-sized, Australia, New Zealand, Japan, and every country we could name in Europe and a few we had never heard of. We weren't just selling tickets at these shows, we were selling massive amounts of merchandise every night (T-shirts, tour programmes, denim patches with our name on them, posters, jackets, you name it). At some shows, particularly in Japan, we were making as much, sometimes more, money from selling official Quo merchandise than we did selling tickets. All of which we shared equally as a band.

Then came the royalties from all the songs. Since the day I had received my cheque for £1,200 for writing 'Pictures of Matchstick Men', I had always been aware of what felt to me like an undercurrent of jealousy in the band about how much money I was making from being the guy who wrote the hits. Now Bob came under scrutiny too, as he was the guy I'd co-written the later hits with. We had tried evening things out by giving four-way credits not just on 'Roll Over Lay Down', but also 'Break the Rules', in 1974. Bob had also started writing with Rick, coming up with great hits like 'Mystery Song', in 1976, which Rick sang. Then there was 'Rain', another all-time Quo classic, which Bob and Rick came up with and Rick again sang lead vocal on. In fact, the next two hit singles we had after that were covers – 'Wild Side of Life', an old Hank Thompson hit, and 'Rockin' All Over the World', written by John Fogerty of Creedence Clearwater Revival.

None of which made Alan feel any better about things as he'd had very little to do with those records, other than playing bass, of course. We would use one of Alan's songs on a B-side, as we did for 'Caroline' when his song called 'Joanne' was on the flip-side – and you earned the same amount for writing the song on the B-side of a single as you did writing the A-side. He still wasn't happy. He had it firmly in his mind that Status Quo was his group, he was the leader, not me and certainly not Rick, and he should get more acknowledgement of that fact – and more money. It was during this period that we all began to drift apart slightly as a group. We weren't at the stage where we would all have separate dressing rooms, though that would come later. But we certainly weren't sharing hotel rooms any more, let alone beds. And when we weren't touring, which wasn't often, we hardly socialised at all.

Meanwhile, I was now starting to enjoy the rewards of our success. At the start of 1975, just as 'Down Down' went to number 1, I bought a big new house in Purley. Still keeping with my south London roots but a million miles from the sort of places I grew up in as a child. This place had eleven bedrooms and an outdoor swimming pool. It also sat in the middle of these beautiful spacious gardens. I didn't know it yet but I was about to discover a love of gardening – or, at least, designing and planning a garden, then paying an actual gardener to put it together. I also discovered I could be a bit of a property wheeler-dealer too on the side. The asking price for the property was £80,000. But, because I was away touring so much and didn't have time to sit around worrying about whether the sale went through, one of our managers played hardball, stringing things out until eventually the price was negotiated down to £50,000. It was still a lot of money in 1975 (approximately £400,000 today, though the equivalent of a few million in terms of what a place like that would cost now) but for what I was getting it was an absolute snip. The main reason I was able to pull this off was because my offer was in straight cash. No banks or mortgages or middle managers involved, just a suitcase full of readies.

It really was a beautiful old house situated on its own private estate. It even had a name: The Glade. Very posh, my son. Boy done good, etc. I loved that house so much I lived there for the next thirty years. Not that I was ever there much to enjoy it when we first moved in. But on those few days off we would get, I would take the phone off the hook and just sit there like a king in my gorgeous huge gardens, or have a dip in my lovely heated swimming pool. No mortgage, no bank loans, a nice new BMW in the drive. It could comfortably get up to 130 mph – I know because I pushed it that far to see what it could do, and then spent the next three weeks telling everyone I met about it. I'd just be enjoying the comforting sound of the envelopes carrying big fat royalty cheques dropping onto the doormat. Gone were the days when a cheque for a thousand pounds looked like a lot. I was now getting cheques every six months, big six-figure payments.

I say this here not to show off but to demonstrate how far I had come as a young man living his dream. But I had so much money I didn't know what to do with it. So I didn't do much, not once I had the big house, big car and big career to work on. My children were still little, just at school. Jean now had money too, and was used to not having me around and built a life for herself around that. There were expense accounts here and there at various expensive West End stores – this was long before Amazon and online shopping, thank God – and she had her own car, her own friends and this huge house to run as she saw fit. I was all right with all of this as long as I could pull up the drawbridge and sit and smoke dope in peace and quiet. How Alan and John spent their money and lived their lives was up to them. I didn't really know and I didn't really care. I already spent more time with them than I did Jean or the kids.

Rick was enjoying a similar spell in a beautiful place he had bought for himself and his wife Marietta and their kids, a beautiful blond boy and a girl. His didn't come with a pool, so he had one built. And rather than enjoy one luxury car Rick, of course, had to have several, from Porsches to a Rolls-Royce at one point.

Apart from my new love affair with my BMW, I also splashed out a few years later on a Porsche and a Range Rover. The Range Rover felt like you were driving a posh tank.

They were still such a rare sight on the streets of London that they hadn't acquired their nickname of Chelsea Tractors, but I already felt funny driving this huge expensive car down the street in Purley, so I ditched it after a while. The Porsche went the same way. I blame Rick for getting me to buy one of those. He was still going on about how cool we would look both turning up somewhere in separate Porches. His did look very cool the first time he drove round to my house in it. But when, in the eighties, every flash git in London started driving one it put me right off. I couldn't bear to be thought of as someone so fashion-conscious. Rick in a Porsche just looked right somehow. Me in one, I felt like a prick. So I got rid of that too and bought a nice new Golf Mk1. Then felt like an even bigger prick when I got it home for doing something simply for the sake of appearances, a kind of inverse snobbery. Since then I've stuck to BMWs. Class will out. And just as important for me – comfort.

People ask: did the success change you? Hoping, I suppose, that you will say no. But when you've come from where we came from, how can success not change you? The truth is you *want* it to change you. Or at least, you want it to change the life you can now afford to lead. Actually, one of the first lessons you learn when you make big money is how little it really changes things. The only thing it really changes is other people's attitudes towards you. Life is life. It doesn't stop fucking you up just because you've got a few quid in your pocket suddenly. The excitement the money rolling in brought me was only fleeting, really. As for fame, that's the biggest lie of all. Fame literally changes nothing for you. It just changes the way everybody else suddenly sees you and acts around you. That can include friends and family too. You're still the same dickhead you always were;

only now people think you have some magic power all because they've seen you on the telly a few times.

That's not to say that I didn't become an insufferable tool for a while there after Quo hit it big. Partly it was the fame. Partly it was the feeling of vindication against all the people that had laughed at us behind our backs all those years we struggled to make it. And partly it was because I had gotten into amphetamines – speed – quite heavily for the first time and thought I knew the answer to everything, like you do when you are out of your head for three days and nights and your mouth is working three times faster than your brain.

While I'd deliberately developed a cocky attitude onstage, Jack the Lad, don't mess with me, and all that bollocks, I'd always been much more sensible offstage. I liked a laugh, of course, and a naughty bit of business in the bedroom now and again, who didn't? But I wasn't aggressive. Now, suddenly, I became aggressive and over-the-top, showing off all my worst qualities in the best possible places. Because Quo were seen at the time as a hard man's band, a gang you didn't mess with, I played that up, mouthing off in posh restaurants, terrorising the waiters and other diners. Really, I was an over-sensitive little twit. You would never have known it, though, if you bumped into me on a night out in 1974.

It didn't help that the band would all go out on the town together as one. We had to most of the time because we were always on the road somewhere. Only now instead of watching porn films in our hotel rooms we were being wined and dined in all these five-star places by record company bigwigs and high-flying promoters. It still makes me cringe when I recall how many really nice people have come up to me over the years since and told me what an obnoxious little prick I was to them back then. The joke was if someone did actually start a fight with me, I nearly always came off the worst. Or if I did manage to get one over on them, I would have ended up in tears anyway. As always, the only truly hard case in Quo was Alan. He didn't have to act hard and show off. Despite that baby face, you just took one look at him and knew not to mess around.

I would think about these things as I sat in my big house looking out on the world. Then be dragged back to reality when the phone rang and it was time to go back to work.

Oh yes, we were living the dream all right.

But soon it would be time to wake up.

(left) The immaculate conception – at least, according to my mother! Halo just out of shot. (Francis Rossi)

(right) You can see by my face how much I believed in Father Christmas. Nice, though, to see my taste in clobber was already highly developed. Dig the double-breasted coat and hipster boots. (Francis Rossi)

(above left) One of the old Rossi's Ice Cream vans, circa 1960. That's me being given what looks like an empty ice cream cone. Thanks! (Francis Rossi)

(above right) Me with my son, Nicholas, circa 1976 on holiday in Climping. (Bob Young)

(left) My mother, me, my maternal grandmother Alice (Nonna), and my younger brother Dominic. In the 1950s, all families were required to have photographs like this taken. (Probably on a Box Brownie.) (Francis Rossi)

Onstage with the Spectres in Catford, summer 1965. *(Francis Rossi)*

What did you do at school today? The Spectres were gigging around London when we were all still at school. Left to right: Alan Lancaster, me, John Coghlan and Jess Jaworski. *(Francis Rossi)*

Groovy, baby. A 'psychedelic' publicity shot from 1968. I look pissed off, probably because I'm the only one who didn't get given a ruffled shirt that day. *(Harry Goodwin/BBC Photo Library)*

(above) High tech sixties style: Bob Young's equipment list and stage plan for a gig in Newcastle, surrounded by some home snaps. *(Bob Young)*

(left) Publicity stills from 1967. Try to look cool. TRY TO LOOK COOL! Oh, never mind. *(Harry Goodwin/BBC Photo Library)*

(above) Yes, I think it's fair to assume we had been smoking some 'funny cigarettes' the day we decided to get dressed up like this. (Status Quo Archives)

(right) Polo neck sweaters, moccasins, purple shirts and stripy blazers . . . We are either extras from *The Prisoner*, or it's 1967 in the Beatles' Apple shop in London and somebody needs to tell John that no boy over five should ever be caught dead in bright green trousers. (Pictorial Press Ltd/Alamy Stock Photo)

Some people went for the double-denim look in the mid-seventies. But I took it a stage further, rocking the fashion world with my unprecedented quadruple denim look. (GAB Archives/Redferns/Getty Images)

We went to Australia for the first time in 1973 – and had some very glamorous shots taken. This isn't one of them. *(Status Quo Archives)*

1973 was the beginning of Quo amassing hundreds of gold records. You never forget your first though. *(Status Quo Archives)*

Written in a Los Angeles hotel room in 1974: the original handwritten lyrics to 'Down Down'. John Peel always used to end his live DJ shows with that song.

(Status Quo Archives)

Art for art's sake, hit singles for fuck's sake. Me and Bob Young in 1976. We co-wrote five hit singles for Quo in the early seventies – then didn't speak for twenty years. We are friends again now and writing together again.

(Status Quo Archives)

The Frantic Three: me, Rick and Alan when we were kings. *(Fin Costello / Redferns / Getty Images)*

Being interviewed somewhere on the road in the seventies. I seem to be the only one talking. Funny that … *(Koh Hasebe / Shinko Music / Getty Images)*

Rocking all over the Wall. Berlin, circa 1977. Left to right: John, me, Alan, Andy Bown and Rick. *(Bob Young)*

Portrait of the artist as a young dog – of two head. (You can tell how much I like this picture by the fact I'm not comfortable giving it a proper caption.) *(Michael Putland/Getty Images)*

Chapter Six

An Offer You Can't Refuse

The peak for the seventies line-up of Quo was probably 1977. We didn't realise it at the time, of course, but looking back now I would probably identify that year as the high-water mark in that phase of our career, and of my life at that time. A year of incredible highs – and also the start of the end of not just that version of the band, but also my first marriage, and very nearly my sanity.

That was the year we released the 'Rockin' All Over the World' single and album of the same name. For me, that was a weird album. It was a real step forward in many ways – it was the first time we had brought in an outside producer since the days of John Schroeder. His name was Pip Williams and there's no doubt he was brilliant for the band. Pip was about the same age as us and had been the guitarist in Jimmy James and the Vagabonds, who'd been signed to Pye in the sixties at the same time as us. Since then he'd become this very successful session guitarist playing on hits by the Walker Brothers and later the Sweet.

Pip had gone from that to producing and arranging sessions for people like the Moody Blues and the Sensational Alex Harvey Band to name just a couple. Pip was a guy who knew exactly where we were coming from but he wasn't crazy, the way we were now becoming from all the years on the road and the drugs and booze that were part of our day-to-day lives. He brought fresh perspective and that was one thing I definitely needed at that point.

In the early years, after I'd moved the family to The Glade, I retreated from the sleazy London nightlife I'd been living. When we weren't touring, I would go home there, pull up the drawbridge, so to speak, and make Jean tell anyone that phoned that I wasn't in. But I was. I never went out. It was like I was in hiding. Jean, meanwhile, had become lady of the manor, always shopping at Harrods, where we now had an expense account. Suddenly the house was full of this very expensive furniture and various antiques. I got into it, too. I didn't like to think I was squandering my fortune. I just couldn't resist going to Harrods with Jean and blowing huge chunks of it on all this . . . stuff.

The trouble was I was hardly ever home. We were at the height of our success, in terms of record sales, and still touring all the time. In 1977 alone, we had spent the first three months doing forty-five shows across seven different countries. Then the next three months recording the *Rockin' All Over the World* album. Then the moment it was finished we took off for a twenty-one-date tour of Australia. As soon as the single and album were released in November, we set off on a thirty-one-date tour of the UK that included three nights at the Glasgow Apollo, three nights at the Manchester Apollo, four nights at the Hammersmith Odeon in London, followed immediately by three nights at the Lewisham Odeon just a few miles away. It was the same everywhere: two nights in Dublin, two in Blackpool, two in Birmingham, two in Southampton . . . We had two weeks off over Christmas then immediately began a three-month European tour. It wasn't unusual for us to play six nights in a row, have one day off, then play another five in a row. It was the kind of pace that makes you into madmen, no matter how successful you are. The Australian tour we did that summer broke all records for British bands that toured there. We headlined – and sold out – all twenty-one shows. Four nights in Sydney; three nights in Melbourne; multiple sold-out shows in every major city in Australia. We had a week off when we got back – then headlined that year's Reading Festival.

It was f–u–c–k–i–n–g c–r–a–z–y.

No wonder we were all going mental. Then Alan decided he couldn't be arsed to fly back from Australia so we could make a promotional video for 'Rockin' All Over the World'. Promo vids were not the norm yet in the music business. Only a label's biggest and most sought-after artists would be asked to make one. So it was a prestige thing for us. More than that, it was also a necessity. The 'Rockin' All Over the World' single was one of the biggest hits we ever had. It was huge in about twenty different countries. To expect us to fly around the world doing TV and radio shows in so many places at once just wasn't feasible. We were mightily pissed off at Alan for not helping us out. These days you could make a video without any of the band in it and no one would bat an eye. But back then in the days before MTV and its ilk, it was all about making an as-live performance video that different TV shows in different countries could play as though you were there live in the studio with them. Alan not being there ruined any chance of that.

Until Colin had a brilliant idea: a life-size marionette of Alan, replete with bass guitar. We all laughed and told him to roll another joint. But he was serious and went ahead and had this thing built. Just like a real puppet it dangled from the ceiling with strings. Colin even acted as puppet-master, operating the strings to make Puppet Alan move as though he was playing. We were laughing so much we had to abandon the first few takes. Then we all got so used to it – Colin was doing such a brilliant job making it move – that we forgot it was even there. During tea breaks Colin would place the puppet sitting down in a chair so that when we came back it was like Alan was actually sitting there waiting for us.

It was comical but we did worry that programme directors would reject the video as a piss-take. Instead, everyone loved it so much they all played it, including *Top of the Pops*, and no one even noticed it was Puppet Alan. That video followed us everywhere on our next world tour. It was only later when word got out to the press that everyone got in on the joke. Everyone thought it was brilliant – everyone, that is, except Alan, who hated it. Whenever it came on telly on that tour, which it did all the time, Alan would leave the room.

On a more serious level, that song became a real calling card for us. A bit like the way 'We Will Rock You' became for Queen (which, oddly, was in the chart at the same time), 'Rockin' All Over the World' was one of those anthems that always got played at sports shows. One of the biggest examples of that was when England won the Rugby World Cup in 2003, and 'Rockin' All Over the World' was what they played through the stadium PA. And, of course, it would also later become the anthem for Live Aid. But we didn't know any of that yet. My main thought at the time was the huge favour we had done John Fogerty, who wrote it. Fogerty is one of the greatest American singer-songwriters ever, but I'm sure he would agree that what Quo did with his song transformed it into one of the best-known rock anthems in the world.

Appearing at Reading that year also underlined for me how much things had changed in the British music scene. The festival that year was a very strange mixture of hippy and punk – onstage and off. We headlined on the Saturday, and just below us on the bill were the Motors (who dressed as punks but were actually a couple of chaps from Ducks Deluxe, a London boogie band from the early seventies) and Lindisfarne, who'd been going nearly as long as us. Wandering around in the crowd were all the usual people we'd seen in previous years there, some naked, most drunk or stoned, or both. There was also a large contingent of punks and skinheads, which I had never seen before. But they all seemed to enjoy what we did. I don't suppose we sounded much different to them than new punk bands like the Damned or the Ramones.

Friday night, though, was headlined by the Jam supported by Sham 69 – and that was a very different sort of crowd. The longhairs and hippies went into shock because the punk and skinheads rioted during the Sham 69 set. I wasn't there but we heard all about it the next day. It sounded very nasty with a lot of people getting hurt, many taken to hospital. I'd seen crazy, out-of-control crowds before but nothing quite like that. It was the first time we as a band had ever experienced what was going on with the whole punk and new wave scene and we were taken aback, to say the least. Musically, it didn't sound a million miles from what Quo was doing. Singing in English accents, playing loud fast catchy songs that didn't outstay their welcome. True, we weren't singing about anarchy, and, yes, we were all now pushing thirty (John had already got there, bless him), and, yes again, we all still had long hair and wore flared jeans. But anyone can get a haircut and buy a new pair of skinny-leg jeans.

According to the music press, though, none of that counted for anything. We were branded boring old farts – along with every other band that had come before including Queen, the Stones, Zeppelin, even the Beatles. We had just returned to London from Australia, where we were welcomed like heroes, so it was all very baffling to us. On the other hand, we didn't care. A week after Reading we began a four-month break from touring: the first lengthy break like that we had ever had. We made an album in the middle of all that. We also became tax exiles. We had to. At its worst in the mid-seventies the British government was taking around 90 per cent of our earnings. 90 per cent! Who in their right mind would consider that right and proper? Especially when you're in a band and you never know from one record to the next when your career might suddenly be over. So it's not like we were just lounging around. Nevertheless, we were now very firmly established in our own bubble, and very little of the outside world was allowed to get in there with us.

I say that, but the truth is that against my better judgement I did still read the music press – or at least the cuttings we would get sent by the record company. We had a lot of good press in places like *Melody Maker* and *Sounds*. But the *NME*, which was now the leading light of the music press, would use us for target practice all the time. Even some of the new punk-era writers on *Melody Maker* and *Sounds* started having a right go. They would treat us like the old geriatrics of rock, and wonder why we hadn't been put out to pasture yet. I kept reading that we were too old to rock 'n' roll any more. The first time I saw that I was twenty-seven. I would read this stuff and not so quietly seethe. I would take it all very personally and think to myself: we'll show you, you fucking pricks! It motivated me to write more hits. Rod Stewart didn't have his first hit until he was twenty-six. Bryan Ferry was twenty-seven when he had his first hit with Roxy Music. Freddie Mercury was nearly twenty-eight when he hit it big with Queen. Even Joe Strummer, frontman of new punk leading lights the Clash, was only three years younger than me. Yet here was I being written off as an old dinosaur. Well, I would show them. As far as I was concerned, I may have had a few big hit records by now but I'd only just begun.

At the same time, our press coverage started seeping across to the national daily newspapers. In those days it wasn't like now where every paper has dedicated pages covering music, celebs, movies and whatnot. There were just a handful of writers from the papers that wrote regular weekly columns about pop. Fortunately for us, we were now one of those higher-echelon groups they liked to write about because, unlike the punks, we were now popular not just with hard-nosed rockers but with a more mainstream audience that liked to watch us on *Top of the Pops*. John Peel was a bit like the music press. He had stopped playing our records after *Hello!* went to number 1. He was onto the next new thing. But you could now hear us on the Dave Lee Travis breakfast show on Radio 1. This was like being in the daily newspapers. Not as cool but far more people paying attention. Meanwhile, we'd made another album with Pip and had another hit single with 'Again and Again', and set off on another six-month tour playing huge arenas in Germany and France, and another massive UK tour that included three nights at Wembley Arena and four nights at the Hammersmith Odeon. We didn't even go home when we played so many shows in London: we just booked into suites at the Dorchester and places like that and kept our 'on the road' mentality going – anything to keep our bubble from bursting. Going home in the middle of that would have thrown the whole thing out of whack.

When people said all our records sounded the same, I took it as a backhanded compliment. You could say the same thing about all the major rock artists, starting with the Rolling Stones, who spent years rewriting the riff to '(I Can't Get No) Satisfaction'. Keith Richards is the first to admit it – 'Let's Spend the Night Together', 'Jumpin' Jack Flash', 'Brown Sugar', same riff to 'Satisfaction', just very slightly reworked – to spectacular effect. By the same token, Rod Stewart spent years living off 'Maggie May', which turned into 'You Wear It Well', then almost every other hit he had in the seventies.

I will happily admit that certain songs definitely carried on where previous hits had left off, put it like that. Like 'Down Down', which has the same propulsive rhythm, right where it counts, that 'Paper Plane' had. Same with 'Don't Waste My Time' and its offspring, 'Roll Over Lay Down', which in turn begat 'Break the Rules'.

Lyrically, though, they all meant something different. 'Don't Waste My Time' was about what we in those days called a prick teaser. I know you can't say that now but in 1972 you could and that's what the song is about. 'Roll Over Lay Down' was about getting home from a stint on the road with the band, it's dawn, and you don't know what to do with yourself, your wife is sleeping and has left a note on the door. 'Break the Rules' was about – well, what do you think? Breaking the bloody rules!

Ironically, the one that didn't mean a thing was our number 1 hit, 'Down Down'. I wrote that with Bob when we were staying at a hotel in Los Angeles on our very first tour of the States. Bob and I always wrote the same way. We would just hang out, roll a joint, talk. I'd always have a guitar on my lap, strumming aimlessly, and Bob would sit there humming. Then seemingly out of thin air would come the idea for a little melody or riff and I'd start messing with it while Bob sat there making suggestions or joining in. We always knew when we had a winner. That's when we would get the cassette player out and record the two of us bashing out this song. Sometimes they were just parts or rough ideas. Sometimes they were whole songs. The good ones would then get taken into the studio and demoed, and after that recorded properly.

In the case of 'Down Down', we didn't need to make a demo. It was all there on the cassette recording we made in LA. I had this fantastic idea for an extended intro that just keeps building until the song takes off like a rocket. I just didn't have any words for it. Even Bob couldn't think of anything and he was supposed to be the poet. We just had this one line over the chorus – dah–dah–de–dah – which we kept repeating over and over. The only word we could come up with to stick in there instead of dah–dah–de–dah was 'down' – as in 'down, down, deeper and down'. Then repeat. I said to Bob, 'There's no way we can keep it like that. It doesn't mean anything.' But the fact is it sounded great. So we kept it. And guess what, it's still one of the most popular records we ever made.

The fact is people bring their own interpretations to song lyrics. Bob Dylan, arguably the greatest lyricist of the twentieth century, would never think to include lyric sheets with his albums, and some of his songs would have twelve or fifteen different verses. It was impossible to hear everything he sang correctly. Even when you could hear them they were so full of symbolism you couldn't possibly know what he was really on about. But it didn't matter. People brought their own meaning to those words.

It's the same with seemingly simple lyrics. T. Rex had a number 1 with 'Metal Guru' when we were having our first hits and nobody to this day knows what that song was supposed to be about. I thought he was singing 'medal gnu' when it first came out. It didn't stop me loving the record. It sounded so cool and sexy it didn't matter what it was 'about'.

It was the same with 'Down Down'. Although I must add that even there I did manage to inject a bit of autobiographical detail in the line, 'I want all the world to see/ To see you're laughing, and you're laughing at me'. That was me thinking about all the haters that put Quo down, but at the same time also thinking about my wife Jean and the times when she would laugh at me, accuse me of dreaming, back before the band finally made it.

The real point is that like U2, the Stones, Bruce Springsteen, Sting and the Police . . . the moment you hear any of their records, you know exactly who it is. That to me is an achievement few artists in the rock sphere have accomplished. Knock us all you like, but as soon as a Quo record comes on you know it couldn't be anyone else but us. Anyway, sod the critics. There are so many records, books, TV programmes, films, ideas that the so-called important critics and I disagree about it, I take everything they say with a pinch of salt, plus or minus. The only critics that really count are the people listening to your music. One small example: for all the micky-taking records like 'Down Down' attracted from the music press, it still remained one of John Peel's all-time favourite tracks. Apparently he used to always close his live DJ sets by playing it. I had to laugh, too, when some years later I was told that Jo Callis, the former guitarist in the Rezillos who later joined the Human League, loved 'Down Down' so much he – ahem – repurposed the riff for the Human League's biggest hit, 'Don't You Want Me Baby'. That speaks to me far more than some hastily written bit of stone-throwing from some know-all with a typewriter. Cheers, Jo!

I see this as different, by the way, to the sampling that would become such a feature of the hip-hop takeover of the pop world in recent times. Sampling a riff or melody from a well-known chart hit takes skill. The German techno group Scooter did an incredible job in 2008 when they took 'Whatever You Want' and built it into their own giant hit, 'Jump the Rock'. That was huge fun. But it's not quite the same as becoming an inspiration to other songwriters to build on something you did first – and make it into something 'original'. Younger musicians are always using older music to reinvent and be creative with. That's the great thing about music – it doesn't have to obey the rules. So when people ask, is it better now or then? I say it is both better and worse. Depending on how old you are. It's like asking who your favourite James Bond is. Depends on how old you are. For some it's still Roger Moore. For me it will always be Sean Connery. (Although Daniel Craig is the exception, as he's going to be best ever, you wait and see.)

But while we were busy congratulating ourselves on how well we had done by the end of 1978, the cracks were appearing, not just within the band, but in our personal lives. I don't want to speak for Alan and John here, as they are still around to tell their own stories. But Rick, who isn't, was definitely burning the candle at both ends. We both were.

Rick had recently had his second child, a beautiful baby girl named Heidi. We were on tour again in Germany when Marietta phoned him to let him know she had gone into labour. Rick was in the shower in his hotel room when Marietta rang – and one of Rick's German groupies answered the phone to her. You can imagine how that went down. Because of the tour, it was another month before Rick was able to get home to see his daughter for the first time. Even then he couldn't stay long as we were tax exiles by then. I'm pretty sure Marietta knew what Rick was like. Not just with other women, but in his whole rock-star lifestyle. Where I would burrow myself away when we were not working, Rick would be out every night, hanging out with other infamous party guys of the era like George Best and Alex 'Hurricane' Higgins. He'd be out night after night, doing coke, drinking champagne, having pretty girls sitting on his lap. Then climb into his latest Porsche or Roller and drive home at dawn at a hundred miles per hour. He had his own big house by then, set in nine acres of rolling fields and woodland in Hambledon, Surrey. Big swimming pool. God knows how many cars. Then there were the various boats he owned along the way. He even had a fire engine at one point. Don't ask me why. Rick just was that wild and crazy guy.

I was the same – but different. Rick, Alan and I were all doing a lot of coke by then. Not John. He was not into it at all. He was still into his beer. Boy, was he into his beer! The first time I'd ever done cocaine was with Rick at this posh party somewhere on tour in Canada in 1975. It was just like you would imagine that sort of party would have been like in the mid-seventies. Coke was king, ultra cool. Offering your guests coke was no different to serving them good champagne. There was actually a big glass bowl on the table in the middle of the room where you would just help yourself, as though you were helping yourself to a punch bowl.

There was a guy there we knew who worked for Manfred Mann's Earth Band and he was the one with all the coke. Rick and I dived in, curious as much as anything to find out what this wonderful substance we'd read about was actually like. The Manfred Mann guy helped fill our nostrils, using a little silver coke spoon, and Rick and I wandered outside and waited to see what happened. The answer, rather disappointingly, was that not much appeared to happen at all. I was standing by the swimming pool with Rick and saying to him, 'Is it me or is this stuff not very good?' Rick was like, 'It's not half as good as speed, is it?' I agreed.

We were both doing a fair bit of speed at that point – white amphetamine sulphate powder that looked much like coke and which you could also snort lines of. Speed, though, had a much more pronounced effect. At its best it definitely aided creativity. When we were making the *Blue for You* album in 1976, Rick Alan and I were all speeding out of our nuts night and day. One night, I left Rick in the studio working on a tune he and Bob had written together called 'Mystery Song'. When I came back the next day there he was still working on the song. I thought, blimey, he's keen. I said, 'What time did you get in this morning?' He just looked at me with these big dilated eyes, sweat running down his face, and said: 'What do you mean? I haven't gone home yet.' Crazy, yes, but the song itself was fantastic and became another hit single for us that year, with Rick singing it. Unlike coke, speed really lasted you.

You always knew when you were speeding. You could be up for days and days on it. But then the comedown would be hideous. Depression, paranoia, insomnia . . . Cocaine was supposed to do all the things speed did for you – keep you going all night, give you extra fizz and energy – but without the terrible comedowns.

That's what we'd been told anyway. But this stuff didn't seem to do anything. We thought, perhaps we need to do a bit more to get us going . . .

By 1978, the speed was only there occasionally. The rest of the time we – that is, Rick, Alan and I again, never John – were doing coke. Rick used to call it 'laughing at spoons' because by then we all had our own silver coke spoons. Coke was such a cool thing in the late seventies you would get ads in *Rolling Stone* selling the paraphernalia. Most sought-after would be this little brown medicine bottle in which you could put several grams of coke. The little silver spoon would be built into the bottle cap. So you could just whip this thing out on a plane or the tour bus or just sitting in a restaurant – not that we were doing much eating any more – and help yourself to a couple of scoops of coke, discreet, like. Classy. Oh yeah.

Like speed, and before that dope, we used coke to 'help' us with our songwriting. Unlike speed, coke was expensive and because the effect was more subtle, you ended up snorting far more of it per day (and night) than you ever would speed. Consequently, while it definitely had an impact on our live performances, which became more and more high-energy, and became our go-to drug in the studio, it was beginning to have all sorts of unexpected, though in retrospect inevitable, effects on every other aspect of our lives, too. Jean said this was when a big change in my personality came about. I'm sure she was right. We weren't able to figure any of this out at the time, though. 'Rehab' was not a word anyone used in those days. Having more than a few weeks between recording and touring was also unheard of. If you felt bad – physically ill, mentally charred – the cure was to do more coke. There was even this private doctor in Harley Street who would give bands these special 'B12' injections in the arse. I've never had a B12 like it. The trick was he would spike these injections with pure pharmaceutical coke. All the big bands knew of him and all of us would go.

One unfortunate side effect of doing mountains of coke every day, for me personally, was that for the first time in my life I became a heavy drinker. I had never been a drinker, beyond sharing a half-bottle of brandy with Rick before we went onstage in the early days. But that was only for a short period. I didn't like the taste. I was always much happier drinking lemonade and smoking dope. As I got older and more successful and found myself in different social situations, I might have some wine. But alcohol was never my thing. Now, suddenly, I began to make up for lost time.

It started as a couple of shots of tequila at the end of the night to help me smooth out the edges of the coke and help me get some sleep for a few hours. Then quickly escalated from there. Rick was the same. At one point, he told me, he was downing a bottle of whisky a day, a couple of bottles of wine and at least three grams of coke. Every day. I don't know how much Alan might have been drinking but he was as knee-deep in 'snow', as we used to call it, as Rick and I were, I'm sure. At least while he was with the band.

The upshot of all this was decidedly ugly. For a band that was used to being accused of sticking to a formula, suddenly it was like all the pieces of the jigsaw got thrown up in the air at once. Where they landed none of us had any say over. At least that's how it felt at the time, though looking back it's pretty easy to see what was happening to us. It wasn't just the cocaine. The success, the break-up of personal relationships, the pressure of always being on the road or in the studio trying to come up with another successful record, all of that would have been enough to finish off most groups eventually. Having three of the four members stoned out of their minds on coke and booze, though, definitely made everything ten times harder than it was already.

The first thing to suffer was the music. Bob Young and I had grown apart – 'grown apart' being a euphemism for starting to hate each other. It all went back to 1976, the year that Colin Johnson and his business partner David Oddie split from Gaff Management and went off to form their own new management operation, which they called Quarry Productions. Their major clients were Quo and Rory Gallagher. I had no problem with it at the time. We were riding the crest of a wave with the *Blue for You* album, which was another number 1, and Rory Gallagher was a wonderful musician and an absolutely lovely bloke.

However, there was also someone new now advising us that became very destructive indeed. I'm not going to name him, just refer to him as Be-Bop. He was supposed to be a financial whiz who was going to make us all more money. Sounds good, right?

Wrong. The only person Be-Bop was interested in making more money for was himself. Unfortunately none of us could see it at the time. Seeing what a bunch of cossetted coke hounds we were becoming, Be-Bop took full advantage. At one point, he suggested giving us chequebooks full of blank cheques. So that we could sign all the pages saving us the 'trouble' of having to sign the cheques every time Be-Bop needed to pay for something on our behalf. We were all so out of it we thought this was a great idea: don't bother me with paperwork, mate, can't you see I'm busy writing songs (read: snorting coke). The only fly in the ointment for Be-Bop was Bob Young, who could see something wasn't right. The fact that Bob had a close personal relationship with me also counted against him, asking awkward questions about this new feller and what he was doing with our money. Bob could tell you down to the last penny where our money was being spent on tour. It's my feeling now that Be-Bop decided he would have to get Bob out of the picture.

That's when the whispering started. In my ear telling me horrible things Bob had said about me. In Bob's ear telling him terrible things I'd said about him. I should have sat down and spoken to Bob about it. Instead, I went straight off the deep end. I've always been that way, whether it was drugs or music or, these days, manically exercising every day. Do I have an addictive personality? That's a definite yes. I see it more as an obsessive-compulsive thing. I like to chop my days up into manageable lines. Coke just really fitted in with that kind of mania. It was also a hell of a lot of fun!

It wasn't much help, though, when it came to dealing with situations like the perilous one we now found ourselves in. At the same time, things between Jean and me were at an all-time low. Marrying so young, and becoming parents so young, would have been enough to put a strain on any relationship. But as I approached my thirtieth birthday, with my coke habit becoming more out of control and my relationship with Bob now up in smoke, and of course hardly ever being home, Jean and I began rowing so much I felt like I had nowhere I could run to for some peace.

When the option to become a tax exile came up, I jumped at it, partly because I did not like the idea that 83 per cent of the band's earnings (down from 90 per cent, gee, thanks, Mr Chancellor) now went to the taxman, but also because I saw it as a chance to escape my worries at home with Jean.

We all chose different options. Alan, whose marriage had broken up, had remarried a beautiful Australian woman named Dayle. They had already decided they wanted to live together in Australia before the tax exile thing became an issue. Alan, I think, also saw it as an opportunity to get himself out of the whole drug thing. It was impossible to escape when the band was working but the rest of the time he was always eager to get back to Sydney and be with Dayle, who he soon started a family with when she had the first of their two sons. John's marriage was also heading for divorce eventually. Meanwhile, he set up home on the Isle of Man, where he would continue to live, off and on, for a quite a few years. Rick took Marietta and the kids and rented a nice big place in Jersey. He was bored out of his mind within the first five minutes. He was always getting one of his pals to get the ferry over to see him, not forgetting to bring a nice big bag of coke with them.

I ended up living in Ireland. No big surprise there given my family connection on my mother's side – and the fact that Ireland also offered tax exemption for artists living there. I also liked the people, who were so open and friendly compared to what I had become used to. I didn't miss not being around the others, not even Rick. Once the novelty of our coke-brothers days were behind us and we were both just full-on self-absorbed coke addicts, I don't think either of us really spared much thought for the other, except when it came time to work.

Jean had given birth to our third son, Kieran, in January 1979. It should have been a joyous occasion, a reaffirmation of our love together as a family. But 1979 was also the year Jean decided she'd had enough and walked out, taking the children with her. I can't say I was deeply shocked when she told me of her plans. It wasn't the first time Jean had left me. In the past, though, she had always come home again eventually. I knew this time was different when she told me she had bought a house for her and the children to live in. Having to stand there and watch her put the children and their suitcases into the car, then drive off without me, was like being knifed in the heart. I had never known such pain. Pain and guilt and regret. I blamed myself, as all good Catholic schoolboys would. Jean knew about the drugs. Knew about the groupies. Had grown exhausted by the fact I was never home, no matter how much money we had to spend.

But it was more than that. She had simply grown tired of being with me, having to put herself second all the time while I was out there living out my dreams and fantasies. I never allowed Jean the space to fulfil her dreams too. I should have realised but I just wasn't thinking straight. I was still young and inexperienced enough to feel somehow that if my dreams were coming true then that meant Jean's were too. That isn't how it works, though. I see that now. Deeper even than that was the fact that we had both known it was over long before. We just hadn't had the courage to end it. It tore me apart having to see the children leave like that. But the brutal truth was I was quite relieved the marriage was over. That we could finally be honest about it.

A few days later I was back in Ireland. I'd booked some rooms at Dromoland Castle, this incredibly beautiful sixteenth-century hotel in County Clare. It was out of season so it felt like I had the place to myself. I didn't but you could lose yourself in those 1,200 acres for days at a time and feel like you were exploring a whole new world. I was close enough to London that my children could come over for visits. I was still able to enter the UK for up to sixty days a year so that also made the transition easier to manage. I mean, I really rationalised the whole thing, laid it all out in my mind as a marvellous step to take. I thought by being in Ireland I was escaping the worst of my problems. In fact, they had only just begun.

I coped with it by doing some more coke. In truth, I don't have many strong memories of that time at all. I know I was in a state, and that it was mostly my fault. That's one of the reasons Jean left me. I wasn't taking care of her and the kids other than by bringing money in. I was never there and when I was I wasn't really because I'd be locked away smoking dope and doing coke and hiding from the world.

Then Rick got ill. It all went back to one typically crazy-Rick night when we were in Holland recording the *Whatever You Want* album, and he took a boat out on this big lake one evening. It was a lovely warm evening so he'd gone out in just a shirt and jeans. But then something happened and the boat broke down and he was out on the water all night, shivering in this thin shirt in the freezing cold. In truth, I don't know for sure what caused him to become so ill soon afterwards but that was always my theory anyway. The upshot though was that, despite numerous tests in the hospital, nobody could tell him exactly what the problem was. They just whacked him with cortisone injections, gave him a ton of heavy-duty sleeping pills and told him to get some rest. So he went home and went straight to bed – for three months. This was to be the start of what became Rick's lifelong reliance on sleeping tablets. The fact is he was in a bad way – his whole body was racked with pain and he was so weak he could hardly stand – but no one could tell him why. He ended up in Germany with Marietta's family, having all sorts done to him in a German hospital. Draining fluid from his knees. Covering his body in these different poultices. Sticking yet more needles in him. He eventually got back on his feet but it took a long time. Meanwhile, we had to cancel a European tour and put the rest of our touring plans on hold while we waited for Rick to fully recover.

I don't know how I felt about this. Annoyed probably. Inconvenienced. Worried about Rick? Not overly. Rick was always getting into scrapes. Rick was always in some kind of trouble. I would sit there chopping out another gram of coke, listening to whatever the latest was with Rick and just get on with my day — which was rapidly spiralling into a kind of permanent midnight. I was beginning to worry about myself more than Rick. That's when I allowed myself to think too deeply about things at all.

Fortunately, we already had a new album in the can, the aforementioned *Whatever You Want,* and, of course, it featured one of our all-time best-known — and most successful — hits with the title track. Rick had written the song 'Whatever You Want' with our keyboard player Andy Bown. Andy had been in the Herd with Peter Frampton, so we knew each other. He'd also been a much-sought-after session player and solo artist in the seventies. He played as a session musician on the *Rockin' All Over the World* album and would officially become a full-time member of the band in 1982. Andy is a great player who deserves more credit for his massive contributions to Status Quo.

What Rick and Andy achieved with 'Whatever You Want' was so good I admit I was a tad jealous. I hadn't come up with anything as good as that as a single since 'Down Down' five years before. Rick sings it brilliantly too. Fair play, it's simply one of those songs that completely defines and reaffirms the Quo musical identity. It's also got that great quality all the best songs have of having universal appeal. It's suggested there in the title, of course — whatever you want, here it is, you can have it. But it's in the glorious rhythm and riff too. Your body starts reacting to it before your brain even knows what's going on. Your feet tap. Your head nods. Your shoulders start to twitch. As a result, it was a major hit in every country it was released in (though not America, where I don't think it was even released) and remains one of the big highlights of any Quo show to this day.

In fact, Rick was absolutely hitting it out of the park in his role as a co-songwriter on that album. With Bob, he also co-wrote the album's other big hit, 'Living on an Island'. If 'Whatever You Want' was archetypal Quo taken to the nth degree, 'Living on an Island' was the exact opposite. Our first proper ballad since 'Are You Growing Tired of My Love' died a death over ten years before, 'Living on an Island' was a soft-as-a-feather, country-tinged ballad that Rick sang like an angel. He co-wrote that one with Bob, and if you listen to the lyrics it spells out exactly what life was like for him at that time living as a tax exile on Jersey: 'Living on an island/Looking at another line/Waiting for my friend to come/And we'll get high . . .'

The painful part was that just as the *Whatever You Want* album went rocketing up the charts towards the end of 1979, the band was nose-diving in the opposite direction. Jean had already left me. Rick was ill. Alan was in Australia. And John was pretty sick of all of us by that point, by all accounts. Then, early in 1980, with our touring commitments on hold while Rick got better, Bob announced he was leaving. He'd had enough of the behind-the-scenes ructions. If I'm being honest, my attitude at the time was very much of the 'good riddance to bad rubbish' variety. I believed he had betrayed me by slagging me off behind my back. Bob believed the same about me. We had both been played for fools.

I don't know if the rest of the band blamed me for Bob leaving, but they were all upset when told Bob was out of the picture. We had all come to rely on him for so long it was hard to imagine touring again without him.

In terms of Bob's input as a songwriter, that was easier to accommodate as by then we were all working with different people, both in and outside the group. It had started with the

Rockin' All Over the World album, where Alan brought in a song he'd co-written with Mick Green, who had been the guitarist in Johnny Kidd & the Pirates, and Rick came in with one he'd written with Jackie Lynton, who'd been one of that generation of British rockers that came up with Billy Fury and Screaming Lord Sutch. Even Pip Williams wrote one of the tracks. In the couple of albums we'd done since then it had become a free-for-all. 'Again and Again', another hit for us, had been written by Rick, Jackie and Andy Bown and, although it became a successful single, always seemed like a piss-take to me; Alan had another with Mick Green; Pip had another. And I had come in with three new songs that I'd co-written with the guy who was to become my main co-writer for the next few years, a lovely chap named Bernie Frost.

By the time we came to *Just Supposin'*, our first album after Bob had gone, in 1980, I was mainly writing with Bernie, Rick was mainly writing with Andy, Alan had teamed up with an Australian singer he'd gotten to know called Keith Lamb, and there was even one song co-written by me, Alan and Andy. I think that was two songs in one, actually; the first time the three of us would be co-credited with a song – and the last. We had also managed to lose Pip as our producer somewhere along the way – as I recall, Alan suggested it would be cheaper for us not to have a producer – and were back to producing ourselves. If that all sounds messy, believe me it was. Very.

All of these typically selfish and over-indulgent band shenanigans were put into perspective, however, by an event so tragic I don't think Rick ever got over it. His two-year-old daughter, Heidi, drowned in the family swimming pool at home one Sunday in August 1980. I was in my studio at home in London recording the guitar solo to a future Quo single called 'Rock 'n'

Roll' and the tape stopped suddenly just as I was in the middle of it. At that precise moment the phone rang and it was Rick. He said, 'Heidi's dead.' I said, 'Don't be daft, she can't be.' He said, 'No. We found her in the swimming pool.'

I still couldn't believe it. Rick was always phoning to let you know about his latest scrape – cars crashed, flights missed, mystery illnesses, endless woman trouble – I had become somewhat inured to it all. I said, 'Are you sure, Rick? It can't be. You've got it fucking wrong!'

But he hadn't, poor bastard. He'd been sitting with his six-year-old son Richard in the lounge watching TV while Marietta had been cooking Sunday lunch. They had taken the cover off the pool because it was a nice day and they were all going to hang out by the pool later. Next thing, Heidi has gone missing. They searched the house and found the poor little mite in the swimming pool. Rick did his best to resuscitate her but it was too late. He was telling me this on the phone and I couldn't believe my ears.

'Fucking hell, Ricky,' I remember saying. 'Now what have we done?'

Chapter Seven

Runny Nosin'

The Rick Parfitt I first knew as a sunny, blond-haired teenager hadn't changed much in the intervening years between meeting him at Butlin's in the mid–sixties and the death of his daughter Heidi in 1980. Now suddenly everything changed.

Rick had always been the starriest member of Status Quo, the most showbiz. Someone who could snap into character when the moment demanded it, no matter what might be going on elsewhere in his life. He lit up every room he walked into. Had friends – and girlfriends – everywhere we went. Was never at a loss with what to do that night, whatever night and whatever place he found himself in. Rick was all about enjoying life. In that respect, he was born to be a seventies rock star. That is, the guy with the gorgeous blonde wife, gorgeous blonde girlfriends on the side, big flash expensive cars, big flash expensive house, big flash expensive tastes. If you needed cheering up, Rick was your man.

But who was there to cheer Rick up when he was down? I don't know if he really had anyone. It certainly wasn't me. Rick and I had been very close in the early years of the band. But as the fame and money and success overtook us, we had grown apart. We were still close. We never lost that tight bond between us, even during those times when we were pissed off with each other, which only made it even more frustrating. We always had that thing that we would never be able to share with anyone else – the mutual experience of becoming famous together, and the struggles, frustrations and many victories that entailed. But we were no longer in each other's lives as much. How could we be? We were both now over thirty, both married (just about, in my case) with kids, and spending most of our time together working with the band. Any time off we ever got, we couldn't wait to get away from each other. That's the same with every band that's been together longer than five minutes.

Rick could also be a handful in other ways. We were like mirror opposites in many ways. A great partnership in the band but very different away from it; it seemed like the more of a recluse I became, the more outgoing and sociable Rick became. The more uncomfortable I became hanging out with other so-called celebrities, the more famous friends Rick collected. He might be hanging out with John Deacon from Queen one night, then out on the razz with Rod Stewart and George Best at Tramp. And, of course, he was a friend to all the models and party girls you find at clubs like that.

He would tell me about the night he was drinking with a group of people until four in the morning, then insisted on driving all the way back to his house in the country, picking up a few of his gold records and driving back to whatever after-hours private club they were in and start handing them out like party favours. No wonder he had so many friends. It would all come crashing down eventually, of course, when Quo's career took a dive in the mid-eighties, but while it lasted Rick was determined to live that life to the hilt.

When Heidi died, though, a big part of Rick died with her. That's how it seemed to me. Sunny Rick was gone. To be replaced by Dark Rick. I don't think I saw Rick smile again – except for the cameras – for at least a couple of years. I don't think I saw him really laugh again for a lot longer than that. Now when he walked in the room he did so like a ghost. No energy at all. No spark. No nothing. He was just . . . gone.

How Marietta coped with it, I will never know. Rick obviously had some time away from the band but it was only a few weeks. I was told later that he spent hardly any of that time at home. And that when he was at home he was in such a state he was no good to anyone. That he would go out into the garden at night and shout for God to come down and take him. Scream at God for being such an evil bastard. I can't say I blamed him. They say there's a reason for everything. But that's not true. The hardest part of having to live through the accidental death of a child must be feeling that they died for absolutely no reason.

We cancelled the tour we had planned for that autumn but of course the record company went ahead and released the album anyway. *Just Supposin'* was another big hit for us. The single released ahead of the album, 'What You're Proposing', was a song I had written with Bernie Frost and it became our biggest hit single since 'Down Down'. It was very nearly our second ever number 1 single, kept from the top spot for three weeks running by 'Woman in Love' by Barbra Streisand, which was a Bee Gees song and went to number 1 in about ten different countries, so fair enough. I suppose.

Definitely cause for celebration, though, except for one thing. It meant we were obliged to promote the single with TV appearances in Britain and Europe. Rick could have easily – and understandably – said he couldn't do it. But he stepped up, bless his heart. I'll never forget him doing his best to be his usual outgoing self when we filmed our *Top of the Pops* appearance. Look at the clip now and you'd never know anything was wrong with him. But as soon as the filming was over and we went back to the dressing room, he was filled with despair again.

To fill the gap we went back into the studio and made another album. We had a fair amount of material already recorded and left over from the *Just Supposin'* sessions. We added a few numbers to that and put it out as *Never Too Late*. It was not the best Quo album ever made but we didn't know what else to do with Rick out of the picture. The songs we had cobbled together weren't strong enough to include a single so we recorded a cover of 'Something 'Bout You Baby I Like'. I remember it was the first time we had experimented with a drum machine. It had been a minor hit for Tom Jones a few years before. The version that inspired our go at it, though, was a fantastic duet Glen Campbell and Rita Coolidge had released a couple of years before ours. It wasn't a big hit either but it had that wonderful honkytonk feel that suited Quo down to the ground. That said, the fact it went top 10 for us says more about how popular we were at that point than how good our version was. The same goes for the album, which hit number 2.

By now Rick was virtually begging for us to go back on the road. Home life was in pieces. Not helped, he was the first to later acknowledge, by the fact he was now very much the worse for wear on coke and booze and anything else he could get his hands on. Marietta ended up putting their son in a nearby boarding school while she tried to build a life for herself again after the death of her daughter. But Rick would be off on another three-day bender or be out on the road with us. It was too much and eventually Marietta told Rick she wanted a divorce. That meant all three frontline members of Quo were now divorced or getting divorced from their wives. Not long after that, John split with his first wife Carol and they were also later divorced. It became one of those strange landmark eras where we all kind of grew into our older selves. A bit like when we came back from Butlin's all those years before. Only now the boys that had grown into men were the men that were easing into a somewhat pained middle age.

After Rick came back we did a big three-month tour: sixty-seven dates between March and June 1981, in twelve different countries. Big runs of shows in Germany, Italy, France, one-offs in Switzerland, Norway, Portugal, Belgium, Sweden . . . you name it, we played it. Somehow in the middle of this we also did two mammoth UK tours that included four nights at the Hammersmith Odeon in London and three nights at Wembley Arena – in London. We could have done a whole tour of London we were in such demand. Were we happy, though, any of us?

No we bloody well weren't. Any of us. Ever.

For me this signalled the start of a bleak period in my life. Just as Quo was at its commercial height, I was sinking fast. While I was tax exiled in Ireland my coke habit had grown out of all proportion. I was now convinced that without it I wouldn't be able to keep writing hit songs. I thought I was proved right when 'What You're Proposing' became such a huge hit. The irony was that the song was almost entirely about doing cocaine. Well, that and getting divorced from Jean – and the general unhappiness now surrounding the band. All that stuff about 'Not disclosing how we're really, really feeling . . .' And that bit about 'If I'm composing, but then I might be runny nosing . . .'

How we were really, really feeling was shit. And part of the reason for that, at least for me and Rick, was that we were constantly 'runny nosing' – snorting coke. For Rick, it was a form of both escape from his feelings of complete devastation following the accidental death of Heidi, and a weird kind of consolation. Like drinking to forget. Only he was snorting and drinking deliberately to try and destroy any feelings he had left.

I would like to have helped him but I didn't know how. No one knew how. I was so deep into my coke addiction I would snort it even when I knew I couldn't get any higher, just to experience it trickling down my throat, the bitter taste as I rubbed it around my gums. The feeling of it as it rushed up my nose. On those exceedingly rare occasions where I had run out of coke, I would find something else to snort – speed maybe. Even snuff, anything just so that I could shove something up my nose.

I was doing so much 'runny nosing' that I started carrying around bundles of handkerchiefs, which I would leave behind, soiled, everywhere I went. When I wasn't snorting coke I was smoking it. I don't mean crack – the synthesised version of coke that addicts smoke out of homemade pipes. I mean I would roll myself a big fat joint and frost it with layers of cocaine. I also took to lacing my tequila with pinches of coke. Big clouds of it, dissolving in the liquid, that I gulped down like a dying man given water. When I woke in the morning I couldn't get out of bed until I'd had a snort of a couple of lines of it. That would enable me to run to the toilet. Then stagger back and have a couple more big fat white lines. Then have a shower, aiming the nozzle up my nose in an effort to clear away the debris in my powder-encrusted nostrils.

This was when my tequila habit became really serious. By the time we came to make our next album, which for tax reasons we decided to record at Mountain Studios in Switzerland, situated halfway up a mountain in Montreux, I was in full swing. We didn't realise until we got there but Queen owned the studios and it so happened that they were all in the country at that moment, too – and almost certainly for the same tax-saving reasons. Rick and John Deacon were already close and I knew Brian May and Roger Taylor. Freddie Mercury was there too but I don't know if anyone ever really 'knew' Freddie, certainly not by that point, when he was at his absolutely most flamboyant peak. So we all went out for a big blowout meal at this Mexican restaurant.

It was an incredibly expensive place, as most good restaurants are in Montreux. I think the bill that night came to a few grand. Queen ordered these pitchers of tequila margarita, which I'd never had before. The waiters would literally stand behind you and the moment you took a sip from your glass they would automatically fill your glass again. I didn't need to be asked twice either. I absolutely loved these pitchers of margaritas. The taste of sweet alcohol always went down well with me, I discovered. God knows how many I personally downed that night but after that it was my favourite drink – and my new favourite pastime. After coke, that is, obviously.

Back in Ireland, getting the landlord of the pub to make you up a pitcher of tequila margarita was not always an option (read: never) so I would get them to mix me a tequila and orange – a tequila sunrise. But they always tasted a bit weak to me. So I would get the landlord to make them doubles. Then trebles. Then quadruples. Soon I told them to forget the orange and just give me straight tequila. I would order a quadruple tequila in a tall glass. Down it. Then ask for another quadruple tequila in a tall glass. Down it. Then ask for *another* quadruple tequila in a tall glass. Down it. Then ask for *another* quadruple tequila in a tall glass – with a splash of orange. That would be the glass I would then carry back to the table where everybody else was sitting.

I would sometimes ask for the splash of orange just so I would appear 'normal' to whoever I was drinking with. But, of course, there was nothing normal about me any more, and everyone could see it. When I wasn't sitting there with my fourth glass of quadruple tequila, I would be in the gents, runny nosing. All the while thinking I had everyone fooled. I will sometimes meet someone from those days now and they will tell me stories of being in the gents toilets somewhere when I was carried in by two roadies, my head hung over the toilet bowl by my hair, as I threw up everywhere. Then lifted up while one of the roadies wiped my face clean. They tell me these stories and I try and feel suitably chastened but the truth is I can't even remember them. They might as well be talking about someone else.

With Rick now deep into his own bottle-of-whisky-a-day routine, and God knows how many grams of coke, the two-month tour we did of Britain and Ireland in 1982 was just a blur. We did a week of sold-out shows at the Hammersmith Odeon on that tour – seven shows in a row at one of the most prestigious venues in London – and I can't remember a thing about it. And if Rick was still alive today, I bet he couldn't either. I'd be out of my brain before we even got onstage. I'd have one of the roadies ready with a few lines already chopped out on a mirror by the side of the stage so I could jog over after a few numbers and top myself up. And a quick glug of tequila. Rick was the same, except for him it was whisky.

By then we had already discovered the joys of Mandrax. In the late sixties and early seventies you could get Mandrax – 'mandies', we called them – prescribed for you from a private doctor, in our case a certain Dr Feelgood in Harley Street. They were super-strength tranquillisers that were meant to help you sleep, or give you what they called 'deep relaxation'. No prizes for guessing what we used them for. Clue: it wasn't for sleeping. They also had a hypnotic effect, which basically meant that you were off your trolley for hours. In America they were known as Quaaludes, or 'ludes'. They were much more prevalent over there and it became a thing that audiences at rock shows would take them along with a couple of bottles of red wine. Mandrax was less well known in the UK, except to famous rock musicians, who ate them like chocolates. We had used them to have a bit of fun when we'd first found out about them in the early seventies, then stopped when we got bored. Now with our coke habits raging out of control, the mandies came in useful again, to help bring you down. When we couldn't get our hands on any mandies we would neck down some reds: Seconal, a powerful barbiturate that would have a very similar effect to Mandrax, only you would hardly remember a thing the next day.

Writing this stuff down here now all these years later I realise how appalling all this behaviour sounds. But in order to fully understand what we were doing you have to recognise what a different world it was back then. All sorts of showbiz types – actors, artists, TV people, musicians, but also their agents, managers, record company people, roadies, you name it – viewed these drugs as either purely recreational or as a useful tool to add to our creativity. Or whatever else they managed to convince themselves they were taking them for. Indeed, some of the greatest music made in the latter half of the twentieth century was made when the musicians involved were out of their brains on one form of drug or another or, indeed, several at once. Including the Beatles, Miles Davis, Bob Dylan, Elvis Presley, David Bowie and anyone else you care to name as the greatest in your opinion.

It has to be said that a great many of the worst records in the world were also made by musicians under the influence of various illicit substances. And again, I include Quo in that list too. So I am aware how all this looks now but the fact is it happened and, along with all the alcohol, that's just where we were in the late seventies and early eighties. Do I regret it? It's a bit fucking late for that now, isn't it? It would be different if I had never learned anything from all this. But hopefully I learned a lot.

We were so far gone on all this stuff I'm not sure we even noticed when John left the band.

Ah, yes, that. It had happened while we were recording at Mountain. The story goes – and it has always been told the same way because neither Rick nor I could really remember exactly what happened, we were so out of it – that John simply sat down at his kit one day as we were getting ready to tape a track, fiddled around with his drums for a bit, decided fuck that, he'd had enough, then kicked them over, then stormed out vowing never to come back.

Well. John had always had a dark and moody side. We knew that. Always had the capability of throwing a wobbly. We had grown used to it. But this was clearly of a different order. Talking to John years later, I'm not sure even he knew for sure what the real underlying reasons for his freak-out was. But I daresay it's no coincidence that it happened at that moment when Rick and I were simply no longer in any state to reassure anybody that we had the slightest idea what we were doing. I'm not saying it was our fault. I'm saying it can't have been easy for John, who never liked drugs to start with, having to put up with a couple of alcoholic drug fiends.

Reading interviews with John later, he talked about being sick of all the tantrums that were thrown. It's true, give three over-indulged musos a sack of cocaine and there will definitely be some 'tantrums'. These could also sometimes turn into fights. Usually, though, just a lot of shouting and finger pointing and door slamming and, well, you get the picture.

Worst of all, when John left, is that none of us tried to stop him. I used to joke that the reason John left was because his pet hates were gigging, rehearsing and recording. Which was not fair. John was a great drummer and long-time fans now understandably regard that line-up of Quo as the classic one. The truth is the whole shebang was out of control at the time John packed it in. We all threw huge wobblers at different times. But nobody ever came over and put their arm around your shoulder. They just left you to it. I was probably the worst for that. I didn't want to know anything about anybody else's problems. I had too many of my own. We all did. Something that was borne out by the fact we all baled out not long after. But I'll come to that.

We replaced John Coghlan with indecent haste, as the saying goes, with Pete Kircher, who was a lovely bloke who'd been in countless bands previously. The song Pete played on that everyone in Britain over the age of fifty will know is 'I Can't Let Maggie Go', which he made while he was in a group called Honeybus. It was in the UK top 10 at the same time we were in 1968 with 'Matchstick Men'. Honeybus were the more famous though because 'Maggie' also became the theme tune for the Nimble bread TV ad at the time. We had first met when he was in a band called Shanghai that once supported us on tour. Since then he'd been in a new wave band called Original Mirrors, even though he was already in his mid-thirties. I'd gotten to know Pete better when he played on an album I produced for former Atomic Rooster singer-guitarist John Du Cann, which Andy Bown had also played on. So Pete fitted right in, no problem at all.

At the time I phoned Pete, he was working as a session drummer for the Nolan Sisters. He said he was ready for something a bit more challenging. But he had no idea what he was walking into. Like John, Pete would become the only non-drug-taking member of the band. Unlike John, he didn't even drink either.

Which is just as well as my memory of the album we made, the dreadfully titled *1+9+8+2*, is foggy, to say the least. To this day, I scratch my head and wonder how that got to number 1. But it did. In fact it became the last Quo album to do so. Let's just say we have made better albums. A lot of *much* better albums. Even the hit single we had from it, a cover of a Johnny Gustafson song called 'Dear John', was decidedly average by our standards. I still cringe when I think back to those days. Like the album, the tour was a huge hit, culminating in us headlining the 1982 Castle Donington Monsters of Rock festival. (Now rebranded for the twenty-first century as the Download Festival.)

The real highlight of our tour that year was when we headlined the first-ever fund-raising concert for the Prince's Trust, at the NEC in Birmingham, in May 1982. It doesn't matter whether you see yourself as a staunch supporter of the royal family, or you think they should all be sacked, the fact is the Prince's Trust is a great thing. A charity founded in 1976, it's all about helping underprivileged young people between the ages of eleven and thirty. The toughest cases involve kids in care. Homeless young people; kids with drug problems or other problems that have brought them into trouble with the law. It's not some wishy-washy thing but a really solid organisation that actively helps these people on a practical level, offering support in all sorts of amazing ways. Thousands of kids benefit every year and they have a hugely impressive success rate, with around three in four moving on to employment, education, volunteering or training.

What a bunch of reprobates like us were doing being there I can't tell you, or hope to justify. Only that we sold the place out and gave all the money to the Trust. We also helped bring a lot of publicity to the charity. So what if we were snorting coke off the toilet seats backstage, as far as we were concerned that was our business. Raising money for charity doesn't mean you have to act like you're some angel. So if and when I do ever get to stand before St Peter at the Pearly Gates I hope he will remember that. I certainly will and so will the thousands of people the Prince's Trust has continued to offer their incredible help and support to over the years since. We also got to meet Prince Charles and I can tell you now, he is a lovely, genuine man.

But these were no longer great days for either Status Quo or me.

The next year was like my own personal Lost Weekend. I'd simply had enough. I couldn't take it any more: any of it. Not the band; not my personal life; nothing. All I cared about was getting as much coke as I could in me, along with a couple of bottles of tequila, a few downers, plenty of hash, with the phone left permanently off the hook. I 'celebrated' my thirty-fourth birthday in May 1983. I have no recollection of how I passed that day, nor do I have any particular recollection of how I passed that year. As a band we had simply stopped. I look back now and I realise that thirty-four is a ridiculously, arrogantly, utterly stupidly young age to be speaking of retirement. In my defence, I will point out that by then I had lived the lives of two thirty-four-year-olds. But then I wasn't really retiring so much as committing a form of suicide, I now realise. I'm not sure there is a right or wrong age for that.

In 1980, Vertigo had released a compilation Quo album called *12 Gold Bars*. It contained twelve tracks, all of them hits of ours from the seventies. It became our biggest-selling album to date, going platinum in the UK for over 300,000 sales. Then, in November 1982, the label released a follow-up compilation, this time called *From the Makers of . . .* This was a double-album package with twenty of our hits and various other tracks. This didn't go platinum but it did reach number 4 and go gold. No reason for us to hurry to make another new album then. Or go back on the road or do anything really except get even more stoned.

I hate to keep on about it. But that's really all that happened during this year or so when the band stopped working. Well, that and the fact that I began another serious relationship. This time with a wonderful Irish woman named Elizabeth Gurnon.

Liz was a streetwise, raven-haired Irish beauty who didn't take shit from anyone, least of all me. She had worked in the music business in public relations and in promotions. When I'd first known her she was working with her brother-in-law, Pat Egan, who was the wonderful fella who promoted all the Quo shows in Ireland. The first time I'd seen Liz in action was kicking the arses of some big hairy louts that had caused some problem for us at one of the shows. The way she dealt with these guys was amazing. I've seen various tough-guy promoters and backstage fixers unload at troublemakers at a gig. But Liz was different class. She virtually had them crying. Liz was beautiful – but she was also hard as nails. When I offered her the job working full-time with Quo she'd originally said no. It was only later, after I'd moved to Ireland to become a tax exile, that I got to know her properly – and fell in love with her.

Liz knew the kind of life I was leading. That is, she had

been around enough successful musicians to understand the life I had been living, constantly touring and recording, constantly having my back slapped by yes-men and my dick squeezed by groupies. Nevertheless, she seemed to like me. And I liked her too. So much so it turned into love. It was certainly a romantic relationship, in that we spent a lot of time together. This was a new thing for me. My years with Jean had been mostly spent away from her. What time we did have together was always taken up with kids, home building and making promises I couldn't always keep. Then feeling rotten about it. Being with Liz felt more open and honest. At least, it did while it lasted and things were going well.

I even managed to persuade Liz to come and work for Quo. The rest of the band had no problem with that. Not that anyone mentioned to me anyway, though looking back now I do wonder. They couldn't argue with the fact that Liz was brilliant at her job, though. Liz was no pushover. She knew her job and she knew everyone else's job, too. She made sure the train ran on time, so to speak. It was knowing Liz would be there that helped bring me back into the fold, in terms of getting the Quo show back on the road.

But there was more trouble to come. Alan and I hadn't been getting on for a very long time. You could say the problems between us went all the way back to when we were still at school. But what we experienced now went way beyond that. I'm not saying Alan hated me at this point. I'm not saying I hated Alan at this point. But if you'd just walked into the studio and seen us going at it to each other in 1983 you'd have been hard-pressed to think any different. That was the year we made *Back to Back*. Though we didn't know it yet, it was going to be our last album with Alan in the band.

After nearly a year off the road, we reconvened to make a new record at Air Studios in Montserrat. This was the former Beatles producer George Martin's luxury new state-of-the-art residential studio in the West Indies. Sun, sea, sand and Status Quo: what could possibly go wrong? The answer: just about everything.

While we had been off the road we had all had a chance to get our bearings in terms of where the music business was these days. It felt like the last time any of us had looked up from our guitars, in that respect, it had been 1971 and we were making *Dog of Two Head*. There had been some slight adjustments to our sound after Pip Williams came in – a lighter touch. But this was no longer the long-haired seventies. This was 1983 and the biggest names in the charts were acts like Culture Club, Eurythmics and Duran Duran. These were groups that focused as much on presentation as music. They certainly had the songs but they also had a very manicured image. Long hair and denim were no longer part of the scene. More to the point, those bands all shared a very contemporary sound that was built more on synthesisers and up-to-the-minute studio technology than anything to do with loud guitars and four-to-the-floor drums.

I knew it was pointless trying to reinvent the wheel with Status Quo. Changes to music come every decade. We were what we were and had been extremely successful at being that way for over a decade. Nevertheless, I definitely felt the need to keep abreast of change, musically at least. The main difference being the sound of the drums. The *Back to Back* album would be the first where we abandoned the live drum sound John Coghlan had perfected and went for a more enhanced, studio-enriched sound. The sort of eighties drum sound that now makes you pull a face because it sounds so dated and, well, eighties. We also brought the keyboards more to the fore, not just tinkling the ivorics but getting Andy Bown to introduce more of a synthesised 'bed'. In terms of image, if you look at clips from that time you'll see I still have long hair and that I'm still inordinately fond of denim and waistcoats. But Rick and Alan have cut their hair. It's hardly the full Simon Le Bon, but it is shorter than before.

Musically, these were cosmetic changes. But I had to fight for them every step of the way with Alan. Rightly or wrongly, Alan had a very fixed idea of how he believed Status Quo should sound: hard, rhythmic, guitar-led, more manly and macho. While my feeling was that we already had that market cornered but if we were to survive in the future we needed to expand our musical horizons a bit. I love rock music but it is far from being the only kind of music I'm in love with. Someone once said to me: 'There are only two kinds of music: good and bad.' I go along with that, in terms of there being whatever music you like, personally, and whatever you don't like, personally. So if I hear a seductive pop song I can swoon over I have no hang-ups about that whatsoever. I also love country music, as became more obvious as my career progressed. My eldest son Simon has grown up to be an opera singer and I now love that, too, particularly because of the Italian connection. Mainly, I just love music.

Alan wasn't having it. Especially after he moved to Australia, where he'd met and married his second wife, Dayle. He seemed to become even more entrenched in his views on how we should sound. Quo made Quo music and that was that, in his opinion. We'd been arguing about it for a long time, for years, but things really came to a head on *Back to Back* when Bernie Frost and I came up with a country-flavoured song called 'Marguerita Time'. Well, you can tell from the title where I got my lyrical inspiration, seeing as it was named after the second most important thing in the world to me right then (after cocaine). Musically, though, in some ways it was like a throwback to our late-sixties period: pure pop but with a twinkle in the eye. A real mums and dads tune, if you like – one for the milkman to whistle on his rounds. It was jolly and catchy and sweet and Alan hated it. Refused even to help us record it at first. And then did so only grudgingly because, I presume, he thought it would never make it onto the album. Rick was caught between the two worlds. Like Alan, his self-image was tied up in being a rock star. He was a born rock and roller. On the other hand, this is the guy who was wearing a lamé suit and singing 'Baby Face' on the ukulele when we first met him. Rick was all for rocking out. But Rick was even more for having a hit. It was doubly tricky for him, too, because he had always tried to maintain a decent relationship with Alan. In the end, Rick did what he always did and left it for me to make the decision.

When we played the tracks we had recorded in Montserrat for Vertigo's label chief, Brian Sheppard, however, he went nuts for 'Marguerita Time'. Zeroed in on it immediately and said it was a sure-fire hit and that we should release it as a Christmas single that year. Alan did not take this news well. At one point he actually said: 'We can't release this as a single. How will I ever face my family again?' I couldn't believe my ears. What on earth was he talking about? Our last couple of singles hadn't made the top 10. Why would we turn down the chance of breaking that run with a song our own record company virtually guaranteed us they could make into a giant hit? For me, we were back to the old adage again: art for art's sake, hit singles for fuck's sake.

There was an argument. That turned into a fight, then a slagging match. Followed by Alan swearing he would under no circumstances play the song live onstage or even mime to it on TV. Fair enough, we would see about that.

What really twisted the knife for Alan was the fact that one of his songs called 'Ol' Rag Blues' had been green-lighted by Brian as the first, lead-off single from the album – but only if I sang the lead vocal. Alan had already decided that he should be the one who sang the lead as he had written the song with Keith Lamb, his mate from the Australian band Hush. Oh dear. Here we go again.

Alan's logic was easy to follow: both Rick and I had sung lead on various Quo singles, usually the songs that either one of us had been the main writer on. Surely it was only fair now for Alan to have a go – after all, he had written 'Ol'Rag Blues'. The problem was that having personally twisted Brian Sheppard's arm into making it the first single, I couldn't now hamper the label's chances of making it a sizable hit by agreeing not to sing on it and front the song. After all, that was my job. Alan was absolutely insistent though. It was *his* song. He should sing it. Accusing me of wanting to hog the spotlight. Even though I was the band's frontman and it was expected of me.

In the end, just to keep the peace, we ended up recording two versions of the song: one with Alan singing lead, one with me singing lead. Then told Brian Sheppard to choose which one worked best as a single. Well, you don't need me to tell you how that went. Three weeks later we were miming to it on *Top of the Pops* – with me singing lead and Alan singing backup into his own mic. We had got to the stage where we even argued about things like who had a mic on telly. Usually Rick had been the one to take the second mic. He was the blond good-looking one who genuinely sang most of the harmonies with me. But Alan was on the warpath and there was no stopping him.

The daft thing is it went top 10. In those days that meant it probably sold around 250,000 copies. So Alan got to make some serious money. But that didn't seem to change things between us. It felt to me like he had been building up this grudge against me for so many years it all just came pouring out like lava from an erupting volcano. He was so pissed off he flew home to Australia. His wife Dayle was pregnant at the time and he said he needed to be with her. Fair enough. But my personal feeling was that there was more to it than that. We had all had kids while the band was working. It was a shame because the *Back To Back* album and the singles we released from it were really good: 'A Mess of Blues', a cover of a great old honkytonk Elvis song, suggested by Bernie Frost, which, ironically, sounded much more the way Alan thought Quo should, and got to number 15; and then, just in time for Christmas, the dreaded 'Marguerita Time', which got to number 3 and became one of our biggest hits ever.

It was farcical. With Alan back home in Australia, we just went ahead and did things like *Top Of The Pops* and *Cannon and Ball* without him. We didn't bother hanging a life-size puppet of him onstage this time, we just moved Andy and his keyboards into the spot stage left where Alan would normally stand, and did the shows like that. The hardcore Quo fans noticed and wondered what was going on. But the mainstream audiences of millions that saw us on TV, none of them blinked an eye. They just saw me and Rick and a band playing next to us and assumed it was business as usual. By then both Rick and I were increasingly aware that this was the state of affairs for the vast majority of the public. It was the start of Rick and me being seen as a double act, by the public and the music business both. Neither of us minded that at all. And as long as it worked and brought the band more success the others were happy with it too. Or should have been. Being musicians, they always railed against it to a degree. But you couldn't argue with the success.

Alan did make one appearance on *Top Of The Pops*. The only other exception to doing 'Marguerita Time' on our own was when we did it on the Christmas *Top of the Pops* and Jim Lea from Slade, who were also on the show that week, stood in for Alan, pretending to twang away on the bass. It was all good fun. People loved seeing Jim on telly with us. It was Christmas. Why not? Besides, the only thing people ever really remember about that show now was how Rick fell over into Pete Kircher's drum kit at the end of the song – while the track kept playing. Rick always swore it was a deliberately silly move. The fact that he and I had both drunk the backstage bar dry that day before taping our performance had nothing to do with it, obviously.

In fairness to Alan, it has to be said that there was a fair proportion of old-school Quo fans that pointedly did not like 'Marguerita Time' either. I still get older fans trying to take me to task for it all these years later, as though I had broken a solemn oath. But for me it's still one of my all-time favourite Quo records. I don't love tequila any more but I will always love 'Marguerita Time'. To me it's a cracking little tune and I'm proud of it. And I'm sure Alan's ill feeling towards it would have softened somewhat too when he received his share of the royalties from it.

The upshot of all this was that I spent Christmas 1983 seriously wondering if I really wanted to continue in Status Quo. Rick was back in wonderland with his new girlfriend, Debbie Ash – a sexy dancer with Hot Gossip, *The Kenny Everett Video Show* regulars that Mrs Whitehouse got into a strop about, and whose sister was the actress Leslie Ash – and God knows how many new cars to either crash or get done for speeding in. He was banned from driving at one point. But drove anyway. That was Rick, a rock and roller no matter what. There was also another beautiful blonde named Debbie Ashby, who was a Page 3 model in the *Sun* who came into his life around this period. It was hard even for Rick to keep up.

Meanwhile, Alan now disliked me more than ever. Andy and Pete were just holding on for dear life. They had both received their first full credits on a Quo album a couple of years before. The last thing they wanted now was to see the whole thing go kaput.

But I was in such a state I was now beyond caring. The way I saw it – as I snorted another gram of coke and downed another dozen tequilas – was that I had given my all for the band for over twenty years, onstage and off. If that was no longer good enough, then fuck them. I was off.

Rick and I had been talking to each other about a life after Quo for a while now. At one point, we reckoned that if we could come away from the group with our mortgages paid off and fifty grand in the bank each we would be set for life. That had been in the early seventies. Now, here in the mid-eighties, it was a different story. Rick had lost his house in the divorce settlement with Marietta. I still had my house but I was rarely there, and my wife and children had long since moved out.

Yes, I now had Liz to consider. But I was now residing so far up my own arse I was about to blow that situation too in a big way. To say I wasn't thinking clearly would be an understatement on a par with saying I liked the occasional small sherry.

To make matters worse, it was now that I realised for the first time that it wasn't just Alan that had felt edged out of the spotlight. It was Rick too. It came out as a casual remark. We'd been talking about what we might do if we split the band. I said I'd probably go solo. Rick looked at me and said something about it being all right for me as I'd always been number one, while he'd always just been number two, and that he was sick of being number two. I thought, what the hell? Did he really just say that? Well, yes, he did. In fact, this would become a recurring theme of our working relationship as the years passed. It used to irk me because Rick was such a star in his own right. The blokes loved him. The girls fancied him. He was great at what he did in the band. I didn't get what his problem was.

Actually, by this point, I didn't care what his problem was. I had too many things to deal with in my personal life. My mother had separated from my father sometime earlier, and so I had moved her into The Glade. At first I thought it would help having Nonna around to look after the kids. But now Jean was gone and my mother was still there. I thought this was fine as I could use the company in that big old house. Only now she had turned into a religious freak. It was her sister in America who did it to her. She went to visit her as a relatively normal middle-aged mad Catholic woman and came home a swivel-eyed religious loon. I was talking to my dad about it one day in the kitchen and he said, 'Me and your mother had a marvellous sex life. Until that cow of a sister spoiled it.'

She didn't even want to be called 'Mum' any more. You had to call her 'Annie'. Even my kids did, all because of religion. When she became hyper religious she'd be lying on the floor convinced she could see something no one else could. She'd be talking about how the Lord was here. I'd be thinking: what is she on about now? She was already convinced that I was an immaculate conception. This was when I was about twenty-one or twenty-two. But I was working away a lot with the band so I didn't get the brunt of it. Dominic, my brother, did. He'd sit with her and they'd read the Bible every night. He was only doing his best to placate her, to stop her from crying. But I was disgusted. What are you doing, brother? What would you fall for that for? But he still can't get over it now, poor sod. As usual, I was far more pragmatic. I loved my mum, but not so much after she more or less vanished before our eyes and insisted I now call her Annie. And definitely not so much when she kept on about me being part of an immaculate conception. I was already in run-for-it mode with the band. This just became one more reason why I was in such a hurry to do so.

I spent a miserable Christmas chewing this stuff over in my mind. Then on New Year's Day came to my decision. I was off. For good. No coming back. Ever.

Of course, being a sly two-faced Gemini, I hedged my bets. I didn't just announce I was leaving the band. I said I wanted to come off the road. Stop touring and just concentrate on making music in the studio.

The rest of the band didn't like the idea. But then the rest of the band – meaning Alan and Rick – had no say in the matter. Our management and record company weren't exactly thrilled either. But I managed to shut them all up by agreeing to do one last massive farewell tour. By massive, I mean highly lucrative. By highly lucrative, I mean spending money as fast as we could make it. Then having to keep going to make some more.

I may have decided I was leaving Status Quo but that didn't mean Status Quo had any intention of leaving me alone. Not just yet anyway.

Chapter Eight

Twelve O'clock in London

Demand for tickets to our farewell, the End of the Road tour, was incredible. That said, a combination of comparatively soft sales of *Back to Back* in Europe and virtually none in Australia, plus the fact that I wanted to get the thing over and done with as soon as possible, meant that our 'final' tour only lasted about three months.

We did five big shows in Ireland. Eight big shows in West Germany. Two in Switzerland, France and Sweden and one in Holland, followed by the forty-two shows in Britain. All finishing with the grand finale in front of 60,000 fans at the National Bowl, Milton Keynes.

I sat down and looked at the tour itinerary and was happy with it. No one else was happy with it. The record company made it very clear to us that they saw the whole thing as a disaster for our career. They were quite blunt in their summation, which they put simply like this: the day Quo stopped touring was the day Quo stopped selling records. The day Quo stopped selling records was the day Quo no longer had a record deal. The day Quo no longer had a record deal was the day Quo was finished.

So what? I was sick and tired of the band.

A fourth single was released from *Back to Back* in the middle of the tour, a version of a song called 'Going Downtown Tonight' by a new guy I'd discovered named Guy Johnson. On reflection it was a piss-poor record, with chirpy keyboards and synths replacing the guitars, and with that heavily processed drum sound that was suddenly popular in the eighties. It wasn't much of a hit, barely getting into the top 20. Alan was clearly disgusted by the whole thing and having to deal with his reaction was just another reminder of why it was the right time to end it all.

Pete Kircher and Andy Bown were going to be OK once the end came. They would no doubt get work with other bands. But poor Ricky was absolutely beside himself. He stood to make a lot of money from the End of the Road tour. We all did. But he was still spending it like there was no tomorrow. I was hardly a role model, in that regard, having split from my wife and kids and taken to shovelling most of my own money up my nose. But Rick took being a spendthrift to new dimensions. He was still always buying cars, Mercedes, Porsches, a Corvette Stingray. Always crashing them then buying new ones. Always throwing parties, always high on life and everything it had to offer him as a rock star. He was also, as usual, embedded in some incredibly tangled relationships with various glamorous women. He had moved in with Debbie Ash for a while, becoming a surrogate dad for her daughter Candie, whose dad was the stunt rider Eddie Kidd. Then that ended and he hooked up again with his former girlfriend, Patty, who he'd known since he was at school but had lately gotten together with after she returned from living for a while in Australia. Then he was seeing Marietta again on the quiet . . . He would tell me this stuff but I had long since stopped trying to keep up. I became like his Father Confessor. I would listen to his complicated love life, tell him not to worry, just to settle down with whichever girl he was most fond of at the time, and he would agree. Then go off with someone else again.

Now for the first time he was forced to think seriously about the future. The trouble was that, like me, Rick was doing most of this thinking with his face hovering over a mirror crowded with big dusty white lines. Ideal it was not.

Then a couple of months before the farewell tour was due to begin in April 1984, I got some unexpected news of my own. Liz was pregnant. Oh wow! Oh God! Oh joy! Oh no! Oh yes! I didn't know how to react. I've always loved having kids. Even when I was at my wildest, in terms of drugs and drink, I always saw myself as a loving, caring father. This, though, was something I had not planned on becoming with Liz, much as I adored her. I had just enough sense left in my head to know that this was probably not going to pan out the way either of us would have liked it to. I still couldn't wait to become a dad again, though. It seemed Rick wasn't the only one whose life had become almost unbearably complicated.

Like everything else that was actually really important right then, I pushed this information to the back of my mind and concentrated on getting through the tour. Four days before the tour started with two nights at Dublin's huge RDS Hall, the band had been presented with the Ivor Novello Award for Outstanding Contribution to British Music. I wasn't sure if this was one of those things they give you when you're about to bow out, as we were. But then I checked and saw that Eric Clapton had won the same award back in 1971 and felt better about it. John Lennon had been given the award as far back as 1964. Suitably convinced it wasn't some sort of dinosaur award, I went to the gents and treated myself to another thoroughly well-deserved line or two (or three).

And that's just about the last thing I can honestly remember of our End of the Road tour, except for flying away in the helicopter after 'Quo's Last Show' at Milton Keynes, glad that it was finally all over. I had taken so much coke, it wasn't exactly the finest performance to go out on.

In fact, it was pathetic. And if you look at the footage that was later released as a longform video, simply titled *Status Quo – End of the Road '84* – it's so doctored to make me look better it's sickening. Lots of shots of helicopters flying overhead and my vocals clearly overdubbed later. I haven't watched it in years. Actually, I don't think I could ever bring myself to watch the whole thing even when it first came out. But when I snuck a little peek at a clip of it the other day, the thing that really struck me was how unhappy Rick looks. He looks angry, baffled, sad, utterly fed up. You might be able to find a shot of him somewhere faking a little smile on the video, but to me he looks completely done in. Later, he told me he couldn't believe what was going on. That this was really the end. But for me, I couldn't wait for it to end. I'm told that Bob Young came and made a special guest appearance, blowing away on the harp for 'Roadhouse Blues', but I honestly can't remember it.

After the show there was no big party or anything. We had had one of those after the seventh and final night at the Hammersmith Odeon a few weeks before. It was held at Stamford Bridge, Chelsea's football ground. It was our official farewell party and the place was absolutely packed with people, many of whom I had no idea who they were. Those I did recognise included genuine old pals like Brian May and Roger Taylor from Queen, Lemmy from Motörhead, Denny Laine from Wings, Rick Wakeman from Yes and John Entwistle from the Who, to name just a few of the famous friends I still don't remember talking to.

Again, I'm pretty sure I spent the night in a private side room, lavishing time on my real best friend, Mr Cocaine, and his good lady, Miss Tequila. I don't think I had properly slept for about three months at that point. I mean my eyes would close, but my brain would not switch off, and my mouth would not stop moving, my whole body on fire. I would get really ill from all the coke I was doing. Then say to myself: God, I feel so bad. What I need is a line of toot to sort me out. Then, feeling good again, I would think: You know what, I feel better now. I'll have another line to celebrate.

Remarkably – foolishly, perhaps – Liz stuck with me through all of this. Liz had never been a prude. She had been in the business for long enough to wear the T-shirt. One of the reasons I fell so hard for her in the first place was that she could hold her own when it came to late-night partying. Except now she was pregnant and had more to think about than just making sure I didn't choke on my own vomit. She certainly couldn't be involved with drugs. Bless her heart, Liz stayed on that tour with me as long as she could, her bump getting bigger every day. But what were once her band duties had rapidly thinned out to simply keeping a weather eye on me. Then towards the end she had to go home – the baby was coming.

For a while, I think we both thought this was it. That we had found our true soulmates and that we would stay together. Especially so after Liz gave birth to a beautiful baby girl, just two weeks after that final awful Milton Keynes show. She named her Bernadette. Only one snag: with three children already, for me the novelty wore off pretty quick. I loved the idea of having a daughter. I definitely hadn't had one of them before. And at first we were all ecstatically happy together, either at The Glade or at the place in Ireland. But we were also spending more time apart. While Liz had ostensibly been working for me and the band, there was never any reason to be apart. But with the band all but finished and a beautiful baby girl to look after now, Liz rightly decided she needed to make that her priority. In truth, I think she welcomed having those breaks away from me. I was a full-time wreck, far more demanding than any baby. Also, my mother, who was becoming more manic and religious by the day, had scared Liz off. Meanwhile, I had started to find other ways of keeping myself happy now I didn't have a full-time band to worry about.

I recorded one last single with Quo, a fairly rote version of 'The Wanderer', which went to number 7. And the label stuck out another best-of compilation, *12 Gold Bars Volume II*, which comprised our eighties hits and also went top 10. But that was the final turning point for me and by Christmas 1984 it was basically all over and I wasn't bothering to hide it from the rest of the guys any more. It's fair to say there was a lot of bitterness on both sides. For me, it was like escaping from prison. For Rick and Alan, it was an act of betrayal on my part. I was sorry that Rick felt that way but less concerned about Alan, who I'd thoroughly had enough of.

The issues in my relationship with Alan went back all through the band's career. Some of it was the sort of stuff that all bands have to deal with. Brian Jones always thought of the Rolling Stones as his band, even after Mick Jagger and Keith Richards had written a dozen major hits for them and Brian had been fired. Roger Daltrey to this day still sees the Who as really his band, even though Pete Townshend wrote all their hits. Ronnie Lane saw the Faces as his group, even though the rest of the world saw them as Rod Stewart's backing group. I'm not saying any of this is fair, or not. I'm pointing out that the whole I'm-the-leader thing causes more problems than it ever solves. As Rick and I were about to discover, it doesn't matter two hoots what you think, it's what the public thinks that ultimately matters.

With Alan, though, there was always more to it than that when it came to our personal relationship. We were always two very different people. One of the reasons I liked him so much as a kid was how full-on and aggressive he could be. How he didn't take shit from anybody, even if he was only half their size. But, as I grew up, that became one of the reasons I started to dislike him. He was immoveable, wouldn't give an inch on anything. He was always right, no matter what. Now, in my mid-thirties, I found the whole thing too overwhelming to deal with. I wanted to push the music into new and more interesting directions – the very thing the critics had always accused Quo of being too thick to even attempt. I didn't want to tear up the script and rewrite history. I loved our music. I just wanted it to develop a little more. Times were changing and I didn't want to get left behind. To me, Alan was the biggest obstacle to that happening. And I simply wasn't prepared to live with that fact any longer. To the point where I was now ready to destroy the whole thing if necessary.

As for Rick, that was obviously a different story. We had first become friends as teenagers. Then forged an onstage partnership that was the equal to any in rock. Some nights it felt almost telepathic between us onstage. We had become two sides of the same coin. Yin and Yang; sun and moon. When it worked it was like a well-oiled machine. You couldn't see the cogs moving, you just felt the heat. I knew I would never enjoy that kind of musical relationship again with anyone else. But Ricky would be the first to admit he was very high maintenance. I am aware, of course, of how pot-calling-the-kettle-black that statement is. Lost as I was, though, in my personal fuck-ups and misadventures, I just couldn't take on Rick's problems too any more. I barely had time for Liz or my new baby daughter. Didn't spend enough time with my three older boys by Jean. And on some level I was painfully aware of all these things even as I was doing them. Ultimately, when I look back now, I see that as probably the real reason why I needed to create some space away from the band: I needed to make a run for it. Like all hopeless addicts, rather than stay and deal with my problems, I thought getting away as far as possible as I could from the whole mess was the way to deal with it. But as I was soon to discover, no matter how far you run, you always bring yourself.

That day of reckoning was still some way off, though, as I contemplated a life after Quo. Even when Alan contacted me to tell me he and Rick were seriously talking about doing a band called Quo 2, I just shrugged my shoulders. I knew it was possible. AC/DC had gone on to even greater success after their original singer Bon Scott had died in 1980 and they brought in Brian Johnson to replace him. On paper, that shouldn't have worked at all. The band had put out several chart albums with Bon. He utterly embodied the AC/DC personality and spirit. Brian had been the singer in Geordie, who'd enjoyed a couple of chart singles in the days when we were also breaking through with 'Paper Plane'. How could he possibly hope to replace Bon? Well, he not only replaced him, he helped take the band to even greater levels of success.

Van Halen, who in 1984 were the biggest-selling rock band in the world, were about to see their singer, David Lee Roth, launch his own highly successful solo career. They replaced him with Sammy Hagar, a great singer in his late thirties who I always got on well with but who'd only previously had one hit – and saw Van Halen become bigger than ever.

So I knew full well that if the boys chose the right frontman they could easily keep Quo going without me. I didn't care. Not one bit. Go for it, my son.

If anything, this just spurred me on to begin building a solo career of my own. As I saw it, my working relationship with Bernie Frost had already proved it could be successful by providing Quo with some of its biggest recent hits like 'What You're Proposing', 'Rock 'n' Roll' and, of course, my beloved 'Marguerita Time'. I saw the musical partnership with Bernie as the ace up my sleeve. Not having been in Quo, and not coming from the same south London backdrop as me, Rick and Alan, he had a totally fresh perspective on things. Unlike Bob Young, I also thought that Bernie would be a good foil for me onstage. He didn't have any musical past to hang onto, or any cares about who was calling the shots career wise. He was just this incredibly talented singer-songwriter who also happened to be the nicest bloke you could hope to spend time with, which also fitted in with my not-so-brave new world as it was unfolding in the mid-eighties.

When I had first gone to live in Ireland, staying at Dromoland Castle, in contrast to writing songs with Bob in hotel rooms, between shows, Bernie and I would carry a couple of acoustic guitars out onto the lush green hills and sit there strumming along just for the pleasure of it. Cows would actually wander over to listen to us.

Another time, later into my time in Ireland, we were staying at a hotel in Dublin where there was a little bar called the Coffee Dock. This place virtually never closed, which suited me down to the ground as I was a night owl. Bernie and I would be there with the guitars again, just seeing what we could come up with, without worrying about studio schedules or meeting a tour deadline. It was one of those places where every other musician in Dublin would turn up at all hours. We would always start the session the same way, no matter what time of day or night it was, with the full Irish breakfast: a big fry-up along with a pot of tea. You could smoke indoors in those days and I would sit there, smoking a joint and writing songs with Bernie. It was idyllic. As soon as we had a couple of new songs finished we'd scoot over to the studio and get them onto tape.

Back in Ireland again in those weeks and months after the band had gone its separate ways, I tried to get the same atmosphere going with Bernie. Only this time it wasn't quite the same as things had changed. Not between me and Bernie, but between me and Liz. After Bernadette was born, obviously Liz was too busy with our daughter to give her big baby – me – all her attention, although she did try, bless her. I was busy, meanwhile, discussing the possibility of my new solo career with the record company. I knew that Rick was also talking to them about a solo deal. The label seemed agreeable and ponied up a new contract for me along with a decent advance. All I needed to do now was get to work with Bernie on a new set of songs.

It seemed almost too good to be true. And you know what they say about when things seem to be too good to be true: it's usually because they are. Well, that's what happened now working with Bernie. It wasn't his fault. It was my fault. Given the freedom suddenly to do whatever I saw fit on an album of my own, I didn't know where to begin. My only guiding principle was that it shouldn't sound like a Status Quo album. Big mistake right there. Not wanting it to be something different. But putting too much emphasis on what it *should* and *shouldn't* be before we'd even written the songs. There is only one way to write a good song and that is to almost let the song find you.

Don't try and restrict yourself. Just trust in your own talent and see what comes out. That was how all my best songs came about. Unfortunately, I was still so wrapped up in the fallout from the Quo split that I couldn't see the wood for the trees.

And of course it didn't help matters that I would spend most of the day on the phone talking to drug dealers, or arranging to go and pick the drugs up, or actually sitting there doing the drugs. What's that you say? How about picking up a guitar? How dare you! Can't you see I'm far too busy getting coked out of my mind?

The coke expenditure was now serious business. Casual cocaine users will buy a gram of coke and make it last perhaps a few days. But there was nothing casual about my coke use. I was now buying it an ounce at a time: twenty-eight grams. That would last me about a week, sometimes less. Or put another way, I was now going through four or five grams of coke a day. Yes, a fair amount of that was going up other people's noses too. I was not stingy with my coke when working. This was also costing me a fair few bob, as my old dad used to say. Maybe a couple of grand a week, maybe more. In the end, my cocaine bill was more than double that of the advance the record company had given me to make the bloody album.

Apart from the damage this was doing to my body – and, even more importantly, to my mind – the rigmarole of simply getting so much cash together every single week proved to be a nightmare. In today's money, I was spending around £20–25,000 on coke every month. This was much more than you could just get out of a cash machine, so I would have to personally go into the bank and draw out the money – a few grand every week. Even though I was that bloke from that pop group, taking this kind of cash out of the bank all the time aroused suspicion. I would have to take two forms of ID, wait for them to check and double-check everything, then stand fidgeting there while they painstakingly counted out the cash. The biggest denomination they had were £50 notes. Sometimes they wouldn't have enough and I'd have to settle for twenties as well.

Because I was always strung out on coke, feeling the world had its eyes on me, and because whatever bank I happened to be in the eyes of the entire staff and other customers were on me, I found the whole thing an ordeal. I took to driving around looking for branches of the bank I hadn't been in before, or branches I hadn't been in for a few weeks. Then, once I'd gotten hold of the cash, I'd drive to whatever coke dealer I was seeing that week, where I would have to endure the other regular ordeal of having to make the trip seem like just a normal visit. Say hi, how are you and would I like a cup of tea? When I didn't really want to say hi, I just wanted to pick up and leave, couldn't care less how they were doing and definitely did not want a cup of fucking tea.

I realise this was what these days we would call First World problems. But this is where I was at while I was trying to make an album with Bernie. It's amazing we ever got anything done but in the end we had eight or ten finished songs, which we parcelled together for a solo album, which we called *Flying Debris* – and, no, it didn't sound much like a Quo album, even though I had both Pete Kircher playing drums and Andy Bown on keyboards. There were the occasional echoes – how could there not be on any record where I'm the singer and co-writer? Tracks like 'That's All Right' had that rolling gait that Quo perfected. In the main, though, this was me and Bernie trying something new.

By then, the plan wasn't even to release it under just my name, but as a joint fifty–fifty collaboration with Bernie. The first single we released from it was 'Modern Romance (I Want to Fall in Love Again), which came out in May 1985, and got to the dizzy heights of number 56 on the UK charts. The follow-up, 'Jealousy', which was catchier, came out in September that year and didn't even get that high in the charts. This despite performing it with Bernie on *Cheggers Plays Pop*, Keith Chegwin's children's TV game show!

As a result of these less than scintillating chart showings, the release of the *Flying Debris* album, which had been scheduled for that Christmas, was 'delayed' by the record company. Delayed as in shelved. To this day, it's never been released, although there are poor-quality bootlegs available.

So much for my budding new career as a solo performer. Looking back now, though, I can see the problem. Rather than come across as a shining new star in my own right, I just came across as Quo-lite. If you dig out the clip of me and Bernie on the *Cheggers* show doing 'Jealousy', the problem instantly becomes apparent. There's me in my blue jeans and waistcoat, same as in Quo, except my hair is now in a ponytail (all the rage at the time). Standing next to me is Bernie, looking . . . uncomfortable. Who could blame him? He was standing in the same spot that Rick Parfitt used to stand. Only where Rick would be throwing shapes and getting stuck in, Bernie is trying to look cool and not quite pulling it off. I'm also trying to look like I know what I'm doing but I can see that I'm not really comfortable either. I was used to miming on TV, had no problem with it, but with no band there to at least pretend we were live, the whole thing comes across as stilted and . . . boring. There, I've said it. It gives me no pleasure to do so. For my money, Bernie and I came up with some good stuff on that album-that-never-was. But it just wasn't meant to be. Worst of all, I knew that if I'd done 'Jealousy' with Quo, it would have been a hit. Plenty to think about then, as I stared down the barrel of a gun, that Christmas.

Fate it seemed had other plans in store for me – and Status Quo. A year before, I had been working in Dublin with Bernie, writing songs and turning into the rock version of Al Pacino in *Scarface*, when Quo's manager Colin Johnson phoned to tell me he'd said yes to an enquiry from the Boomtown Rats singer, Bob Geldof, for Rick and me to take part in a single for a charity project he was working on, which he was calling Band Aid. Colin was a bit vague on the details, just that there would be tons of other major league stars involved and that, on that basis, he thought Rick and I shouldn't pass up the opportunity to be involved.

I wasn't sure what I thought about that. But with the *12 Gold Bars Volume II* album steaming up the chart, I agreed on the basis that it would be a good bit of promotion to do for the record.

The record, of course, was 'Do They Know It's Christmas?', written by Geldof and Ultravox singer Midge Ure, and it was about to alter the course of music history. Not that any of us knew that the day we all assembled to record our vocals and be filmed doing so.

Geldof was moved to act after seeing a harrowing Michael Buerk report on BBC News showing the effects of famine on starving children in Ethiopia, which sent anyone who saw it into shock. Geldof conceived of a simple but brilliant plan – to gather together as many big names as he could from the world of pop and make a one-off single, sales from which would be donated to the various charities operating in that part of the world, to try and help feed these poor people and their children. I was later told that it was Geldof's then partner, Paula Yates, who had really been the driving force behind getting all the names together. But in the end, it doesn't really matter who did it or even how, the cause was undeniable, and the potential money that could be raised inestimable. It's worth remembering that unlike now, where your record can go to number 1 with less than 5,000 sales, in 1984 a hit single could still generate millions of sales.

So it was that on 25 November 1984, a Sunday, Rick and I and about forty other pop and rock stars turned up at Sarm West Studios in London's Notting Hill Gate, and did our bit for Band Aid. Four days later 'Do They Know It's Christmas?' was released and went straight to number 1, selling more than a million copies in that first week alone. It stayed at number 1 for about five weeks and eventually sold something like four million copies.

You can't argue with a phenomenon like that. Nevertheless, I have to confess that Rick and I were nervous turning up at Sarm West that day. We knew Phil Collins and Sting, so that was all right. We also knew Paul Weller, or rather Rick did. He had actually known Paul since he was a young unknown and had been a Quo fan. His father would bring him to Quo concerts and Rick would show Paul his guitar. But we had only met Geldof once before, bumping into him at the offices of Phonogram. We didn't know most of the others, all these young guns like Simon Le Bon, Boy George, Bono, Tears for Fears, Paul Young, George Michael, Tony Hadley from Spandau Ballet and various others. We wondered if they would just see us as these incredibly old farts, like Mum and Dad turning up and ruining the kids' party. We needn't have worried though. Everyone was as nice as pie. It turned out that the first gig Paul Weller ever went to was to see Quo perform. He said it was so loud and exciting it was the final clincher in him deciding to form his own band.

The future Sir Bob was another kettle of fish, obviously, running around, looking as frayed round the edges as he would soon become famous for. He was very stressed out to find Phil Collins setting up his full drum kit, telling Bob, 'We've got to give the song some bollocks.' He was right, too. It's Phil's drums that really drive that song. I'm still not too sure how many of the other people in the room could actually play a musical instrument. (Kidding!)

What I hadn't expected was how much many of us had in common when it came to cocaine. Naturally, Rick and I had ensured we would get through the day feeling as little pain as possible and brought our own not inconsiderable supplies. Very soon, our little corner of the studio became the go-to hangout for quite a few others.

The only one that I took a dislike to was Marilyn, Boy George's 'companion'. Marilyn was living proof of what an air stewardess once told me: that it's not the ones in First Class nor the ones in Economy that give you any bother – it's the bastards in Club Class. They have made it just far enough to escape Economy, but not far enough to fly First. And for some reason it eats them up and they become the most demanding pains in the arse on any flight. That was Marilyn. He'd had exactly one hit single – what in the business we call a two-for-one: his first and his last. But the way he carried on you'd think it was the real Marilyn Monroe standing there. He was making such a big thing about being gay and being unsure which toilet to use I felt compelled to give him my own personal suggestion. I told him to use the gents but to put the seat down and sit on it. That way he could have the best of both worlds. Oh, the look he gave me! Like I'd never had 'dealings' with a gay person before. Never mind that I was the father of a beautiful gay son.

One of our 106 appearances on *Top of the Pops* — more than any act in the show's history. No wonder I can't remember which one this was. Sometime in the early nineties … maybe.
(John Jefford/BBC Photo Library)

Celebrating being awarded the Ivor Novello Award for Outstanding Contribution to the British Music Industry at the 1991 Brits. Left to right: Rick, Roger Daltrey from The Who, Andy Bown, me, John Edwards. We later ripped those suits off to reveal T-shirts and jeans underneath. You can take the boy out of Forest Hill …
(Status Quo Archives)

When we released *Don't Stop: 30th Anniversary Album* in 1996 it was our biggest hit for years. It was a fun album to make, featuring various friends. Queen's Brian May guested on our version of Buddy Holly's 'Raining In My Heart'. Then there's us with the Beach Boys, performing the single from the album, our version of their classic 'Fun, Fun, Fun'.

(top: Martyn Goodacre/Getty Images; bottom: Brian Rasic/Getty Images)

Rick and I receiving our OBEs in 2010. It might not sound very rock'n'roll but we were both tickled pink to meet the Queen. Amazing how far three chords can take you.
(John Stillwell-WPA Pool/Getty)

Outside the Rovers Return on the *Coronation Street* set in 2005. That's Sam Aston on our shoulders. He played Chesney Brown, the tearaway stepson of Les Battersby – who me and Rick ended up chinning in the episode. I still love playing the theme tune to *Corrie* on my acoustic guitar. Such beautiful chords.
(Matt Roberts/PA Archive/PA Images)

Face-off. At Madame Tussaud's Rock Circus in 1991. I like my wax head. It's got more hair.
(Francis Rossi)

In the army now. *(Steve Parsons/PA Archive/PA Images)*

Rick and I at the Leicester Square premiere of *Bula Quo!* with some of the players from the movie. That's the lovely Laura Aikman in the middle. *(Ian West/PA Archive/PA Images)*

Glastonbury 2009. Everybody kept telling us how great it was to play Glastonbury. When we got there we found out they were right! *(Christie Goodwin/Redferns via Getty Images)*

Onstage during the Aquostic tour. My driver, who has been with me for years, said to me: 'I never knew you could play acoustic guitar.' *(Christie Goodwin/Redferns via Getty Images)*

The aptly named Frantic Four. It was fun getting back with the original foursome while it lasted. Thankfully it didn't last too long.

(top: Christian Behring / Geisler-Fotopr / DPA / PA Images; right: Kevin Nixon / Future Publishing via Getty Images)

Onstage with Quo's newest member, Richie Malone. Rick sent Richie a note after he joined, saying: 'You're the one!' *(Brian Rasic / WireImage / Getty Images)*

Me and Rick in 1983. I was already thinking about leaving Quo. But not for long …
(Michael Putland/Getty Images)

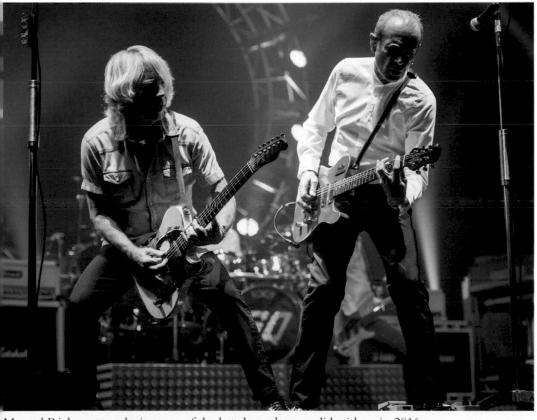

Me and Rick onstage during one of the last shows he ever did with us in 2016.
(David Jensen/PA Archive/PA Images)

The Rossi clan at the *Bula Quo!* premiere. Left to right: Simon, Nicholas, Kieran, Bernadette, Francis, Eileen, Kiera, Fynn, Fursey and Patrick. *(Francis Rossi)*

I love this shot from 2015, mainly because it proves what I've been saying for years: that I always photograph better from the back. *(Christie Goodwin/Redferns via Getty Images)*

As the day flashed by and Rick and I were finally called to add our vocals, poor old Rick had shoved so much powder up his hooter his voice had cracked. So I ended up overdubbing his part. It didn't make any difference. I'd had Rick's voice singing in my ears for nearly twenty years so I could do a passable imitation. Being Rick the rock star, he did manage to push himself right to the front for the group picture afterwards though, standing next to Sting like they were the best mates in all the world. Or maybe it was Sting making sure he got his picture taken with Rick.

What I don't think even Geldof had realised that day was quite how enormous this whole Band Aid thing would quickly become. The record became a hit all over the world, raising millions for the famine relief organisations. Then America got in on the act with its own USA for Africa single, 'We Are the World'. That sold more than ten million copies worldwide. At which point Geldof was back asking if we'd open up a Band Aid themed live concert he was organising for the following summer. He was calling it Live Aid, he said, and we were one of the first bands he had approached. Though I know he said that to all the older bands.

As you might have learned by now, I can be a cynical old sod at times, always questioning everybody's motives, including my own. I admit I wasn't too sure about agreeing to Geldof's latest idea. It was one thing to organise a single day in a recording studio where everybody – including all the artists, roadies, the studio and the video crew – gave their time for free, but a daylong concert at Wembley Stadium? That required a much greater leap of imagination – and an even greater organisational skill. I loved Bob for what he was trying to accomplish. I just wasn't sure if he was going to be able to accomplish something like that.

Well, as we all now know, Bob Geldof pulled off the seemingly impossible that day in July 1985. And I am so thankful that Status Quo was able to be such a unique part of it. At first, we had told Bob, 'But we're not really a band any more. We haven't even been in the same room for a year.' Typical Bob, he just yelled back at me: 'It doesn't matter a fuck! Just get back together for the day. It doesn't matter what you sound like as long as you're there!' I thought, that's easy for you to say. Or yell. I wasn't at all sure how Alan would react, though, being asked to fly over from Australia for a fifteen-minute gig with a singer he couldn't stand.

Fair play to Alan, though, he seemed to grasp the importance of the event before I did fully, and immediately agreed to come and join in for the show. He was happy to pay for his travel arrangements too. He was a complete gentleman about the whole thing. So now we had to do it. Colin phoned Bob with the news. He seemed unimpressed. I think in his mind we had already agreed to do the show. He had told us to be there and we bloody well better be. It was exactly this upstart Irish punk attitude that forced so many other stars to come out of their shells that day for Live Aid. Whatever you may think about Geldof, he was a king that day.

By the time it was announced that we would be joining the show, Bob had lined up an American Live Aid to take place simultaneously at the JFK Stadium in Philadelphia, and persuaded the cream of the world's musical talent to also appear: Queen, David Bowie, Paul McCartney, Bob Dylan, the Who, Led Zeppelin, Mick Jagger, Elton John, U2, Madonna . . . the list was long and hugely impressive. He had also somehow managed to oversee other twinned Live Aid events in the Soviet Union, Canada, Japan, Yugoslavia and West Germany. By the end of the show in London it was officially one of the largest-scale satellite link-ups and television broadcasts of all time. According to the stats — they still take my breath away — almost two billion people watched the live broadcast. Or put another way, nearly 40 per cent of the world's population.

What memories!

Or rather: what memories? Yes, you guessed it. I vaguely recall the marvellous brass section of the Coldstream Guards regiment blasting 'God Save the Queen' just before we went onstage. And I think I remember the late great Tommy Vance — a Quo fan of old and a good mate — booming out the words, 'It's twelve o'clock in London, it's seven o'clock in Philadelphia. This is Live Aid. Will you please welcome — Status Quo!' Though that might just be because I've now seen the footage on TV so many times.

We had met up that Saturday morning at a pub in Battersea, just down the road from the flash, new riverside flat where Rick now lived with his girlfriend, and soon to be second wife, Patty. Next thing we were on a helicopter heading for Wembley. We had helicoptered in to our final show at Milton Keynes Bowl the year before. We had headlined several big outdoor festivals over the years. But this was definitely a very different experience. The buzz wasn't just confined to that huge Wembley Stadium crowd of over 70,000, it was everywhere you turned that day. The TV, radio, people on the street, everywhere and everyone was talking about it, vibing on the whole thing — and it hadn't even started yet.

At the time we hit the stage I was still straight. I saved my bingeing for afterwards, but the whole thing went by in such a flash I really don't remember much about it now all these years later. The rest, as they say even though it almost never is but in this case absolutely was, is history!

Credit where it's due, it was Mike Appleton, then producer of *The Old Grey Whistle Test* TV show and the guy who was organising the BBC's live coverage that day, who had been absolutely adamant that we should open with 'Rockin' All Over the World'. I know Bob has since usually claimed it was he that came up with that idea, and for all I know, he may well have. But that's not how I remember it. I just know Mike Appleton virtually threatened us with termination with extreme prejudice if we didn't do it. And of course Mike was absolutely spot-on.

Keeping with Bob's stated aim – repeated over and over until it felt like he had tattooed it on your face – to make the concert a 'global jukebox', we stuck to the obvious crowd-pleasers, following 'Rockin'' with 'Caroline', finishing up with 'Don't Waste My Time'. I know this because I've seen the footage. That is, watched it through my fingers covering my eyes. Don't get me wrong, that short but sweet set is one of the proudest moments in the career of Status Quo. But what a state I was in for the rest of that day. What a state Rick was in, too.

Or at least that's how it felt to me. After we came offstage people were going ballistic – and in the days that followed, even more so. For a band that didn't officially exist any more we were suddenly famous in countries that had never even heard of us the day before. It was the same for Queen and U2. Queen, our mates, had been on everybody's shit list after playing at Sun City less than a year before. Now they were one of the most loved bands in the world again. U2 were already big but Live Aid made them into global superstars.

After our set, and the obligatory round of breathless interviews where I did my best to hold it together long enough to seem at least semi-coherent, I headed for the VIP enclosure set up by the Hard Rock Café backstage. Rick jumped straight back on the helicopter and headed back to his local in Battersea, the returning hero.

Back at the show, Freddie Mercury treated me to a bear hug that nearly broke my ribs, then picked me up and swung me around like a rag doll. I remember thinking: if Freddie decides to shag me now there will be nothing I can do about it. He was so strong. Freddie had no intention of wasting his charms on the middle-aged likes of me though, at least not in that regard. He just told me how well we'd done going out there first and braving the storm. Bless his heart.

At the end of a very long and crazy day we were all rounded up and taken to the back of the stage, ready to try and find a place for ourselves onstage to sing the final song, 'Do They Know It's Christmas?', which I really didn't want to do. I was sitting with David Bowie and Bruce Springsteen's guitarist – and, years later, one of the stars of *The Sopranos* – 'Miami' Steve Van Zandt, when they came to round us up. Then just as we stood up all the lights went out and the table we were sitting at collapsed. We were all laughing hysterically, bumping into each other trying to make our way to the stage and only just getting there in time. As I got onto the side of the stage I saw Rick, who had helicoptered back to the show with Patty. He seemed to be having the time of his life. Meanwhile, I was stood at the back, very uncomfortable. At least, I assume I was, as once again I couldn't remember much about it when I woke up the next afternoon, or whenever it eventually was.

It was only after reading about it in the Sunday newspapers and seeing my picture that it started to dawn on me what a great day it really was. We had fed the world. And somehow revived the name Status Quo in so doing. What we did next to the world was another thing.

One I would now have to think about long and hard. As would the others . . .

Chapter Nine

Army of Two

I always look back now and think of the career I've enjoyed with Status Quo as falling into two distinct categories: Before and After Live Aid. In the decade and a half before that incredible show, Quo had enjoyed its greatest successes, in many ways. We released sixteen new studio albums in that time, almost all of which were hits all over the world, selling more than fifty million copies along the way – more if you included all the hit singles we had too. And we wrote and recorded some of the songs that are still the fans' favourites to this day, from 'Caroline' and 'Down Down' to 'Rockin' All Over the World' and 'Whatever You Want'. But what a miserable time we ended up having when it was all over. Long before it was officially all over, actually.

In the nearly thirty-five years now that have passed since Live Aid, we have also released sixteen new studio albums, selling another fifty million copies – and more, again, if you include the combined sales of all the singles. We have also pushed the boundaries far more musically, and we have toured in more countries around the world and sold more tickets to our shows than ever before. And, by and large, we've been a bunch of incredibly happy people. Well, there are always a few moans and groans, that comes with the territory as you get older – the occasional moments of you–must–be–joking! But by and large this has been the golden age of Quo for the guys in the band, me especially, and for a whole new generations of Quo fans.

And yet it so easily could have gone another way. If Rick and I had stuck to our guns and absolutely insisted that Quo was behind us and that we were now determined, come hell or High Court action, to continue with our solo careers . . . well, you wouldn't be reading this book now. Because I wouldn't have had a very interesting story to tell, other than how I had once been a famous musician in the seventies, but blew it in the eighties big time.

Not that I was sure I knew what I was doing in the crazy weeks that followed Live Aid. The pressure to reform the band and cash in on our new sky-high profile was being applied from all quarters. I got word once again that Alan and Rick were up for it, and had even let it be known to the record company that they were prepared to get someone in to replace me if necessary. But that wasn't what the label executives wanted to hear. Nor was it what the various big-name tour promoters were interested in either. They all made it abundantly clear that the only line-up of Quo they thought could still be successful was one with both me and Rick in it. That they weren't that bothered who played the other instruments, as long as the two of us were there to front the band still.

I got all that but I was still holding out. I knew Rick was hurt and confused by all this, could never really see what my problem was. But I didn't care. I wanted a clean break. Or thought I did, anyway. My second single with Bernie, 'Jealousy', was scheduled for a late summer release and we still had the *Flying*

Debris album ready to go. I decided that at the very least I owed it to myself to see that project through to its logical conclusion. What if those records were hits but I'd already committed myself to doing another Quo album? I didn't want to shoot myself in the foot. That's what I told myself, not realising how close I was to shooting myself in the head if I didn't reconsider the Quo situation.

I even agreed to do a handful of 'evening with'-style shows with Rick, billed as 'An Evening with the Music of Status Quo', in which we just pitched up and sat there talking to fans, answering questions and just hanging out and having fun. We weren't required to sing and play. We were just there to chat. How we got talked into this I really don't know. But somehow Rick and I were on the road again together – at least for a few days. It was fun, talking to the Quo fans. They really know their stuff and certainly had plenty of questions to ask. The main one being: why did we break up? Followed even more urgently by: when were we getting back together?

Ricky told me about the solo album he was working on. It was to be called *Recorded Delivery*, and from the few tracks he played me on cassette it sounded, somewhat eerily, a bit like my own attempt at a solo record. Lots of echoes of Quo, but at the same time a quite determined effort to do something new – lighter, more pop. The guitars submerged beneath a more 'contemporary' bank of swirling keyboards. Except for the fact he was now doing his gruff rock voice, which I never liked, much preferring his real voice, which was lighter and much easier on the ear. I played Rick some of what I'd recorded with Bernie and he was very polite about it, though probably thinking what I was thinking about his stuff: wouldn't it all be just so much better if we had Quo doing this material?

In the end the record company forced our hands. Or at least that's what we were told. They said the label had produced a legally binding document that demonstrated that as a band Status Quo still owed the label one more album. And that they would sue us if we refused to deliver one. Not only that, but they were going to sit on Rick's and my solo albums until we gave them this so-called missing Quo album.

Truthfully, I don't know if I really believed this at the time. Lots of bands have broken up owing their record labels an album or two. The usual way of dealing with it was for the label to stick out another compilation or a live album. The fact that they also had both Rick and me signed as solo artists was another reason to be nice about it. In the end, I agreed to get Quo back together for one album, then that really would be it, finished. One thing I absolutely would not budge on, though, was working with Alan Lancaster again. There was just too much bad blood there still. Alan had been one of the main reasons I had walked away from Quo in the first place. I was damned if I was going to allow myself to become entangled again in that kind of toxic situation.

I would get together with Rick and make another Status Quo album – but not if Alan was involved. It complicated things but no one bothered to fight me over it. The label had made it clear that as long as they had both Rick and me in the band it would always be regarded by the vast majority of people as de-facto Status Quo. I knew Alan would hit the roof when he found out. But I also knew that Rick would be over the moon, even though it was only for one album.

Rick had blown through all his money, even the windfall from the End of the Road tour. But then Rick always blew through his dough then relied on the next tour to sort him out.

Only this time there was no next tour. He told me that at one point he was so skint he didn't even have anywhere to live. So he checked himself into a suite at the Holiday Inn in Chelsea, where he stayed for a few months, telling them he would pay them at the end of his stay – which they believed because he was Rick, the blond one from Quo. He must be a millionaire!

Like me, Rick had picked up a sweet six-figure advance from the label for his solo album. Once he'd paid off his huge hotel bill and rented himself a flat, then hired Pip Williams and some top-notch session musicians to help him make his album, he was heavily in debt again. The prospect of getting together with me to make a new Quo album and do a tour – and the kind of sizable advances that would immediately become available to us as a result – meant he didn't have to think long about it.

I could hear the excitement in his voice when I spoke to him on the phone. But then he started whispering. I didn't realise it but Alan was staying with Rick at his flat at the time. He had gotten wind that something was afoot. And yes, he would have given his right testicle to be involved. But it was either him or me and, truthfully, I didn't feel like I owed Alan anything. I'd given him twenty years of my time and my best efforts. And through that we had both made a lot of money and enjoyed a great deal of success.

Rick, meanwhile, had to tiptoe around like he knew nothing about it until Alan had gone back to Australia. Then the minute Alan was told what was going on, he got straight on the phone to everyone he could think of to tell them what fucking bastards we all were. It was water off a duck's back to me. I'd been listening to Alan having a go at me since I was a kid. But Ricky was quite shaken up when Alan phoned him and had a go at him too. As far as Alan was concerned, Rick and I had betrayed him. He immediately launched a very expensive lawsuit against us over the ownership of the name Status Quo.

This is where things got really messy between Alan and me. He didn't like it that Rick had sided with me, but he was most upset with me, and now tried to do everything in his power to stop me making an album under the name Status Quo. He started with an injunction, but when that didn't work he shelled out for some very expensive lawyers to take the whole thing to the High Court. Meanwhile, having obtained a preliminary ruling in our favour until a date could be set for the High Court hearing, the record company stuck a lucrative new contract under our noses and told me and Rick to get on with making a new Quo album. Fair enough, but who were we going to get in the band to play the bass and drums?

Andy Bown was more than happy to sign up for the new line-up. But I didn't ask Pete Kircher if he wanted to be involved. I know that this has been a source of pain for Pete over the years, wondering why I didn't ask to bring him in. The answer is that Rick had already found the perfect rhythm section, and it was one that already worked in tandem. You hired one, he came with the other, sort of thing. It was nothing personal – or professional – against Pete. He was a lovely bloke and a great drummer. But at the end of the day it was our choice to make. What I will hold my hands up and apologise for is that I didn't phone Pete personally and explain my reasons. I didn't feel I had to, actually. It was nothing personal. On the other hand, I admit now that perhaps I could have handled it better. I was still doing coke, still super paranoid, and wasn't talking to anybody outside of the band at that point. I was somewhere else, somewhere not at all good. Though I wouldn't allow myself to admit it yet.

The names of the new guys were John Edwards (bass) and Jeff Rich (drums). John was nicknamed Rhino from his time in Judie Tzuke's band, because he was such a clumsy sod. I never did like the nickname though, so instead I always called him John Boy, from *The Waltons*. He had real pedigree though. He'd been trained as a classical violinist as a child and won a scholarship to the London College of Music when he was just eleven. Since then he'd played with an impressive array of different artists, including Peter Green, the Climax Blues Band and, most memorably of all, Dexys Midnight Runners during their chart-bossing 'Come On Eileen' era. That's John with the bog-brush hair in the 'Eileen' video, pretending to be happy wearing farmer's dungarees and chewing a blade of grass.

Jeff Rich was a few years younger than me and Rick but he had a similar sort of background, in that he'd been a professional musician since the sixties, when he'd been the drummer in Billy J. Kramer's backing group. He'd also played for a time in Jackie Lynton's band, so there was that connection too, and several other bands. He and Rhino had first hooked up as a working rhythm section in Judie Tzuke's band, which is how Pip Williams got to know and work with them.

Pip Williams had brought them both in to play on Rick's album and now Rick couldn't speak highly enough of them. The fact that Pip would also be working with us now on the new Quo album also helped seal the deal. They were great players, already completely locked in to each other's style as a rhythm section, and they were available right now.

The only question in my mind when I went down to meet them and have a jam for the first time was how would I get on with them? I didn't want to be boxed in with a bunch of people I couldn't stand just for the sake of convenience, that would have been like going back to square one. So I played it cool to begin with, just leaning against the wall, acting nonchalant, twirling away on my guitar. The atmosphere soon thawed though. Rhino and Jeff were a hoot. And they could really play. Jeff was a phenomenal drummer and Rhino was incredibly versatile and open to musical ideas.

I soon got the vibe from Rhino that he could be a band leader in his own right if he wanted to be – something that he did in fact become when he formed his side-project, named simply Rhino, in the following years. I didn't mind that at all. It meant he was very comfortable coming to the front of the stage alongside Rick and me and giving it some welly, as we say, during a Quo show. Jeff was simply a brilliant drummer with a lot of feel. He also had an unusually sunny countenance, which meant he was always very easy to work with.

However, I was not so sunny during the making of that album because outside the actual writing and performing the rest of the period was incredibly stressful. I thought I had my personal life in control – which just shows you how messed up I was. It was the band situation that had me on the ropes. Even as we came to finishing the album and discussing which singles we should release from it, Alan's High Court action was looming ever nearer, which meant we still weren't even sure if we would be able to release it under the name Status Quo.

In the end, the judge decreed that Rick and I could keep the Status Quo name and Alan was left in the unenviable position of having spent a lot of money achieving the opposite of what he'd been hoping for. I take no pleasure in this fact. But that was Alan: a born fighter. He thought he had the right so he took it all the way. He underestimated how much right Rick and I felt we had to the name too, having written most of the big hits between us and become the public face of the band over nearly twenty years. When Alan then offered to sell his rights to the name to us, we accepted, agreed a fair six-figure price, which he was more than happy with at the time, and breathed a sigh of relief as we began to look forward to a brand new chapter in the Quo story.

Of course, the bitterness on Alan's side didn't end there. Over the years he has made some outlandish claims about the manner in which he left the band. In one interview I read he said something about how we had 'stolen' his 'children's inheritance'. Well, there are different ways to respond to that. I could point out that without the songs I wrote that became huge worldwide hits for Quo – particularly 'Pictures Of Matchstick Men', which started the ball rolling – none of us would have any sort of 'inheritance'. But I don't like to say that. I prefer to point out that as a band, we were all in it together, all working equally hard to make Quo a success. I didn't ask John Coghlan to leave. He was the one that decided he wanted to leave. It's not my fault that his solo projects never took off or that his career never really recovered, leaving him to rely on his connection to Quo to keep things going.

Similarly, I didn't ask Alan to leave us in the lurch every time we had a hit that he thought made him 'look bad'. I didn't ask Alan to throw his weight around and start yelling if he thought he didn't have enough of his songs on a Quo album. Frankly, he could make our lives a misery sometimes. And if he had been given the chance to carry on the Quo name without me he would have jumped at it. He tried. No one wanted it. That's not my fault. The fact that he still talks about how unfair the whole thing was over thirty years later says it all. In fairness, Alan went back to Australia and joined the Party Boys, having great success there for some years. The fact is, Quo were going far longer without Alan than it did with him. So when I still read the stuff he comes out with, like the most recent old bollocks about it being my years of involvement with drugs that somehow turned me against him – and still interferes with my capacity to think straight – well, I'm flabbergasted. As you'll see as you read on, drugs and booze would play no part in my life after the eighties. For Alan to suggest that my reasons for not wanting to work with him again were because my brain is somehow still addled from cocaine is offensive, frankly. But that's Alan. Always up for a ruck.

The sad part is that right at the end of all the legal bullshit, Alan took me to one side and told me: 'I know you're the main bloke in this band.' I said, 'It's a bit fucking late to be telling me that now, isn't it?' Alan officially resigned from Status Quo in January 1987. Of course, that wasn't the last of our dealings with Alan – or John – but we will come to that in due course.

Rick, meanwhile, had not allowed the petty backbiting to get to him. The moment he got his hands on his share of the advance money for the new Quo album, he'd splashed out on a new car. Not just any car, of course, being Rick, but a two-tone champagne-and-walnut-coloured Rolls-Royce Silver Shadow. Not a new one – he hadn't been paid that much. But it was still a lot of money second-hand, about fifteen grand I believe. You had to hand it to Rick. He was just a born rock star. He also went out and bought Patty, who he was about to marry, a fur coat. The funniest part was he was banned again from driving at the time, for four and a half years this time. He didn't care. He simply got Patty to be his chauffeur. The message was: Rick Parfitt is back!

I was fine with that because it meant so was Status Quo.

Our first single with the new line-up was 'Rollin' Home', a real rock and roller in the classic Quo style. It went straight into the charts and we did *Top of the Pops* for the first time with the new line-up. No one complained. No one rioted. In fact, we got a ton of great feedback from people, old and new Quo fans, people in the business, telling us how glad they were to see us back. Looking at the clip now, you can see how much fun we were having again (even if I am starting to look just a little bit bloated from my excesses, which were still raging not so quietly in the background) and how into it Rhino and Jeff obviously were. Talk about a whole new lease of life.

We didn't write 'Rollin' Home'. That honour fell to John David, who was a bassist and multi-instrumentalist who worked with Dave Edmunds. Dave came in and produced the track, along with another David song called 'Red Sky' – which became our second single by the new line-up. 'Rollin' Home' went top 10 and 'Red Sky' went top 20. Why we didn't release an original number from the album was more down to the record company deciding what they thought they could turn into a hit. After a couple of flops on my own with Bernie, with songs we had written, my confidence was not high in that department, either. The fact is Quo hadn't released an original song as a single since 'Marguerita Time' three years before. Looking back now, though, I think we could easily have released 'Calling' as a single and seen it do very well. It was written by me and Bernie again but it sounded more Quo than Quo, while at the same time sounding up to date with modern eighties tastes. I didn't say anything at the time, though. The feeling in the business now was that you let the record label choose the singles – and if they didn't hit they only had themselves to blame. That's still the way it works to this day.

Pip Williams produced the majority of the album and did his best to continue what Rick and I had started when making our now-forgotten solo albums: make it more contemporary sounding, but bring even more of the recognisable Quo signature sound to it. I'd say we were only semi-successful. Tracks like 'In Your Eyes' still make me gag. A song I wrote with Bernie, it doesn't sound like it belongs on the same album as the rest of the material, though I do like the guitar parts. Mostly it was a hotchpotch of different things. Good stuff like 'End of the Line', which was a sort of Bryan Adams-type rocker that Rick had co-written with a friend of his, Ricky Patrick – good but not really a Quo track. 'Invitation', which was a song I had written with Bob Young back in the day, which might have been a follow-up to 'Marguerita Time', only even more country-sounding. Again, good – but probably not the sort of thing our fans were longing to hear. Even a song I co-wrote with Rick, 'Save Me', which was very Quo-sounding, was still guilty of trying to sound too modern.

The best of the new songs was probably 'Overdose', which Rick co-wrote with Pip, and for all I know had originally been destined to be on his solo album. A good song, though, and Rick sang it really well. Kind of like the Who meets Status Quo meets ELO.

The rest were cover versions: the John David singles plus an Ian Hunter song called 'Speechless' – which I liked at the time but admit I'm baffled by now. The original sounded like Ian doing his best to distance himself from Mott the Hoople by coming up with something that might fit better into the charts in 1983 – the year he recorded it. Our version sounded like a faxed copy of that, only even more contrived. Us trying to sound like Ian Hunter trying not to sound like when he was successful.

There was, however, one really good cover of a song we did – called 'In the Army Now'. I'd actually fallen for the track back in the early eighties when I was living as a tax exile in Ireland, and the original record, by a group called Bolland, was played a lot on the radio. I looked into it and discovered that Bolland was two Dutch brothers – Rob and Ferdi Bolland – and that they'd had a big hit with the song in Norway where it was number 1 for weeks on end. The record had never gone beyond that and I thought it would make a great track for Quo. But when I brought it to the boys for the *Back to Back* album it was rejected out of hand. Alan wasn't budging after having to give in on 'Marguerita Time'. He also wasn't having any song on a Quo album that spoke out openly about the iniquities of war or being a conscripted soldier. Even Rick thought it was a bad idea so that was that.

Now, though, in 1986, with everything up for grabs, I suggested it again. I had been planning on keeping 'In the Army Now' for my solo album. Now things had changed. I felt sure it was a sure-fire hit and that's what we needed for this new Quo album. Rick still didn't like it. But everyone else did, so we had a crack at it. Its mix of Quo-style guitars and harmony vocals, and that new keyboard-synth production polish that Pip was aiming for – plus our drum tech belting out the line, 'Stand up and fight!' in his most gravelly voice – turned it into the best track on the album. As soon as we had finished it I knew we were onto a real winner. Lo and behold we ended up having our biggest international hit single since 'What You're Proposing' six years before. It went to number 2 in the UK, where it stayed in the charts for over six months, and went to number 1 in West Germany and some other countries around Europe. That was in September 1986. As a result, the *In the Army Now* album went top 10 and gave us a handful more gold records. It was big everywhere, in fact, except Russia, where conscription was still in force; therefore it was viewed very poorly by the authorities, we were told.

By then we really felt like we were back in the groove. It was a relief for all concerned. Mainly, though, for me and Rick. The band was now the band. But it was Rick and I who were now fronting everything. The band was so good as a unit Rick and I began to enjoy ourselves onstage again like we hadn't done for years. We had spent the summer touring football stadiums and Britain and Europe as special guests of Queen and Rod Stewart. The idea was to reintroduce us to the world with as big a splash as possible and it certainly did the trick. In the middle of the three-month tour Rick and I were invited to take part in a special show at Wembley Arena to celebrate the Prince's Trust tenth anniversary. It was billed as the Prince's Trust Rock Gala, and the idea was that we would become part of an all-star line-up including Phil Collins, Eric Clapton, Mark Knopfler, George Michael, Elton John, Tina Turner and others – with Paul McCartney singing up front – performing a set of three songs by the Beatles: 'I Saw Her Standing There', 'Long Tall Sally' and 'Get Back'. It was a great night and the show was filmed and later shown on TV. The main thing I remember about our actual performance, other than standing next to Rick doing that Status Quo dance we do, then seeing the other guitarists lined up next to us doing it – Midge Ure on Rick's left, Mark King from Level 42 on my right. Next thing, there's Mark Knopfler doing the same thing standing next to Paul McCartney. Sorry, lads, it must be catching!

What I do remember is being introduced again to Prince Charles, who was lovely as usual. And to his wife, Princess

Diana, who most definitely was even lovelier, and quite stunningly beautiful, much more so in person even than on camera. What did we talk about? That would be telling. Mainly I just remember staring into her gorgeous blue eyes.

On the final day of the three-month tour we managed to do shows in three different countries in one twenty-four-hour period. We started with an early morning appearance – 12.30 a.m. – at a festival in Denmark, before flying to London and making our way to the Knebworth Festival, where we were special guests for Queen. We then flew straight to Switzerland, where we headlined the Seepark festival.

Two months later, with the 'In the Army Now' single riding high in the charts and the album having similar success, we set out on our real 'comeback' tour: fifty-two shows in nine countries, including eight nights back at our old home-from-home, the Hammersmith Odeon in London, with the final night on Christmas Eve 1986. It really was just like old times. Multiple nights at big venues everywhere we went. At the start of 1987 we kept up the pace. Beginning in February we did another twenty-four shows in just thirty-one days, finishing with shows in Bahrain, Oman and the United Arab Emirates. This was genuine new territory for the band. We had played a few shows in the UAE the year before to see how they would go down. The answer was: spectacularly well. We loved it there, too.

It really felt like there were whole new worlds now opening up to us. The other thing that made this new on-the-road life much easier was that with the new line-up I no longer had to battle with three other equal members to get my musical ideas across. The show was now being run exclusively by myself and Rick. It didn't mean we didn't listen to what the others had to say. We still wanted it to be a band. And on our next album, Rhino, Jeff and Andy would all get songwriting credits. I just wasn't going to fall into the trap of having another strong voice in the band when it came to making any of the really important decisions. Everyone would have a say – but Rick and I would have the final say. End of.

Unfortunately, my personal life was far less simple to control. It was like trying to keep a row of spinning plates from toppling over. Just as I'd fixed things with the band again, I now found myself at the mercy of two unforeseen events in my life – though, in retrospect, they were pretty inevitable, one way or another.

The first concerned my health. Well, what a surprise. Rhino later told me that he was deeply shocked when he first began working with the band at how much coke Rick and I were doing. I would wake up sometimes on tour with the phone in my hand, halfway through a call back home to England. The phone bill would be more than the price of the room. Rick was the same.

Awake I wasn't that different, sitting in my hotel suite with the curtains drawn, living in a kind of permanent midnight, either doing coke or trying to score more coke. Now at the ripe old age of thirty-eight, after nearly ten years of doing mountainous amounts of cocaine every single day throughout the whole of that time, my nose broke. That is, my septum – the thin partition that separates the channels of your nose – began falling out. Bit by bit.

I was in the shower at the time. I'd already had a snort of the white powder just to get me out of bed and into the shower, as I did most mornings. By now I'd taken to 'washing' my nose in the shower. Getting the showerhead and pointing it up my hooter, jetting hot water up there in order to give it a bit of a clean. My nose had been slowly disintegrating for a long time. I had taken to pestering my doctor for all sorts of different nasal sprays and gels to help it stop hurting, help it recover from the abuse it was getting from my constant cocaine use. Recently, I'd been shoving a vitamin E capsule up before I went to bed, with the ridiculous idea that it would have a soothing, efficacious effect on my nose while I slept – which was about the only time I wasn't snorting coke up there.

God knows why I thought showering my nose was a good idea. It wasn't the coke residue left in my nose that caused me problems, it was the coke that had already been absorbed into my bloodstream. Nevertheless, I had got it into my head that this was a good 'healthy' thing to do every morning. Give my poor old nose a clean – ready for me to start shovelling more stuff up there again.

This particular morning I was standing there, pointing the showerhead up my nose, when I suddenly heard an unexpected sound. A little thunk: something landing at my feet. I looked down and there was the bloody membrane of my septum, like a chunk of chopped liver on the floor of the shower. I realised what it was immediately – or, rather, I had no idea what it was, just that it had come from my nose. I reached down and picked it up, gave it a quick rinse under the shower and tried to shove it back up my nose. Then – thunk! It plopped out again. I tried again. Same thing – thunk! Then another little piece. Then another . . .

Oh dear.

I got out, towelled down, then went and chopped myself out a few more lines of coke, snorted them and sat there on the edge of the bed wondering what to do next. I rang my manager.

Of course I did. I was a rock star and anything – anything at all – that went wrong for me, I called my manager. But when I told him what had happened he didn't know whether to laugh or cry.

Eventually, he said, 'We better get you to the doctor's. Sit tight. I'll come and pick you up.' Then added: 'Have you still got them?'

'Got what?'

'The bits of your nose that fell out?'

'Yeah. Why?'

'In case the doctor can sew them back in or something.'

That's when I knew my life had reached a level of farce bordering on tragedy.

Oh dear. Oh dear, oh dear.

So I went to the doctor's, and from there to the hospital, where I learned what every other dickhead rock star with a heavy-duty coke habit has learned the hard way. You can't actually 'fix' what was politely referred to as a 'deviated septum'. You just have to live with it. These days it's become a parlour trick for me. Showing how I can thread a cotton-bud in one nostril and weave it straight out of the other nostril. It looks gross because it is gross. It always used to make Rick gag. I have done it for the children of friends who want to demonstrate to their kids just what a rotten idea cocaine really is. I've even done it on telly a couple of times to really make the point. Don't try this at home, kids – or at school or at play or anywhere else in the world.

Oh, and you really do have to stop shovelling snowploughs' worth of coke up your poor ruined nose. Or rather, you really *should* stop. You would have thought your hooter falling to bits might have been some kind of major turning point. In fact, I still hadn't quite learned that lesson yet but it was coming.

The other lesson I hadn't learned yet was how to keep my dick in my trousers. I'm not talking about one-night stands on the road. This was far more serious than that. This was the real thing.

It began when Rick and I had done those few 'evening with' shows on the road a couple of months after Live Aid. We were booked to do one of these shows in a big room at the Portland Hotel in Manchester, where we were also staying the night. They were odd occasions, these shows. Huge fun with the real Quo fans. But there were always a few nutters asking the most obscure, bizarre stuff. There were always a few over-excited women in the audience too, mainly middle-aged ladies throwing bras and panties onstage. Usually at Rick, it has to be said, who enjoyed all that thoroughly. I didn't mind, as I wasn't looking for that kind of action.

After the show, Bernie and I, who was along for the ride, went into the bar at the hotel to have a drink. As soon as we walked in my eyes lit on this incredibly beautiful young woman sitting with a friend at a table. When I say incredibly beautiful, I don't just mean good-looking or sexy or yum-yum-yum. I mean that to me, at that moment, she looked like the most beautiful woman I had ever seen in my life. She was Indian, with glowing skin the colour of golden cocoa butter. Dark flashing eyes like mysterious beacons. The face and body of a goddess. I found myself being pulled toward her like a magnet at the North Pole. Her name was Page Taylor and my life was about to change again and I knew it. I sensed it would not end well. You can't wake up in heaven and not know there is a hell around the corner. But I didn't care. All I knew was that I wanted to be with her and that suddenly nothing else mattered. Not even half as much. I was gone.

The friend she was sitting with was also stunningly attractive, and blonde. Thankfully, Bernie couldn't take his eyes off her – leaving Page for me to talk to and get to know. I just walked straight over to their table, introduced myself and Bernie, then sat down and ordered champagne. We drank that, then ordered another. Then after that we all went out for dinner together. I don't remember where we went. I just remember being unable to take my eyes off Page. I had always had quite a thing for beautiful Asian women. Page had been born in Delhi but her family had emigrated to Manchester when she was a child. The offspring of immigrants – just like me. With a strange tangle of different accents – just like me. If you haven't guessed yet, I was talking myself into what I was already convinced would be the perfect, ultimate relationship before I'd even taken my shoes off.

By the next morning I'd already made up my mind. Hell, I'd made up my mind the moment I first laid eyes on her: Page was the new love of my life. And my relationship with Liz, and by extension our daughter Bernadette, was over. I'm shaking my head in shame as I write this. What a dickhead!

So began another episode in my life that I don't look back on with any pride. Indeed, the guilt and shame I would feel when it finally arrived, as I knew it would eventually, was so intense it nearly finished me off. None of which was of any help to Liz. I was baling out. We had always promised each other that if either one of us ever met someone else we would always tell the other, be upfront and honest rather than cheating. The pain of losing someone was bad enough without all the lies that usually go with it.

But when I sat Liz down to tell her about Page, she was absolutely furious. That's when I realised that certain lies can actually help ease the pain. I should have found a way to lessen the blow. Made her feel, perhaps, that it was probably just a fling, not something so big it would destroy our own relationship. I never, ever wanted to hurt that woman. The truth is, although I was head over heels about Page, a part of me knew it was probably not going to be a lifelong relationship. But another part didn't. I told Liz everything and when she saw how smitten I was she exploded. She handed in her notice with the band, took Bernadette, and not long after she moved to Canada and understandably refused to have anything else to do with me.

It was a bad time. I was a complete arsehole to Liz. Although we were parents to our daughter, who I loved dearly, because of the life I was living – in Ireland one minute, back in London the next, on the road or in the studio again for most of it – Liz and I had never really lived as a so-called normal family with Bernadette. It was one of the things that I loved most about being with Liz while it lasted. The idea that we wouldn't allow so-called norms to dictate to us how we should live. Liz was not a homebody. She'd been around, knew the scene, didn't get on my case if I was doing coke or whatever. At least, that was what I had always told myself. I was so out of my tree 24/7 during those years I was telling myself all sorts of things that decades later I would sit and think about, and realise I had not been truly honest about. Not to Liz or to myself. Ultimately, Bernadette was the one that suffered. I don't like regrets but that is something I do very much wish could have been handled better. On the other hand, I had just enough brain cells left to know her mother would always do a much better job of bringing her up than I would.

Liz was understandably deeply wounded by my abandonment, while I had disappeared so far up my own bum I simply refused to acknowledge it. Worst of all, I disappeared from our daughter's life so completely that it would be many years before we were able to reach any kind of emotional and practical resolution. And I still regret that.

The fact is I had met Page and I couldn't help myself. Not only was she staggeringly beautiful but she was unlike any woman I had ever been with before. Bright, wealthy in her own right, super confident and at the same time crazy – but in a good way. She wasn't into drugs. But she was exciting, full of mischief and adventure, I never quite knew which way she was going to go on anything – and that made her unpredictable, dangerous even. I simply couldn't get enough of her.

Page was a lethal combo to a frazzled old rocker like me back then. She wasn't about to move in with me or even allow me to treat her as my 'girlfriend'. When we were together we were totally together. But she made no promises she couldn't keep. She was still only in her early twenties and settling down with one person was the farthest thing from her mind. She certainly wasn't interested in my money. Her father was a very successful gold bullion dealer, and owned a big jewellery business. When Page went out with me on the town she was dressed to kill in forty-grand pearl necklaces and twenty-grand gold-and-diamond rings. And, of course, gorgeous as she was, when she came out on the road with me she brought more luggage than the rest of the band put together.

In some ways, she was with the wrong Quo frontman. With her couture-designer clothes, gold and diamonds, Page was more the sort of girl you pictured being seen in the tabloids on Rick's arm than mine.

But she wasn't. She was with me. It really shouldn't have worked but for about two years it worked better than it had any right to. Nothing could go wrong.

Until one day it just did.

Chapter Ten

Deeper and Down

I admit it. I was lost. I'd gotten everything I wanted – a successful new line-up of Quo that I had complete control over; a drop-dead gorgeous young girlfriend, intelligent, wild, sexy; and all the cocaine and tequila I could consume without actually having a heart attack and dying. I was still rich, despite a divorce and four children by two different mothers. The only thing I didn't have was the sense to know what to do with all this good fortune. I was a wreck. A walking, talking, singing, playing, permanently fucked-up mess. Deep down I knew it. But I still hadn't gathered up the strength and courage to do anything about it. I still had my coke blinkers on. Anybody that tried to remove them from me was going to be in trouble. Anybody.

It was exactly the cliché they talk about in drug rehabs. That you have to get so low before you finally decide you have no choice but to help yourself out of the hole you've dug yourself. Except, I didn't go into 'recovery'. I just went mental instead. Let everything slide. My relationship with Liz: my relationship with the band; my ability to tell fantasy from reality. I ran away from it all, hid in my darkened room with my best friends coke and Page.

You can see how far off the pace I was by some of the disastrous decisions the band made over the next year or so. The biggest fiasco was our trip to South Africa, in October 1987, for a week of shows at the notorious Sun City resort, the entertainment complex located in Bophuthatswana, one of ten South African Bantustans: tracts of low-quality land supposedly enshrined as independent black homelands that were in fact one of the struts of the apartheid regime. I write this now because I've since done my research but at the time we were talked into going I hadn't the faintest idea about any of this stuff. No Google to look this stuff up on back then. And not enough brainpower left in my head to really care.

Back to my research: when the United Nations imposed a cultural boycott on South Africa in condemnation of apartheid, the organisers of the Sun City resort simply went out with truckloads of money and offered it to any entertainers willing to take it. Among the many musical acts before us that couldn't resist the temptation to earn millions for a few shows were the Beach Boys, Cher, Liza Minnelli, Frank Sinatra, Rod Stewart, Elton John and our old mates Queen, to name just the most famous. Most of them did their shows without anyone batting an eye. But Queen got pilloried in the press and ended up with a fine from the Musicians' Union and inclusion on a United Nations blacklist.

Now this we definitely knew about. And it would have been hard to pretend we didn't, seeing as Bruce Springsteen's famous guitarist and my backstage mate from Live Aid, Steve Van Zandt, had just made Sun City the focus of his music-industry activist group Artists United Against Apartheid. Dozens of big-name artists had appeared on his song, 'Sun City', pledging never to perform there while apartheid stayed in place.

Why didn't we take note of this before we allowed ourselves to go there? Well, one: there was the money. One of the upshots of our getting back together as Quo was that we now discovered that as well as owing the record company an album we also had a huge unpaid tax bill to take care of. We also liked money. Two: Rick and I were just too out of it to give little details like apartheid our attention, while the rest of the band just did what they were told. Three, and most pertinent: we were stupid enough to believe that, following Queen's shows in 1984, the reins had been loosened and it was now all right to play there, as long as you insisted on non-segregated audiences and ensured you employed as many black people backstage as white. What they didn't point out was that ticket prices would be so high the local population would never be able to afford to go anyway.

Well, we did the shows. I can't pretend we didn't enjoy it. South Africa is awe-inspiringly beautiful, and so are most of the people. But what we did was wrong. Sure enough, we came home to a shitstorm of abuse from the media. The United Nations publicly condemned us and we were duly blacklisted in parts of Europe and Scandinavia. Of course we were. We should never have gone. Then a second shitstorm began. We may have been sleepwalking through our career at this point, but Rick and I had recently woken up enough to begin openly questioning where all the band's money was going. We were more or less forced to, after the legal separation from Alan. That was the first time it hit us that while Rick and I were fighting off the taxman and picking up everyone else's wage bills, a certain former advisor was living high on the hog. Rick and I, though now leading separate lives, suddenly had a new common enemy to bond over.

My belief now is that South Africa was meant to be this person's *coup de grâce*. A trick to finish us off while waltzing off with the money. Later on, the more I thought about it the more I came to believe that the tabloid press had even been tipped off about the whole thing. It was a terrible way to end what should have been a triumphant year for the band, and foreshadowed a decline in my own fortunes, personal and professional.

It was in this sort of desperate headspace that I approached the making of the next Quo album. After making the comeback of the year with *In the Army Now*, we should have been set fair to take Quo to a whole other level. The late eighties were a great time to be in a rock band again. The biggest-selling bands in the world in 1987 were Bon Jovi, Whitesnake and Def Leppard. They all had long hair. They all played loud guitars. They were all selling millions of records all over the world. This could so easily have been a great new era for Status Quo. But I was too far gone to recognise any of this, or to even care. As long as I had my toot and my tequila and my sweet little poppadum girl, I was happy not to sweat the small stuff. Or the big stuff – which is how we came to make, as our follow-up to *In the Army Now*, one of the worst Quo albums ever.

It was called *Ain't Complaining* – a very Quo-sounding title for the least Quo-sounding album we had ever released. That in itself was not a crime. I was the one who had long pushed for the band to be more musically adventurous. The problem was that it was so dire. Worse even than that, so derivative.

Take the title track: a nice-enough catchy tune that became a modest hit single for us. Rick and Pip wrote it and it sounds like a Def Leppard outtake. You look back at the time and you can see where they were coming from. Leppard were having huge hit singles with tracks like 'Pour Some Sugar on Me' and 'Animal', both taken from their squillion-selling 1987 album *Hysteria*. These were great records that relied totally on their technologically driven production techniques. They used sophisticated electronic drums and bass synthesisers. They used multiple layers of harmonised vocals. The guitars were brilliantly produced too, to within computeised parameters. These records were the future of rock and pop, way ahead of their time – and about as far from the kind of as-live rough-around-the-muzzle sound of Quo as it was possible to imagine. Yet this was seen as the new gold standard for rock bands to record by. Certainly, hip producers like Pip Williams thought so, and you can completely see why. They weren't wrong. They just weren't right for Status Quo.

So we ended up with tracks like 'Ain't Complaining', replete with electronic drums, multi-layered harmony vocals and little production tricks, like that irritating-after-two-listens intro. The thing is, this was one of the best tracks on the album. The rest of the album sounded even less like us.

The real fault, though, was mine. That's how I see it now. I should have had the presence of mind to question what was going on. Not allow Rick and Pip to virtually hijack the album. But I didn't because I was too fucked up on drugs and my own personal problems. I completely abdicated responsibility. I didn't even write that many songs for it. Of the twelve tracks I co-wrote two with Bernie – 'Cream of the Crop', a fairly standard mid-period Quo number I could have written in my sleep, which was smothered in keyboards and full overcoat production; and 'Magic', which wasn't too bad, I suppose, but magic? Not with all those fake synthesised horns and by-the-yard melody.

I also co-wrote one with Rhino, 'Don't Mind If I Do', which was forgettable. And one with Andy, 'Burning Bridges', which I thought was the best thing I'd done for years, but went down with hardcore Quo fans the same way 'Marguerita Time' had five years earlier. They hated it. Fortunately, the mainstream audience also felt the same way as they had about 'Marguerita Time' and turned it into one of our biggest hits.

Ain't Complaining was one of those albums made by committee: you start by wanting a horse and end up with a donkey. Everybody pitched in. Everybody did their best. Pip bent over backwards to try and bring us into the contemporary rock scene. And it just all backfired. 'Who Gets the Love?', a horribly average 'power ballad' that Pip co-wrote with John Goodison, who'd written hits for Brotherhood of Man and the Bay City Rollers, was the second single, and it was a flop. The album didn't do too well, either, becoming our first not to make the British top 10 since *Dog of Two Head* seventeen years before.

The only bright spark was the success of 'Burning Bridges', which we released towards Christmas 1988. I still love that song. It's the only one from that album we still play live. It's one of those tracks that has always worked better when played live too. It's a real show-stopper.

They say bad news always comes in threes. Well, if playing South Africa was the first sign of things falling apart, and the relative disappointment of the *Ain't Complaining* album was the second, my now failing relationship with Page was the third. I find this one harder to talk about even now, all these years later. They say karma is a bitch and it does occur to me that perhaps I simply had it coming, after the way I had treated Jean and then Liz. In those relationships, I was always the demanding one. The one that only did what he wanted to do when he wanted to, how he wanted to and bollocks to you if you don't like it. Now I got a taste of my own medicine.

Not that Page was cruel to me. She was just . . . Page. When she was with me, she was with me. But when she wasn't, well, she wasn't. And in the end, that's how it went. At the time, I saw it as a case of me dumping her. But really it was a mutual thing. It was a wrench at first but mainly I was relieved. You could say the age gap between us was too great. But it was never simply that. Page had her whole life ahead of her while I seemed to have put my best times behind me. How else to explain all the drugs and booze and loose living? I didn't want to face up to it at the time, but when I look back now I can't say I blame her. We had a lot of fun together while it lasted. But I just wasn't very much fun any more. Nothing for me was. Not even the drugs. But my God she was beautiful.

The beginning of the end to all that came in Russia, of all places. Despite our recent travails, we were having a pretty good summer. Our Sport Aid '88 charity single – a rejigged version of 'Rockin' All Over the World' retitled 'Running All Over the World' – had rehabilitated our reputation after South Africa and in August that year we were booked to perform for fourteen nights at the Olimpiysky National Sports Complex, a massive indoor arena built specifically for the 1980 Moscow Olympics. That makes it sound quite glamorous. In truth, the venue was a dump, like a condemned building. I remember the building was partitioned into two venues and Torvill and Dean were doing their show on the other side of the partition.

This was before the Berlin Wall had come down but the Soviet Union was now under the control of Mikhail Gorbachev and his new glasnost philosophy – meaning openness. It's a shame this didn't apply to many of the shops or restaurants, which were nearly always closed. I don't mean this flippantly. I mean I was appalled by how bad things were. We were lucky in that we had our own catering facilities at the shows but on those few occasions when we went exploring – chaperoned by our own over-friendly KGB team – it was shocking to discover the level of iniquity the local people suffered. Everywhere was closed, basically. There was the odd shop here and there open but they would be closed again the next day. Apart from one burger-and-chips van parked outside our so-called luxury hotel, where the restaurant only sold pickled cabbage and the bar only accepted US dollars and gave you change in any currency you can think of except roubles, which you wouldn't have wanted anyway, there was nowhere that was open more than a day at a time. When one of the crew asked our KGB minder how come the burger van could stay open but none of the restaurants could, he replied: 'Why do you think there are no dogs on the streets of Moscow?' Charming.

The other problem for me personally was the sudden lack of cocaine. Moscow in 1988 was not an easy place to score good coke. I was told I could buy some awful shit masquerading as good coke that would have made the rest of my nose fall off, or I could go without and just drink more. I chose the latter.

But this is where things slowly started to change. The first few shows we did, I was drinking before, during and afterwards as per usual. Then going back to the hotel and carrying on until six in the morning. Then one night when we got back I couldn't be bothered going to the bar. I put it down to the lack of coke at the time, but I see now that I was actually just . . . tired. So I did something I hadn't done before and simply went to bed.

The following night I didn't really feel like having a drink before we went on. No biggie. I still had a couple during the show. But again as soon as we got back to the hotel I just went to bed. Rick asked me if I was feeling ill maybe? I didn't know. I just felt . . . tired. Sick and tired.

And that's how it continued through the two weeks we were in Moscow. I was drinking less and less each show until one night I didn't have anything to drink at all. I didn't see this as anything particularly momentous at the time. As soon as I arrived back in London I had another ounce of coke waiting for me. It wasn't a conscious decision to stop drinking. In my head I would have been happy to have a few tequilas any time I wanted. I just didn't really want one that day. Or, as it turned out, any of the days and weeks that followed.

The other thing I gave up without realising it at first was my relationship with Page. I had brought her with me to Moscow, and we had planned to see each other again as soon as we got back. But I just didn't get around to calling her. No big decision. Just waiting for the right moment to call and it simply never came. I did notice, though, that she wasn't trying very hard to see me, either. And that's when things really began to drift between us. The band had a couple of months off after Moscow, until we went back on the road again in November. By then 'Burning Bridges' was in the UK top 5 and we were booked to do a week of shows leading up to Christmas, finishing with a sold-out night at Wembley Arena. Normally, this would have been one of those occasions where Page and I partied away the whole of the Christmas and New Year holidays. Not this year though. We didn't see each other at all. Nor did we speak. In fact, we never saw each other again. It was a bleak way to bring what had been a very intense two-year relationship to an end.

Instead, I spent the next few weeks alone, wondering how things had come to this, doing coke on my own, not even drinking. It certainly gave me time to think. I don't like to use that word 'regret'. But that doesn't mean I don't feel it over certain things; or if not regret then remorse. I know when

I've fucked up. But to say I regret it makes me sound like I'm asking for sympathy. Whereas, remorse – genuine sorrow for something I've done or not done – feels more accurate. I didn't regret my marriage to Jean not lasting longer, but I was sorry for the pain it had caused her and my children. I didn't regret leaving Liz for Page, but I was sorry for the pain it caused her and Bernadette. I didn't regret my wild affair with Page, but I was sorry for the way it spun out of control.

It was while I was thinking through all these things that I realised there was one other regret I didn't have – for all the years I had spent getting wasted on booze and drugs. But now, suddenly and very powerfully, I was immensely sorry for it. I was also looking for a way to make things different, better. I had just outgrown the guy with the coke and limo and gorgeous model girlfriend. Hello Earth, this is Francis. I want to come down!

As I'd stopped drinking, not just tequila but anything with alcohol in it, the coke wasn't having the same effect on me now. I was doing much less coke anyway by then. The two things used to balance each other out. Now when I did coke I was just permanently razzed-up, my brain whizzing like a runaway train. I was aware that stopping dead from the coke was probably not the best idea. When I'd first done it back in the seventies, the whole spiel was that coke was good because it was completely non-addictive – unlike its evil twin heroin, which was totally addictive.

In the decade-and-a-half that had passed since, however, there was far more information available about the dangers of cocaine use. Yes, it was addictive – highly addictive. Well, I was the living proof of that. How did you stop though? I looked into it, spoke to the usual private doctors, and what I learned was so scary it was nearly enough to put me off trying

– possible hallucinations, psychosis, almost certain depression, even suicidal thoughts . . . all kinds of lovely things. I needed a line just to take it all in.

None of those nasty withdrawal symptoms happened in my case, though. All I knew for sure was that I wasn't going to put myself into one of those posh rehab joints for broken-down celebs. I saw them as a con, which is probably unfair. I'm sure the Priory has done a lot of good for some people. I just wasn't sure how it would work for me. So I decided I would simply taper off in my own time. Just do less and less coke until I got all the way down to not doing it at all.

For anyone that knows anything about drug or alcohol dependency, you will be thinking that this is the worst possible way to try and beat a serious addiction. And you would be right – except in my case it actually worked. I stopped. Eventually. And once I'd stopped I stopped for good. None of this one-day-at-a-time stuff. Once I was done I knew that was me finished for good. Granted, I still enjoyed smoking a joint. But I never drank again and I never did cocaine again. That was nearly twenty years ago. I even stopped smoking dope – eventually.

In case all that sounds too easy, I should add that it wasn't easy at all. Bad habits die hard. Drugs are the worst habits of all. And yes, it was hard. For weeks I couldn't sleep properly. For a long time afterwards I suffered from depression. I've always been a very wiry, excitable sort of chap, so instead of leaving me flattened and exhausted, going without cocaine for the first time in years turned me into a nervous wreck. I couldn't rest, couldn't eat properly, and would then binge-eat and sleep for eighteen hours straight.

Mostly, I just felt lonely – desperately alone and empty. Without the booze and the drugs, without the companionship of a relationship, I had nothing to help me fill the gap. Inevitably, my 'tapering off' would slide back and forth into full-on addiction. In the end, I just wasn't going to be able to get the job done on my own. Who to turn to, though?

I was so desperate for company that one day during a visit to my chiropodist, a wonderfully warm and lovely Irish lady, I asked her if she would marry me. She laughed it off, of course. What else could she do? 'I'd love to, Francis,' she said, smiling, 'but I'm married already.' I was perfectly serious, though. If she had let me I would have whisked her off and married her that same day. She must have seen it in my face because she suddenly looked at me very strangely: very concerned, as though I had just shown her a new scar I had. I suppose in some way that's exactly what I was doing. I didn't learn, though. A few days later, I asked the same question of a music teacher friend. She also tried to laugh it off. She was married too. And again, I saw that same look in her eye. Pity mixed with confusion. They thought I was mad. I think I was mad. Mad, and desperately alone and looking for some sign of where I was to go. But none came.

Driving home at night sometimes, I would think about picking up a hooker. There were plenty of them on the high streets of Streatham and Balham in those days. I would slow the car down and they would look at me hopefully: 'You looking for business, love?' Not really. But I was looking for something. Female companionship. Human warmth. Someone to sit down with, just be with, quietly, and talk to. A brass on the streets of Balham will sell you a lot of different things, but she can't give you any of that. It was no good looking to the band for company, either. They had quite enough of me on tour, and we were now always on tour again. And Rick didn't want to hang out with some screwed-up lunatic that didn't even drink or take coke any more. Where was the fun in that? I couldn't blame him.

Instead, I'd go home, stick on the TV, try not to think about coke, or much of anything, just try and zonk out in front of the telly. Bored, unhappy, unable to figure out what my next move should be. Or if I even had a next move still in me.

Then one night, completely out of the blue, a name popped into my head, someone from my cloudy past. Someone I hadn't thought about in years, who now, as I thought about her again, suddenly seemed like the one person in the world I really wanted to see again.

Her name was Eileen Quinn and I had first met her in the early seventies, during one of Quo's tours of America. We had just opened for Peter Frampton at a show in Long Island and were now having a few days off in New York. Bob Young and I hired a car and took a drive up the interstate to a small city called White Plains, in Westchester County, upstate New York. White Plains is where my cousin Patrick Arnone lived.

Patrick is gay but had a very close girlfriend named Eileen. When Bob and I arrived at Patrick's place, Eileen happened to be there too. We stayed there all day, just talking and eating this delicious food that Eileen had prepared. She was just sixteen but she was already so together and mature for her age. The band was riding high at the time. We'd just had our first number 1 single back home with 'Down Down' and our album that year, *On the Level*, had also gone to number 1 in Britain and several other countries. I had met a lot of different girls by then. All shapes and sizes, all types of personality. I thought I was actually quite jaded on the subject. But there was something different about Eileen. Something really easy and refreshing and warm and true that I simply hadn't encountered in a woman before.

She didn't really know me. Quo were not a big hit in the States. Eileen only knew the long-haired guy who happened to be the British cousin of her friend Patrick. I was nothing special to her except that Eileen seemed to have this gift for always seeing what was really special about people. Not how much money they had or who they thought they were. But who they really were, when you stripped away all the bullshit. These days you'd say she always saw the positive, but it was something more than that. Eileen always somehow saw the real, good and bad, and was always very accepting of it.

When Bob and I got in the car to drive back to the city I felt really sad that I would probably never see this incredible young woman again. However, I did finally get to see Eileen again when she accompanied Patrick on a visit to London sometime in 1986. I had just started my tempestuous relationship with Page and I invited Patrick and Eileen to stay with me at The Glade. My main memory of this time was sitting in the garden just hanging out with Eileen, talking about anything and everything. Again, no sexual tension, just a genuine satisfaction at being in her company. I don't know where Page was at the time, but instead of getting screwed up over it, I forgot about her while I was in Eileen's company. We just hung around the house, eating in the garden and chatting, and had a really lovely few days. Until then, my groin had always led me. Because I didn't have that immediate yearning below the belt, I saw our burgeoning friendship as just that – really warm, increasingly close, never dull, always amusing and quite gentle.

That had been a few years ago now though. I had thought about Eileen occasionally, always with that warm glow you get when you are remembering really good moments. But my life had become such a shitstorm of career malfunctions, drug abuse and relationship breakdowns that it was only now that, out of the blue, Eileen's name and face suddenly jumped back into my consciousness. I found myself smiling as I thought about her. This was a revelation. I don't think I had smiled much at all for months at that point. Something was going on, something was different, and then I realised. It was me. I was different.

Suddenly I was all action. I knew I only had a very short timeframe to make something happen. The band was going back on the road in a few days for some Christmas shows. I couldn't bear the thought of waiting until the tour was finished, then trying to find Eileen while it was Christmas. I made some phone calls and got the band's travel agent to book me a flight the very next day to New York. When I got there I had a driver waiting and got him to take me straight to White Plains. It was winter, snow on the ground. I had left without bringing a coat. I didn't care.

As soon as I got to Patrick's place I told him everything. That I had come for Eileen. That I would not be returning home without her. That I was in love. I was sure of it. He looked at me sadly. 'But Francis,' he said, 'Eileen is married.'

'What? No!'

'Not only that,' he said, 'she's pregnant.'

I nearly fell down with shock. Here I was, having finally figured out where my true love lay, only to discover I was too late. Much too late . . .

Patrick tried to console me, offered me a drink. No, this couldn't be. I couldn't have come all this way for nothing, could I? Then he told me to look closely at the wedding pictures he had of the so-called happy couple. Eileen was sobbing her eyes out in most of them. She had already known that the wedding was a mistake.

That's when I decided. I would not accept that Eileen wanted to stay where she was. Or at least, not until I heard it from Eileen herself. Patrick kindly agreed to help, even though he thought I was probably wasting my time. He phoned Eileen, told her I had come to visit unexpectedly and invited her to come and have a meal, just the three of us, at this quaint old American diner.

All perfectly innocent – until Eileen arrived, that is, and Patrick immediately made some excuse and left. Eileen looked at me and knew immediately there was more to this than simply grabbing a bite and catching up. I just blurted the whole thing out. I just knew I wanted to be with her. And that, well, I wanted her to come with me back to London, and marry me. I told her that I wanted her in my life, even if it was just as a friend. That if she agreed to come back to London with me and things didn't work out between us, she could still live there and I would help bring up her baby as though it was my own.

She looked at me again. Was I serious? I was. Hmm. But she was already married, and pregnant, and who was I to come here and talk about giving all that up? Was I crazy? I was. Crazy serious. Hmm.

Really she should have stormed off and told me never to call her again. But then she wouldn't be my incredible Eileen. Instead, she stayed and we talked calmly for hours. Hours and hours and hours. It was like this wasn't really a surprise to her at all. We just got along together, it was easy and good and real and fun and thrilling and . . . well? Would she run away with me?

To my immense relief and joy, Eileen confessed that she had always had strong feelings for me too. That she had always thought that I had been ignoring her signals deliberately, because I was always off with some gorgeous rock chick. I listened to all this with growing hope and passion. Nevertheless, it was all too late now, surely? Or was she really as crazy as me and ready to come and start a whole new life?

She told me that she would need to go home and speak with her husband first but that I was to go back to Patrick's place and wait for her. That she would be packed and ready to leave with me for London that night.

I was so shocked I went back and sat waiting at Patrick's place in silence for the next two hours. I felt sure this was a dream. That she had told me to go and wait for her while she went home but probably made plans to never see me again. Either that or her husband would be next through the door, looking to kill me. Patrick was equally bemused. He had been through some pretty tangled relationships in his own life but nothing quite like this.

Then suddenly there was a knock on the door and there she was. Eileen. Come to run away with me. At this point everything took on the quality of a dream. A mad dream in which I some-how managed to win the heart of the queen and was now on my way home to London and the start of a whole new life.

No sooner had we arrived back at The Glade than the enormity of what we had done began to really sink in. It wasn't just Eileen's husband that had been left in turmoil. Eileen's whole family thought she had lost her mind, giving up a good life in America for God knows what kind of life with a serial philanderer and drug-addled musician in England.

But that wasn't how Eileen and I saw it. We knew we had a very real connection, and that if we didn't at least give it a chance to grow into something we may regret it for the rest of our lives. We weren't trying to hurt others or ruin lives. We just felt we had a real opportunity here for the kind of once-in-a-lifetime happiness most people never get to experience. My personal life hardly existed at this point. I wanted to be with someone I could love and trust, with whom I could try to rebuild that part of my life, of my psyche. Eileen, having made a clean break of it by flying off with me to London, saw things the same, from her own perspective. We both took a chance on each other in the hope – the belief – that somehow life had offered us this one last chance at true happiness.

And fortunately for us, that's how it turned out. Eileen's family and friends eventually came around. Any fears they had over how I would behave towards Eileen's baby were soon dispelled when they saw how little it mattered to me that Eileen was having another man's child. As soon as she had the baby in February 1989 – a gorgeous little blond-haired boy she named Patrick – I was as delighted as I had been when fathering my own children. It had already been decided that Patrick would be brought up by his mother and me, and that we would also bring him up to know his real father. It worked out well, in fact. I treated Patrick just as I did my own children, and Eileen treated them just as she did Patrick.

Don't get the wrong idea here, though. We were still far behind in the happy-ever-after stakes. We had only been back for twenty-four hours before I had to leave for the Quo Christmas tour. My mum knew Eileen already, from the previous visit, but also through the family connection with Patrick, so she was happy to have her at the house. Nevertheless, that must have been a strange time for Eileen. Heavily pregnant, thousands of miles from home suddenly, having just said goodbye to her husband and the father of her child. I brought her out for some of the shows and thankfully the tour was not a long one, just a week or so. But still, I wouldn't have been hugely surprised if she had changed her mind during this period. Nor would I have blamed her.

But she didn't, and we spent a wonderful Christmas together. Being with Eileen also helped give me the strength to really try and shake off my coke habit. With Eileen pregnant, and never having been a drugs person anyway, time at home was now time off the coke. Outside of our relationship, though, things were still hard for me to deal with. Thankfully, and I have no idea why, I honestly don't, Eileen somehow saw all this, grasped the truth and gave me the strength to believe in myself, in us, in a better way forward.

It didn't help that the band's business affairs were still in such disarray. We now had a chap named Iain Jones as our acting manager. Iain had been with us as our tour manager and we trusted him but he wasn't an experienced band manager, per se. That is, he was great on tour, but stepping up to be the guy in charge of the entire operation was not something he was used to yet. He didn't even have his own office. He was just doing his best to help us as best as he could while we tried to work out the financial mess we had been left in. This, however, was proving to be almost impossible. We needed some heavyweight help.

In the meantime, we were scheduled to write and record a new Quo album. This proved to be a blessing in disguise for me, as it gave me something to focus on each day while I was trying to build a new drug-free life with Eileen. I set to work with Bernie, determined to fully contribute to the new album. I hadn't really been present on the last few Quo albums. Or rather, I'd been there in body, but not always in spirit. We had already arranged to record the album at Compass Point Studios, on the beautiful Bahamian island of Nassau. Built by Chris Blackwell, the owner of Island Records, Compass Point was known as a luxury destination for big-name bands looking to mix a little rest and relaxation with their rock 'n' roll. Again, I saw this on a purely personal level as being the ideal place to make my first Quo album without drugs for over ten years. In fact, it turned out that the island was the easiest place in the world to get coke. I managed to stay well away from it though. It also allowed me some proper space when we weren't working away from Rick, who was still surviving on the old rocket fuel. I was afraid that if I spent too much time in his company, especially after dark, the temptation would prove too great.

We had Pip Williams there producing and again we felt obliged to try and keep the band's sound as up-to-the-minute as possible, without sacrificing too many elements of what constituted the signature Quo sound. Again, though, I'm not too sure how successful we were at that. It was better than on *Ain't Complaining,* where I barely recognised us on some of the tracks. But the emphasis on keeping up with the Def Leppards and Bon Jovis was definitely still there, I thought.

This, though, was not helped by the fact that – hand on heart – the songs really weren't there this time either. Unlike with the last album, though, I had no one to blame for this except myself. Of the twelve tracks, I had co-written eight of them. Of those eight, there aren't any that I really dislike. I can hear the effort and thought I've put into them all, the genuine desire to get the band back to where it needed to be. But the fact is there aren't that many that are what you would call really memorable. They are all decent, nice, not bad at all. The sort of things you say when something doesn't truly grab you. I knew all this but let it slide. It wasn't like I had written anything better lately.

This time the public weren't so easily fooled, either. We called the album *Perfect Remedy* but it had the opposite effect on our recording career, barely getting into the top 50. Even the singles from it – 'Not at All' and 'Little Dreamer', both written by me and Bernie – were flops. It was the first time an album of ours hadn't gone gold in Britain since *Piledriver*. It seemed that in our attempt to keep Quo's music up to date we had managed to leave the fans behind.

This became even more obvious when the touring side of the operation now suffered. We had to shelve plans to do another big European tour and ended up doing just one solitary eighteen-date tour of the UK. Yes, we finished the tour with two (almost) sold-out shows at Wembley Arena but things were suddenly not going to plan at all.

Enter our knight in shiny smile and well-coiffed hair, David Walker. It's fair to say that, without David Walker, Status Quo may not have survived the nineties. That's how much of an impact he had on our career. David had first made a name for himself in the music business when he was the business manager for the Sweet and negotiated a huge new deal for them with Polydor Records. He then formed a management company with former talent agent Lindsay Brown, named Handle Artists Management, where they managed Barclay James Harvest. Lindsay took care of the live work. David took care of the business contracts.

At the time we first got involved with David he had branched out into managing pop acts like Pepsi & Shirlie and other musical artists, including Pip Williams, which is how we got to know him. David was a larger-than-life character who brought sparkle to any social situation – but it was all built on a solid business background. David knew his stuff and for the first eighteen months or so he was really good for us.

He was one of those guys you heard coming before you saw them. Big, loud, upfront; tons of energy. In the years to come, Rick and I would look at some of the decisions we made with David as our guide and wonder if we had really done the right thing. But the reality is, if it hadn't been for David we wouldn't have had much of a career left at all, at that point.

David wasn't interested in the music. He left all that to his artists. He took care of the business – all the things the artists are rubbish at. We poured our hearts out to David, told him of the mess we were in. He took it all in his stride – he had obviously heard many similar tales before – then told us not to worry. He would take care of it all. We had nothing to worry about now he was involved. Except for one thing. As he told us straight out at that very first meeting: 'Remember, I don't come cheap.'

And he didn't. The good news was that when it came to making money, David Walker was exactly the man you needed in your corner to help you do that. The upshot of this was that the nineties became some of the most successful years Quo would ever have. We didn't always make the kinds of records that our hardcore fans thought we should. But we did build our career up again, bringing in a whole new generation of fans to the party. We have David to thank in large part for that.

The first thing he did was to cancel all our plans for 1990. There had been a shorter, remixed version of 'The Power of Rock' from *Perfect Remedy* that we had talked ourselves into thinking might be a hit. David pulled the plug on that immediately. His point: another modest hit single would do nothing for us. We needed a slam-dunk top 5 hit, no argument allowed. But the problem was we didn't actually have one to hand. Don't worry about it, said David. We'll find you one. Which is exactly what he did.

Or rather, he found us fifteen rolled into one.

One of the biggest-selling singles of 1989 had been by Jive Bunny and the Mastermixers, the father and son DJ team of Andy and John Pickles, who had released a novelty record they titled 'Swing the Mood'. This was a cut-and-paste collection of cover versions done as short clips from a dozen different hits, mainly from the fifties – Elvis, Bill Haley, Little Richard, all that – sandwiched between bits of Glenn Miller's 'In the Mood', all set to the same dance tempo. It came in regular 45-rpm format, which is the four-minute track radio played, and also 12-inch format, which lasted six minutes and became the track they played in clubs and at parties. You could also get it in various CD formats. The critics hated it. I didn't much like it either. But the public absolutely loved it. So much so the record went to number 1 in Britain, where it sold nearly a million copies, and dozens of other countries too. It even went top 10 in America, where it sold over half a million.

This did not escape David Walker's attention when he decided we needed a sure-fire, solid-gold hit to resuscitate our career. As a marketing genius, he especially loved the fact that the image of Jive Bunny wasn't even of the people that had constructed the record: a cartoon 'Jive Bunny' rabbit starred in the videos, while there was a man dressed in a costume at live promotional appearances. By the end of 1989 it was the second-best-selling single of the year, just behind 'Ride on Time' by Black Box. By then they had released an identikit follow-up – another twelve old rock 'n' roll hits dressed up as disco that they called 'That's What I Like'. When that went to number 1 all over the world again, it looked like a bulletproof winning formula.

David had already been working on a plan for us to spend the latter half of 1990 'celebrating' the twenty-fifth anniversary of Status Quo. Personally, I hate anniversaries. And if you wanted to be finicky about it, you'd have to point out that our summer stint at Butlin's in 1965 wasn't actually when we first started using the name Status Quo, or even when Rick had joined the band. But none of that got in the way of David's good idea. Which, in a nutshell, was simple and sweet: to mark Quo's twenty-fifth anniversary, the record company would release a special compilation called *Rocking All Over the Years*, a double album containing twenty-two tracks, all of them major Quo hits.

The cherry on the cake, as he put it, would be the inclusion right at the end of the album of a new Quo single, to be called – wait for it! – 'The Anniversary Waltz'. The title was mine. Not to be confused with the old Vera Lynn hit of the same name. But everything else about the record was really David's idea. This was to be our very own Jive Bunny-style collection of old rock 'n' roll hits all given the heads-down no-nonsense boogie Quo treatment. Our single would also be released in various lengths and formats, including a monster ten-minute-plus version on the 12-inch, which included eight extra covers to the original seven. This also comprised a Part 2 to the single, released in its own shorter, radio-friendly, multi-format.

The way David saw it, we didn't need a cartoon bunny to front it – Status Quo was already a well-established brand in its own right. We just needed the right product to rejuvenate the brand. I'm half-wincing as I write this because all this talk of 'brands' and 'product rejuvenation' was all new to me. But I trusted David to know what he was doing. What with Eileen coming back into my life in a big way – and discovering, early in 1990, that she was pregnant with our own baby – plus my own ongoing 'issues' trying to stay on the almost straight and nearly narrow, frankly both Rick and I were happy to have someone strong like David lead the way.

One thing about David Walker: he didn't pull any punches when he spoke to you. He sat us down and told us straight that the old Quo formula had dried up and that if we didn't make a major pivot and try something different we may as well pack up and go home – or get used to the idea of playing in clubs and holiday camps again. He knew that would frighten us. Neither Rick nor I wanted to listen to this. But neither of us could really argue with him. The slackening sales figures told their own story.

So we put everything into David's hands and watched as he did his stuff. And boy did he go to town!

Chapter Eleven

Davey Rock It

David Walker was our hero. He was going to make everything all right for us again. And for a few years that's exactly what he did.

Having recorded what would be released later in 1990 as the singles 'The Anniversary Waltz Part One' and 'The Anniversary Waltz Part Two' – both of which were also mixed into the mammoth ten-minute full-length version, which David Walker had a field day promoting as 'the longest single ever released' – he then set up some huge outdoor stadium shows for us that summer: four in Germany, two in Malta and two in Finland. Then right bang in the middle of those, he got us onto the bill at the Silver Clef Award Winners charity concert at Knebworth Park, in front of over 120,000 people. Sharing the bill with Cliff Richard, Robert Plant, Eric Clapton, Mark Knopfler, Elton John, Genesis, Paul McCartney and Pink Floyd, it felt a bit like Live Aid all over again, the show being filmed and later broadcast by the BBC. Only this time we got to do an hour-long set – and I actually remembered everything about it when I woke up the next day. This felt good, really good! All that high on life stuff – sorry to disappoint any old rockers out there, but it's true. Especially the fact that the sun came out and shone for us while we were onstage. It had pissed with rain all through Tears for Fears' set, who were on before us. More seriously, if you compare the clips now, of us at Live Aid and at the Silver Clef show five years later, the difference is remarkable. Live Aid, we were ramshackle and hanging on for dear life. The Knebworth show, Rick and I and the whole band were absolutely on fire.

A month after Knebworth, the announcement went out about us doing a twenty-fifth anniversary tour – thirty shows around Britain, including no fewer than four sold-out nights at Wembley Arena, the final one the night before Christmas Eve. Along with this came news of the release of our new single – the 'Anniversary Waltz Part One' sing-along – and the new double-album compilation, *Rocking All Over the Years*.

Suddenly everything went from doom and gloom to unicorns and rainbows. Despite my concerns about the single being seen as too gimmicky, it flew up the charts, getting to number 2 – our biggest hit since 'In the Army Now' four years before. It was followed by *Rocking All Over the Years* going to the top of the album charts, becoming officially the biggest-selling album we had ever had, going double-platinum at home in Britain and becoming our first big hit in places like Australia, France and Germany for years.

As if I wasn't getting my fair share of good news, Eileen gave birth to another child – a beautiful boy we named Fynn – at the same time that we released 'The Anniversary Waltz Part One'. True to form with all my children, I barely had any time to be with my newborn son. At least, not at first. But Eileen coped in her usual incredibly confident way. She came out with the baby on certain legs of the tour and we built in more time at home so that I could be there at least part of the time. Between TV and radio appearances promoting the single and press interviews talking about the new compilation album and the whole subject of Quo reaching its silver anniversary, I did manage to get home far more than I used to.

That changed, though, as soon as the tour kicked off in October 1990. Again, David Walker surpassed himself with his event planning. He arranged for us to perform a special one-off show at Butlin's in Minehead – the place where it all began (sort of). David arranged for a special Quo Express train to take hundreds of press, TV and radio people down to Butlin's from Paddington. Despite the popular notion that Quo was much maligned in the media, we had actually made a lot of very good friends there over the years. Fantastic characters like Chris Tarrant and the Radio 1 DJs Alan 'Fluff' Freeman and Tommy Vance. There was also the gorgeous actress Vicki Michelle, who'd become famous through her role in the classic TV comedy *'Allo 'Allo!* I can't remember how Vicki ended up on the train but let's just say I do know she has always been a genuine Quo fan.

Rick and I weren't on the train down from Paddington. We were already at Butlin's, getting ready for the show. How very weird that was to be back there, actually in the same room as the one we had worked in as the Spectres all those years before. It wasn't called the Rock and Roll Ballroom any more. It was now the Grand Ballroom. But I swear the dressing rooms hadn't changed at all. Same mousetraps hidden in the corner. Very different crowd, though. In truth, it didn't really bring back that many memories. The rest of the camp had changed so much since those days, though I did notice they were still playing Dusty Springfield and Gerry & the Pacemakers out by the fairground.

After the show the huge media contingent all partied long into the night, as did Rick and the band. I stayed for a while but as I was no longer drinking it wasn't really my scene any more. Instead, I went back to my hotel room and had a bowl of cornflakes and a cup of tea, and had a look to see what I could find on TV. I enjoyed being told about it the next day, too. Apparently a 'suitably refreshed' Chris Tarrant had to be helped into a chauffeur-driven car and sped back to London in time to present the Capital Radio breakfast show that morning.

The band and I all joined the media people on the train back to London. I think I was the only one on the train that didn't have a hangover or wasn't doing coke. Instead I tucked into what I still recall as the best-tasting scrambled eggs and smoked salmon I've ever eaten. Meanwhile, the champagne came out and the party for everyone else just carried on again, with Rick and me doing back-to-back interviews in a special carriage together. It was such a free-for-all I did wonder if we were actually going to get any press out of it. I needn't have worried, though. David Walker and our longstanding PR man, Simon Porter, made sure we got the most over-the-top news coverage for anything we'd done since Live Aid. Maybe even more than Live Aid. Everything after that seemed easy. The tour was a sell-out. The records sold millions. Even the 'Anniversary Waltz Part Two' single went high in the charts. The turnaround from exactly twelve months before when it looked as though the band was on its last legs was incredible.

What I hadn't realised was that David had only just got started. He showed me this thing about market research, which was a subject no musician had even heard of before then. I remember sitting there gobsmacked, reading this. Market researchers know what car we all drive. They know what television show we're watching. And that was then. These days they know what we're thinking! That's what it feels like to me sometimes. And please don't get me started on Twitter and Facebook. I won't know what you're talking about. Or rather I will but I don't want to. Back then I just had to trust what David told me.

As a result of his strategy and planning, he had us booked solidly on the road for the next two years. We had a few months off at the start of 1991 – during which he had us booked into a studio to make a new album. No running off to the Bahamas this time, either, but knuckling down to some serious graft at Bray Studios in England and ARSIS Studio in Surrey. Things to do other than work: none.

It was like the old days again, back in the seventies when the band never stopped working. Well, we needed that. A shark dies if it stops swimming. That's a bit how it felt to me suddenly. That the moment I took my foot off the pedal with Quo would be the moment it all fell apart again. And I needed to keep going. My life had changed so much since Eileen had become a part of it and I wanted to make the most of every second.

I was now completely free of cocaine addiction. I knew that for sure the last time I ever did it. I had been taking a break with Eileen and the children in Amsterdam. Known as that city is for its legal marijuana and liberal attitude to drugs in general, this may not have been the wisest place to go, but the truth is I still enjoyed smoking a little hash or weed. Not as much as I used to. I would restrict myself to what I called the six o'clock joint – meaning a puff at the end of the day, perhaps.

We were all strolling around, looking at the canals and shopping, when I bumped into someone I knew, a waiter from an Italian restaurant, and had stopped to shake hands. As we did this, he slipped me a little gram packet of coke. Once upon a time I would have received this as a wonderfully thoughtful gesture. I didn't say anything because I didn't want to make a big deal of it in front of Eileen and the kids. But I did make an excuse and ran back to the hotel. In my mind, I was going to give the gram to someone else I thought might like it. But of course as soon as I got to his room, I talked myself into having a toot. Hadn't had one in ages. Surely one can't hurt! The usual addict's logic. Except it did bloody hurt. It was potent stuff and by the time I hit the street again my whole body had gone cold and numb, my teeth grinding. I stopped at a bar and ordered a double tequila to try and calm myself down. By the time I found Eileen and the kids again I was in full self-loathing mode. I felt I had betrayed Eileen's trust – which I had – and really let myself down. I said to myself there and then: never again. That's the last time I do coke ever!

And this time it really was.

The same, of course, couldn't necessarily be said for everybody else on the team – least of all Rick, who was still going full throttle in those days, and David Walker, who apart from being like an attack dog when he needed to be, already had a significant coke habit. In Rick's jovial life's-a-party way, his coke habit was just another string to his bow, so to speak, in terms of always looking on the bright side, even when he was in the deepest shit. But with David, who was naturally hyperactive and full-on, the extra coke dimension could make him a fearsome prospect for people to deal with. He wasn't just an ideas man, he was a make-it-happen-NOW man. Or else.

In truth, Rick and I loved this approach at first. Even though we didn't have much to do with each other when Quo wasn't working, in our different ways we both needed a protector. For Rick, that person was often me. Although he was in the early stages of what later became a recurring theme – his whole boring 'Why am I always number two and you're number one?' routine – he had pretty much given up on actively wanting to lead the band's career after he realised what a pain in the arse the day-to-day responsibility for that was. So every now and then he would take me aside and say: 'We are going to be all right, aren't we, Frame?' The answer was I didn't know. But the only way to get any peace was simply to tell him, 'Yes, of course, Ricky, we are going to be fine.'

Going all the way back to the days of Pat Barlow, we had always liked having a strong father-figure-type running the band's business affairs. David, though, took it to a whole new level. He was protector, saviour, bodyguard and soul-survivor. As the years went by this became something I enjoyed less and less. But while it lasted David was our hero, absolutely.

The trouble was it meant we would spend the rest of the nineties pretty much looking for new and ever more gimmicky ways to sell the group. In David's defence, the music industry was moving in that direction anyway, but he really made the most of it. We still recorded the occasional new album, and a couple of them like *Rock 'til You Drop*, which I produced, I still really like. But which, it's only fair to mention, Rick most decidedly did not like. All that gets remembered from that campaign now, though, are the surrounding publicity events. In fairness, David had absolutely bust a gut making this one happen and again it was on the grand scale and it certainly did bring us a lot of media attention.

The shtick was that we would celebrate the release of *Rock 'til You Drop* on Saturday 21 September, 1991, by Quo achieving a new world record by performing four shows in four different British cities, all on the same day – with 50 per cent of all the proceeds from ticket sales being shared equally among the Nordoff Robbins Music Therapy Trust and The Brit Trust. David then also made a deal for the Britannia Music Club to sponsor the event. We would start at 2 p.m. sharp with a show at Sheffield Arena, then hop on a plane to Glasgow, where we would be onstage at the SECC arena by 4.30 p.m. Then fly off straight after that show to Birmingham, where we would be onstage at 7.15 p.m. at the NEC arena. Then jump straight onto yet another plane after that to take us down to London, where we would hit the Wembley Arena stage at 9.50 p.m.

Everything was timed to the second. The whole idea was we would – wait for it – rock 'til we (literally) dropped. Geddit?

Of course, this was just the icing on the promotional cake for David. He had begun the whole build-up to that album earlier in the year when he had arranged for us to appear at that year's Brit Awards, where we were presented with a special inaugural award in recognition of our twenty-five years in the business. All very nice, thank you, I love you too. Except I had come up with another twist. We went up to the podium and accepted the award dressed in dinner suits. Then as soon as we'd finished thanking everybody we ripped them off – they were those specially made theatrical suits dancers can just rip off in one move – revealing our usual T-shirt and jeans underneath. Cue: huge applause and much laughter. It was one of those stunts that showed we were in on the joke. It worked too as the next morning's front page of the *Sun* ran a picture of us tearing off the suits with the caption: 'The highlight of the show.'

Although we didn't go back on tour until June, David kept coming up with new things for us to do, anything to keep us in the public eye, from me and Rick appearing on *Aspel & Company*, along with the late John Hurt and the irrepressible

Dawn French, to a highly publicised visit to the prison workshop at Pentonville Prison, London. Again, there were pictures of me and Rick in all the papers next day as David sat there congratulating himself, and rightly so. Rabbits were being pulled non-stop out of hats.

In May, Rick and I attended the official unveiling ceremony of our two waxwork dummies at Madame Tussauds. Again, this was all David's work. He may not have been able to claim credit for Quo being so famous, but he was definitely the one responsible for doing everything in his power to consolidate that position here in the nineties. The dummies, by the way, were placed in the Rock Circus section and were very weird to look at. My dummy, I thought, was better looking than the real-life me. He certainly had more hair. Rick's didn't really do the real-life him any favours. Not that he seemed to notice. He was too busy hamming it up for the cameras. Rick was simply one of those people born to be in front of flashing lights and cameras. If he'd been born twenty years later he'd have been a natural for reality TV shows like *I'm a Celebrity . . . Get Me Out of Here!*, but he wouldn't be passed as medically fit by the time all that came around. He was a show-off and lived for the attention. The way I looked at it was, thank God one of us is, because I am the exact opposite.

There had also been a jaunt over to Monaco to attend the World Music Awards, where we were presented with the award for Outstanding Contribution to the Rock Industry by Prince Albert of Monaco. We then spent the summer doing big outdoor stadiums again. In Britain, we co-headlined a seven-night tour of football stadiums with Rod Stewart, starting at his beloved Celtic Park and finishing two weeks later at our home-from-home Wembley Stadium.

Nothing had quite prepared us, though, for the four-shows-in-one-day malarkey on 21 September. The whole thing had begun the day before at Newbury Racecourse, where Nordoff Robbins staged a special Music Therapy charity race day. David organised for Quo to be the official sponsors of the two o'clock race, called, oh yes, the 'Rock 'til You Drop' Stakes. The BBC showed the race live with us seen handing over the Rock 'til You Drop trophy to the owner of the winning horse. Then at midday the following day Rick and I were guests on the Saturday morning kids' TV show, *Going Live!*, bigging the whole thing up, before flying off to Glasgow.

Onstage at Wembley Arena that night we were joined by Norris McWhirter, the co-founder of *The Guinness Book of Records*, who presented us with certificates for performing the largest number of British arena shows in under twelve hours. Towards the end, I actually did think I was going to drop. Tired doesn't even begin to describe it. All this without any chemical assistance to pick me up: I really must be a new man now, I thought to myself. When I was then told we had managed to raise over £250,000 for the charities we had nominated, I got a lump in my throat.

There was still one last twist to come, though, which David had arranged without our knowledge: Michael Aspel was going to be strolling onstage, followed by the TV cameras, to surprise Rick and me for a joint *This Is Your Life* show. No way, Aspel! That really was the last thing I fancied doing at that precise moment. Or ever! What, have your past rolled out before you and the watching millions? Fortunately, David tipped us off at the last minute — at which point we told him in no uncertain terms what Aspel could do with his big red book. If the show had been about Quo, we'd have probably done it but David warned us the programme makers just wanted to get up close and personal about our private lives. Sod that! Our lives were complicated enough as it is, let alone talking about them in public. (That said, Rick of course did do a similar show some years later called *Stars & Their Lives*, with Carol Vorderman. He was brilliant on it, too. Obviously.)

It was all to the good, though. *Rock 'til You Drop* went straight into the top 10 and a week after that Quo was back on the road, starting out on what would be one of our longest tours ever. Twelve solid months, playing all over Britain, Ireland and Europe.

Before we said goodbye to each other though, Eileen and I made time to finally get married. It was just a few days after we'd done Wembley Stadium with Rod Stewart. As an odd coincidence, the date of the wedding, Wednesday 19 June, 1991, was almost exactly the same date I'd married Jean nearly twenty-five years before. How the world had changed for me since then. My three boys with Jean – Simon, Nicholas and Kieran – were all now young men. And the wedding ceremony, such as it was, hardly carried the same meaning it did first time around, when I was still a God-fearing Catholic boy still dreaming of making it big one day as a pop star. I was now in my early forties and I'd been to the top and right back to the bottom, and was now on my way up again, thanks to David – but mostly thanks to Eileen. Without her, I'd never have had the energy or motivation to keep going. Eileen allowed me the freedom to follow my obsession. We didn't need some bit of paper to tell us that, though. I just did it to provide her with all the legal rights of being my wife.

We kept it all very low key. We set off from home that morning for Croydon Register Office and were back home in time for lunch. The driver I'd hired for the day and our lovely housecleaning lady were our only witnesses. I didn't even have a best man. I did remember to kiss the bride though! No honeymoon afterwards, either. As far as Eileen and I are concerned, every day we spend together at home is a holiday. I can see a lot of you grimacing at that but it's true. We did try going on holiday now and again, somewhere hot by the beach. Then came home again a few days later because we were bored.

Quo's career established a pattern throughout the nineties, under the tutelage of David Walker. It was still about the music, but in a very heightened sense. Everything was geared up to turn whatever we did into a major event. We would headline the End of Race show at the TT races on the Isle of Man. Or we would be on TV messing around with some comedian. We were always playing lots of big events, like the twenty-fifth anniversary party for Radio 1, in front of 125,000 people at the Party in the Park, in Birmingham. Hale and Pace did take-offs of us on their TV shows. *Alias Smith & Jones* did take-offs of us on their show. Bobby Davro did impersonations of us on his TV show. When Rick and I turned on the Blackpool Illuminations, in September 1993, more than 25,000 people turned up to see us, the biggest crowd for over thirty years. That same morning we had done a live Radio 1 Roadshow set, followed later the same day by a *Daily Star* Roadshow. We were no longer just rock 'n' roll musicians, we were showbiz entertainers. Rick was living his dream. I wasn't complaining either. Well, not as much as I let on in the press. The fact is, we were earning more money than ever, and becoming more well known than ever. You can't deny that David was doing his job. It used to be that when I walked down the street I might get recognised by some hairy rockers or obvious music fans.

Now I was treated like a mainstream entertainer, him off the telly. Rick would lap it up and get put out if it didn't happen. I would tie my hair back, and try and not be noticed. At the same time, of course, I still craved the recognition. I still needed that affirmation. In my job, the day people stop noticing you is the day your career is over.

There were now Royal Doulton mugs of me and Rick, which were sold in limited editions of 2,500 at the Royal Doulton Fair, and are dreadful. Then in 1994 we went to make a record with Manchester United, who were about to win the first Premiership and FA Cup double. We recorded a proper-bloke football terrace version of 'Burning Bridges', retitled 'Come On You Reds'. Brian McClair, one of their main players, had seen us at Old Trafford on the tour with Rod, and he suggested adapting 'Burning Bridges'. Being Scottish and partial to a good bagpipey knees-up, he thought it would be brilliant. The public agreed and sent the single to number 1 – our first number 1 single since 'Down Down' nearly twenty years before. I don't care how cheesy everyone who isn't a Man United fan thought them, I still love the way we adapted the lyrics: 'Busby Babes they always made me cry/Thinkin' 'bout the teams of years gone by/Charlton, Edwards, Law and Georgie Best/We're United, you can keep the rest . . .' That said, as I don't really know much about football, it was Rhino who came up with the lyrics and Andy Bown who worked out how to make them fit.

Around the same time we did another Prince's Trust show, this time billed as 'The Appointment'. We did the show at the Albert Hall and Prince Charles was there. We raised over £70,000 for the Trust and afterwards Rick and I presented Charles with miniature versions of our trademark white and green Fender Telecaster guitars for his boys, William and Harry, who were eleven and nine, respectively, at the time. Oh, the joy of show business! I don't know if they ever got to play them together, or which one of them was me and which one Rick, but we also brought another Telecaster, which the whole band signed and put up for auction in aid of Capital Radio's 'Help a London Child'.

Even on those increasingly rare occasions when we did just put a new record out because we just wanted to put a new record out, David was always able to find a way to turn it into something just a little bit special – or hammy, depending on how you looked at it. When, two months after 'Come On You Reds' went to number 1, we released a new single, 'I Didn't Mean It', and were booked back to appear again on *Top of the Pops*, David somehow figured out that it would be our hundredth appearance on the iconic show. Not only that but it meant we had now been on the show more times than any other act in the show's long history – a record we still hold to this day. Naturally, David turned this into another publicity blitz, along with the other fact he had unearthed that 'I Didn't Mean It' was the forty-sixth Quo single to make the UK top 30.

Any hopes I had, however, that *Thirsty Work*, the album that followed on the heels of the single, would also prove to be a success were quickly dashed. It was our first all-new album since *Perfect Remedy* had fallen at the first hurdle five years before, and went top 20, but only as high as number 13, which made it our second, worst-selling album since *Dog of Two Head* nearly twenty-five years before. When the other two singles lifted from the album – a nice enough song by Andy and Rhino called 'Sherri, Don't Fail Me Now!' and a cover of a truly beautiful Jennifer Warnes love song called 'Restless', which I now confess we completely murdered – barely scraped into the top 40, any hope I had of convincing David Walker that he was wrong to push us in the direction of novelty hits and compilation albums had vanished.

By now the music world had moved on without us. In 1994 Oasis and Blur were the two biggest British acts in the world. Britpop was the newest of the new waves. It seemed the only way old-fart seventies stars like Quo could get back into the charts was by releasing what were essentially novelty records. Elton John was the best at this: he had big hits in the nineties by doing singles with George Michael (Elton's old hit 'Don't Let the Sun Go Down on Me'), Kiki Dee ('True Love'), even Ru Paul (a version of the original Elton–Kiki hit, 'Don't Go Breaking My Heart'). Rod Stewart was the same, having joint hits with Tina Turner, Sting and Bryan Adams. He even tried covering hits by Oasis and Primal Scream. (It didn't work. Sorry, Rod.) Some of the older acts had the 'integrity' not to be tempted down those paths – and most of them subsequently spent the nineties languishing in oblivion. We survived.

Sure enough, the following year found us making the *Don't Stop* thirtieth anniversary album. David really went to town this time, with a truly 'high concept': a fifteen-track CD, all cover versions of songs that had really influenced us over the past thirty years. That was the party line anyway. Well, we bent those rules a bit, as you do, but it ended up a real cross section, from out-and-out rock, like 'Proud Mary' by Creedence Clearwater Revival and 'Get Out of Denver' by Bob Seger and his Silver Bullet Band, to old sixties-style pop, like 'I Can Hear the Grass Grow' by the Move, 'Fun, Fun, Fun' by the Beach Boys, and 'Get Back' by the Beatles. There was a range of stuff from the fifties – Chuck Berry's 'You Never Can Tell'; Buddy Holly's 'Raining in My Heart' – to the seventies – 'Don't Stop' by Fleetwood Mac; 'All Around My Hat' by Steeleye Span – to the eighties – 'Johnny and Mary' by Robert Palmer; 'The Future's So Bright (I Gotta Wear Shades)' by Timbuk3.

On paper, looking at it now, it sounds like a right shambles. But here's the thing. We really enjoyed making that album. It was probably the most fun record we ever made in many ways. Every track killer: absolutely no filler. My personal favourite remains our version of 'When You Walk In The Room', which was written by Jackie DeShannon and had originally been a big hit in the UK for The Searchers. I still think that's one of the best tracks we ever did. Pip Williams really excelled with his production. Then there was David's touch of genius by bringing in the Beach Boys to duet with us on 'Fun, Fun, Fun'. I had wanted us to do 'Wouldn't It Be Nice', which I always loved. But it just didn't sound right. 'Fun, Fun, Fun' just worked from the off. Then we had Brian May from Queen to add his unique sparkle on guitar to 'Raining In My Heart', and Steeleye Span's great Maddy Prior, who I love, duetting with me on 'All Around My Hat'.

Released with the heavy-duty promotional fun of the fair under a highly lucrative new deal David had cleverly put together with Polygram TV, the album came out early in 1996 accompanied by a massive TV ad campaign and me and Rick appearing on every TV and radio show that David could 'persuade' into having us. A lot of these decisions were also chewed over with Simon Porter, the brilliant PR man who was becoming more and more influential. I always liked Simon. He had all the right instincts but was also someone I knew I could trust. The result was our biggest-selling album since *Rocking All Over the Years* – our early 'anniversary' album five years before. None of the singles we released from it reached the top 20 but the album went straight in at number 2, selling nearly half a million copies in the first six weeks. I'm not saying David said I told you so. I'm saying he bloody well yelled it in our faces. Deservedly so. He had been proved right again. Who were we to complain about silly things like 'credibility' and 'critical acclaim'? Sod all that.

When we released 'Fun, Fun, Fun' as a single, David had the Beach Boys fly into London and take off with us on a big promotional tour of Britain. The Beach Boys were legends, of course, but they hadn't had a hit in Britain for years and the interest in the joint record was huge. We ended up performing together on dozens of TV shows and radio shows. Everything from *Top of the Pops* and GMTV to *The Des O'Connor Show* and Cilla Black's *Surprise Surprise*. The whole thing was surreal. I'd been a Beach Boys fan since I was a teenager. We first met them a couple of years before when we both appeared at 'The Last Tattoo' concert in Berlin, to mark the withdrawal of the last of the British and American troops from the city. We all went out afterwards and had a good time, swearing allegiance as you do on those very late nights and early mornings. But when David suggested getting them in for a track on the *Don't Stop* album, we told him he was off his head. But he did it. Don't ask me how. I still have no idea. But that was David – *very* persuasive.

Meeting Brian Wilson was a little bit different, though, as you might expect. In the mid-nineties he was only just emerging still from decades of being a drug-damaged recluse. He became a lot better as the next few years went by and began doing his own solo tours. But at the time it was very sad. I would be having a little chat, getting on with him well, then suddenly he would just switch off, not know you were there, go wandering off somewhere in that genius mind of his. The first time we met I said: 'Hello, mate. How are you?' Brian just looked at me and said, 'Who are you?' He had no clue. And why should he? Our career path had been steered by David into so many new directions by then, I wasn't sure I knew who I was either. The mid-nineties had seen a massive resurgence in guitar-oriented rock, from Nirvana and grunge to the whole Britpop phenomenon, with Oasis and Blur leading the charge.

I'm not foolish enough to suggest that Status Quo might have found a new connection to those bands, but it did make me wonder if we were even still thought of as a guitar-oriented band, in the same way we had made our name as back in the seventies. Of course, I was just a couple of years short of my fiftieth birthday. Things had changed whether I liked it or not. I should just be thankful Quo hadn't gotten completely lost in the shuffle. We had certainly come close before David Walker came along and set us on a whole new and more successful path.

But still . . . we were no longer just about the music and I began to clash more and more with David over this. In his usual too-shrewd way he tried to keep me happy by arranging things like a separate solo deal. The result was *King of the Doghouse*, an album comprising some songs of mine that I'd done with Bernie and a batch of new tunes written for me by Tony McAnaney, a talented musician who'd written with me and Bernie on a track on *Thirsty Work,* but was best known for writing the Jimmy Nail hit 'Crocodile Shoes'. Tony was great. He'd been introduced to me by Iain Jones but David Walker was less keen on the idea of Tony and me working together. I liked the album – at least, while I was making it. It had a lot more of the folky, country, melodic stuff that I'd never had the chance to explore very much with Quo. I still think the title track, which I love, would have made a great Quo track.

Who knows, I might have to revisit that idea one day. But the album died a commercial death when it was released in 1996. All it did, in fact, rather than 'keep me happy', was make David Walker seem even more correct in his summation that Quo's days as original music makers were over and now it was all about – dreaded phrase – 'extending the brand'. The trouble was we still had one foot in the old music business model of only gauging success by sales of albums and singles. Whether they were actually any good or not – that is, albums that would stand the test of time the way all the original Quo albums have – didn't matter. Thankfully, the pendulum has swung again in more recent times. Now, because nobody sells albums any more, it's all about how good they are, musically: it's not about first-week sales or any of that. It's about having them out there ready to be discovered at any time.

What none of us knew was that all the major rock bands of the seventies and eighties were about to follow us down that road, with the advent of what is now recognised as the classic rock market. Within a few years all the rules would be rewritten as bands reformed, sometimes as original line-ups, but most often with a couple of original members and some other well-known names grafted on. Queen and Paul Rodgers or Adam Lambert immediately spring to mind. Or gigantic American rock bands like Foreigner and Journey. Or Black Sabbath – both with and without Ozzy Osbourne. Or Deep Purple – both with and without Ritchie Blackmore. Look at the Rolling Stones and Guns N' Roses – only three original members left in each band but no one cares as long as the singer and guitarist are there.

The music world hadn't gotten to that stage yet, though, and with Quo I found myself caught between totally getting what David was doing for us, and pining for a time when it was just down to how good were the riffs the boys and I could come up with. Except we weren't boys any more, we were middle-aged men, with all the attendant issues that brings too. In my case, that was putting on weight – without the drugs to comfort-consume, I had become very partial to really good food. Having Eileen as my wife also helped with this, as she was one of the best cooks I had ever known. I would deal with this in time by developing a daily fitness regime, which I would become even more addicted to than I had been to coke all those years.

I was also going bald, or thinning on top, to put it more kindly. I decided I also had the answer to this with the arrival of the new 'hair technology' of the time. In my case that involved getting a hair transplant at a fancy (read: very expensive) hair clinic in London. Losing your hair has always been a nagging problem for us aging rockers. Years ago, you had to do what Elton and so many other singers did like Frank Sinatra, and simply get a wig. In more recent times it has become more acceptable to simply shave the whole thing off, like Michael Stipe from REM did when his garden stopped growing.

Neither of those things ever appealed to me. Instead, I opted for the hair replacement route – plug-ins. Again, this is something Elton also tried but not terribly successfully. There have been many other cases of famous rock stars getting a little 'work' done on their hair, some well known and some not so well known – I'm thinking here of Chris Martin from Coldplay and Bono from U2, and let's say 'rumours of' Mick Jagger and Roger Daltrey also having a 'rug rethink', as the author Martin Amis once so eloquently put it.

In my case, I decided honesty was the best policy and invited the cameras in to see what I was having done. Sure enough, the next day's newspapers were full of the top of my head having clumps of hair stitched into place. None of this bothered me in the slightest. It would have bothered me more to pretend I'd never had it done and lie about it in interviews. The only thing that hurt was the procedure itself. It bloody hurt a lot! Still, it did improve the thickness of my hair. If not the colour, which I have allowed to grow ever greyer as the years have rolled by.

Rick had none of these problems. Rick's health issues were far less cosmetic and much more serious. The way he had always lived his life, I knew it was surely only a matter of time before he crashed. But even I was shocked when it happened as quickly as it did. Rick was forty-eight when he had his first heart attack. I nearly keeled over myself when David phoned me with the news. Officially, we tried to play the whole thing down. Some story went out that Rick had been having chest pains so checked himself in for an appointment with his doctor, who advised him he needed an urgent heart op.

The truth is, Rick had nearly died before he even got to the doctor. He told me that he just got up one morning (or probably one afternoon, knowing what a night owl Rick was) and was on his way to make a cup of tea when he felt like he'd been hit by a thunderbolt that left him gasping in pain on the floor. When he finally recovered enough to drag himself to the phone he didn't call for an ambulance like anyone sensible would, but dialled his private doctor – who told him he was busy and to come in and see him tomorrow. In the meantime, he told Rick to take a couple of aspirin and go back to bed. So that's what Rick did. That might sound odd, unless you knew Rick. He had this habit of having what he called his 'second kip.' He would get up in the morning, make himself a cup of tea, then go back to bed for his 'second kip'.

In fact, Rick said, he felt so much better the next day he nearly cancelled the appointment. But somehow he had just enough sense to see the doctor – who took one look, told him he had almost certainly had a heart attack, and promptly sent him to Wellington Hospital in St John's Wood, where they took him in and prepped him for an immediate quadruple heart bypass. They told him that if they didn't operate immediately, he would be dead within twenty-four hours.

He used the phone in his private room to call his mum. Followed by David Walker, whose next call was to me. He told me what had happened and that Rick might not survive the op. Bloody hell, Ricky! I thought. What have you done this time?

Fortunately, Rick pulled through. Of course, David made sure he made the news and Rick's room started filling up with cards and flowers from Quo fans all over the world. He also had a string of visitors. I went and had my picture taken with him grinning from his bed. All for tomorrow's newspapers thank you, David. There was a bit of a kerfuffle, I found out later, when both of Rick's wives turned up to see him. Marietta, who Rick had been seeing again for a couple of years on and off, and Patty, his second wife, who he had divorced the previous year but who he was also seeing again. Apparently they had to sneak one out while the other one was waiting to come in. Very Rick, that scenario, I thought.

The other thing that was very Rick was his response to all the medical advice he was now given, in terms of recovery but also in terms of avoiding having another heart attack. When one consultant told him that a glass or two of good red wine might be beneficial – something to do with the tannins in red wine – Rick took that to mean he could have one or two *bottles* of good red wine a night. When they told him he would need to rest for a few weeks, he took that to mean a roadie would have to carry him home to his couch, where he could lie around smoking sixty cigarettes a day, drinking red wine and snorting coke. He told me all this with a straight face, by the way. When he saw how I looked at him, he tried to turn it into a joke but I knew he was telling the truth. 'The thing is, Frame,' he told me, 'after being in hospital for so long I thought I owed myself a couple of big nights.' In fact, he'd only been in there for eleven days before checking himself out.

The truth is, Rick was very ill for a long while afterwards. Although he made his comeback onstage with us just three months later, for a while I did wonder if he would ever be fit enough to work again. Then his first show back, at Norwich City football ground, he was jumping around like a spring chicken. Like nothing had happened. The place was packed with about 25,000 fans and there were 'Welcome Back Rick!' banners everywhere. One read: 'Rick Parfitt's got more bypasses than Norwich!' Rick was so chuffed, just revelling in the attention. Afterwards, he tried to explain it to me as what he called 'a midlife refit'. Like a car, he saw it as having 'worn out the valves in the old engine, so I've had some new ones put in'. He also told me he felt so good that he expected to live to be a hundred. That any 'repairs' he needed he would get fitted along the way.

And in fairness, that's pretty much what he did for the rest of his life. I may not have agreed with his analogy. Whether he liked it or not, Rick wasn't a car. I knew he was kidding himself. I couldn't fault his work ethic, though. Which was just as well as the next eighteen months saw us touring constantly. In 1998 alone we played to more than two million people around the world. David Walker's never-ending campaign to turn

Status Quo into part of the family furniture was still paying big dividends. When we released the *Under the Influence* album in 1999, David organised a ten-date tour of British pubs, giving a right old knees-up to a couple of hundred people a night. This time the shtick was that the ten pubs had all been nominated in a competition held in the *Sun*, under the banner headline, 'Get Quo to Play in Your Boozer', which they announced had attracted over 10,000 entries. David did a similar pub-tour promotion for us in Holland and Germany.

The thing is, none of this actually translated into record sales, with *Under the Influence* selling less overall even than *Perfect Remedy*. It was also galling on a personal level, as the title *Under the Influence* had absolutely nothing to do with alcohol or pubs. It was just something David the marketing whiz had glommed onto as a way to publicise the record. Simon Porter really fought David on this one; he could see it was a bad idea. I remember Neil Warnock, our brilliant booking agent, also warned me it was a bad idea. Neil was someone who had been around as long as us, starting out at NEMS before forming his own companies, most notably The Agency, in the early eighties, which is when we started working with him. These days Neil is the head of UTA (United Talent Agency), one of the biggest talent agents in the world, with over a hundred agents working for him. Neil knows his stuff. So when he took me to one side and had a serious word with me about David's latest brainwave, I had to take it seriously. David was unstoppable though. I got it that in the absence of major radio play, which we had stopped getting in the late nineties, David saw the tabloids and the mainstream TV entertainment shows as the only media left where we could get word out about our latest records. But the pub promotion left me feeling very disenchanted. Not least as I now hated going into pubs and hated drinking. The song 'Under the Influence' had been inspired by a recurring dream I was having about an old girlfriend – and two of her best friends – while the melody actually came from something I wrote on the piano when I was thirteen. But when I told David this, tried to explain that the song meant something different but real, he just pulled a face and said, 'I can't build a marketing campaign about that!'

Most of all I was starting to hate all the fakery involved. Showbiz and promotion I am fine with, it has always been part of the music business game. But it felt to me like Quo had now gone way beyond that. You need to find the right balance. Without it we were becoming a laughing stock even to some of our longstanding fans. Even, if I'm honest, to me. Something had to change, but what? And how?

David, meanwhile, was full steam ahead. And bless his heart for it. One thing about David: he was absolutely unstoppable. And the truth is some of what he came up with was brilliant still. Our 2000 Australian tour was launched with a trip on the Australian version of the Orient Express, the Great South Pacific Express. It was like the Butlin's trip only bigger. Much bigger. An amazing, historic vintage steam train that carried over 250 fans and media to one of Australia's grandest old railway stations, Grandchester, located deep in the outback. When they got there we were waiting to play a free show on a flatbed railway carriage. It was pretty incredible, if unbelievably hot.

Then there was the flip-side, like the time just a few months later when we became 'the first outsiders ever to enter a *Big Brother* house' when we played a gig for the housemates in the Norwegian version of the show. God, did it smell in there! I mean whoop-de-doo, do you know what I mean?

But then there were also glorious events like making our first appearance on the Night of the Proms tour. Full classical orchestra and choir, featuring classical and jazz musicians and rock artists, including Simple Minds, Meat Loaf, UB40 . . . We did two months of shows in Belgium, Holland and Germany and it became the most enjoyable experience I'd had as a performer for many years. It was also the easiest. We only had to do four songs a night and we were sequestered in luxury private accommodation throughout as the shows all took place in one grand venue per country. I took to bicycling to and from the show every day. That and the unique experience of hearing 'Rockin' All Over the World' and 'Caroline' being thumped out by a full orchestra and choir made this a truly memorable time for the band.

The stretching of the Status Quo 'brand', to use one of his favourite words, continued apace throughout the last couple of years we worked with David. For all the good things he did, there were now other things that were truly getting me down. David had tried to turn not being played on Radio 1 any more into a publicity opportunity by having us sue the BBC. Simon Porter was going, 'No! It's suicide!' We all knew it was a huge mistake but David went ahead with it. I read my quote – written for me – in the official press release and felt like an old granddad spoiling the kids' party: '"Someone seems not to like us at Radio 1," said Francis Rossi. "But the staff are not paid to be taste-makers. They should play the current Top 40, which is their remit."' I was made to feel like an even bigger fool when the whole thing backfired so spectacularly the judge ruled against us, which ended up costing the band upwards of £500,000. Note: costing the *band* not the *manager* half a million quid!

Meanwhile, we were all over the telly in other ways. Argos had been using 'Whatever You Want' in their official ads for years. 'Down Down' now became the theme to a Kwik-Fit ad, while 'Whatever You Want' also started being used by everybody from Hoseasons Holidays to the theme tune to a Saturday night TV show called, wait for it, *Whatever You Want*. We got paid very handsomely for these things and we were very happy about that. But how it left me feeling inside was wretched.

Everything reached a head – or rather a new all-time low, at least for me – with David's plans for our next album, which he had already come up with the title for: *Famous in the Last Century*. He had the whole thing figured out. Released early in 2000, it would comprise twenty of our favourite songs – again – from the twentieth century. Yes, it was the *Don't Stop* album over all again, with the spirit of 'The Anniversary Waltz' thrown in. I hated it before he had even finished selling us on the idea. I hated the album even more when we'd finished making it. Not because it wasn't good. The songs were ace, the band was great; it was just the whole concept that broke my heart. People used to chide us in the seventies for always releasing the same record, but back then we had originality and imagination on our side. This, though, wasn't even our own material. It wasn't even our own idea. And in the end it wasn't even a hit. Both singles from it flopped and the album popped into the charts at number 19 for a week in April 2000 then popped out again.

We were all having that sinking feeling, more or less. Jeff Rich quit the band the month the album was released, right at the start of what was to be another gruelling eighteen-month world tour. Jeff's replacement was Matt Letley, a great drummer with a lot of experience playing with a varied bunch of people like A-ha,

Bob Geldof, Vanessa Mae, Hank Marvin and Kim Wilde. Matt was a very technical drummer and could play anything and play it really well. He was also a very quiet, calming influence in the dressing room. Something I was grateful for as we ploughed on gamely through the *Famous in the Last Century* tour. The irony was that, without the drugs to hold me down, I was feeling fitter and more ready to work than for years. But I was bone tired of David's methods of keeping us 'relevant'.

By the end of it I was seriously having thoughts about jacking it in. Well, not seriously. I had tried that once before and look where it had got me. But I was thinking about an escape route. Rick came to me in his familiar fearful way and told me that David had said to him at the end of the tour: 'You realise that you two have probably only got a couple of years left and then it's all over.'

You couldn't say something like that to Rick without completely freaking him out. He still remembered with a shudder the aftermath of our first break-up, back in 1984. He came to me in a complete panic over what David had said. I was disgusted and angry. How dare he say that, and not even to me but to Rick, who he knew couldn't handle that kind of thing?

Years later, thinking about it, analysing late into the night yet again, I realised that David was probably thinking of himself more than us. He was a very wealthy man, not far off his sixtieth birthday, and as someone who was always thinking two steps ahead, he was probably already planning for his retirement. And under those circumstances he simply couldn't see how we would ever be able to carry on without him. In reality, he didn't want the band to carry on without him, such was his ego.

In the end, the whole thing became academic. David Walker suffered a heart attack while attending his son Charlie's eighteenth birthday with the family at home, in Gerrards Cross. He was taken to hospital but died in the early hours of the morning on 30 August 2001. The following Wednesday we were all there for his funeral at Chilterns Crematorium in Buckinghamshire. He was only fifty-seven and had only recently come out of a drug rehab. He was looking in the best health I'd seen him in years. He'd been in rehab before but it had never taken. This time it really seemed like it had. He came out very anti-drink and drugs. He wasn't the kind of guy who liked to exercise, though, and he was still smoking God knows how many cigarettes a day. Still, fifty-seven is no age to go. I was deep in shock for a long time afterwards.

Deep in shock – and suddenly free.

Chapter Twelve

The Double Act

When Simon Porter took over as manager from David Walker, the plan was very simple as far as I was concerned. I was going to reach my fifty-ninth birthday in 2008. That would be the perfect time to retire, I told Simon. I'm not sure he believed me. I'm not sure I really believed me. But that seemed a sensible sort of deadline to set, to see if we could keep the band going at the level we'd become used to. In the end, I didn't retire at fifty-nine. By the time we got there, Simon had already proved himself several times over and the band was in the best shape it had been in for decades.

In the beginning, though, I asked Simon to basically do two things for us: allow us to start making the kind of records we could be proud of again; and keep whatever good things David had brought to the band during his time with us, while ditching the bad. That is, have our cake and eat it. Why not? After all, we had earned it surely, after everything we had been through all these years together?

Fortunately, Simon has been exactly the right man to deliver exactly that. Having worked as Quo's publicist throughout the David Walker years, Simon knew all the tricks in terms of promotion. It may have been David that dreamed up all those gimmicks for Quo, but it was Simon who had been the man on the ground organising them. On the other hand, Simon had also had a long career working with credible bands like Motörhead, Uriah Heep and the Damned, to name just a few. Simon knew exactly what I was talking about and, good as his word, that's exactly what he has done for us ever since.

A good example was the first album we did with Simon managing, *Heavy Traffic*, in 2002. For me, this was the best, most authentic-sounding Status Quo collection since the heyday of albums like *On the Level* and *Blue for You*. We sounded like a real band again, guitars upfront in the mix, all but one of the tracks a band original, including half a dozen brand new songs written by me and Bob Young. And what an unexpected joy that was. Bob had simply shown up at one of our shows a couple of years before and suddenly it was like we'd never been apart. We were finally able to sit down together and talk through all the bullshit that had ruined our friendship back in the bad old days. We were older and had a much greater sense of perspective – one of the few benefits getting on a bit actually has. That was the most important thing. The fact that we were able to pick up our songwriting partnership again just like that was an added bonus.

I was now writing with everyone in the band again, in fact: Andy, Rhino, just not Rick. But then Rick only came up with one song on the album, something he had done with Rhino, called 'Creepin' Up on You' – which, ironically, was one of the most Quo-like tracks on the whole album, like something from the *Dog of Two Head* era. Brilliant.

The only track we didn't write was the single 'Jam Side Down', by Terry Britten, who'd written huge hits for everyone from Tina Turner to Meat Loaf, and his co-writer Charlie Dore.

Looking back now, I wish we'd gone with one of our original tracks. Not because it wasn't a good song – just because we had more than a few candidates. I couldn't argue though when it became our first top 20 hit in Britain for nearly ten years.

Simon did everything he could to push the boat out with the publicity, emphasising the fact that as a band we were back on true-blue Quo form. He also showed us he could 'do a David' when he organised a big promotional party on the decks of the navy aircraft carrier, HMS *Ark Royal*. We did a special set and the whole thing was filmed for TV. We also found ourselves back on *Top of the Pops* again doing 'Jam Side Down'. When *Heavy Traffic* was released it also made the top 20, becoming the best-selling Quo album of original material since the eighties. It seemed we had found a new formula with Simon – just being ourselves. Who'd have thought?

In the years since we have pretty much done as we pleased. Yes, we've had our share of new compilations, live collections and box sets, but that's become par for the course for every major band of our generation. Contractually there is nothing you can do about it anyway. What has made it an even more popular course of action for the major labels is that with record sales having shrunk to the size of a mushroom all their main business these days is centred on repackaging back catalogue. When you've got a back catalogue like Quo's that goes back half a century you can have a field day.

At the same time, we've also made some of our best original albums ever. We went on a roll after *Heavy Traffic* did so well with more great chart albums like *The Party Ain't Over Yet* and *In Search of the Fourth Chord* (see what we did there?). Both albums featured great new songs from every member of the band. We still brought in outside writers like John David on occasion for singles like 'The Party Ain't Over Yet', in 2005, which made the top 10 and gave us our best-selling hit for ten years. But we also mixed things up, with Bob and me coming up with two of my favourite singles from those times, both of which did well in the charts: 'You'll Come Around' and 'Thinking of You'. Both of them were cut from the same cloth as all our classic hits and for me were further confirmation that Quo was still a serious rock band to be reckoned with.

This also underlined how much I still loved that moment when you get the phone call saying your new record has gone in the charts. For twenty years I think we all more or less took it for granted that anything we put out would get in the charts. We were already thinking ahead to *Top of the Pops* even as we made the records. Now, though, here in the twenty-first century, there were no such guarantees. The record business hardly exists any more with the advent of streaming of music direct to your phone, computer and so on. Most of the record stores have disappeared. There isn't even a *Top of the Pops* any more.

I've been told more than once that Quo doesn't really need to make records any more. Look at the Stones, they say, they have released just one new original album in the last twenty years yet they are one of the biggest touring bands in the world. Or how about the Eagles, one of my own personal all-time favourites, they have released exactly one new original album since 1979 – and, as I write this, they are selling even more tickets than the Stones.

So I get all that. And the upside is that Quo has always been considered an absolutely killer live band. But I still love the whole concept of an album. Yes, the days of side one and side two have long since disappeared. I know they keep banging on about the so-called vinyl revival, but that's like saying people still make black-and-white movies. It's a fetish. A cult. Nice if you are into it, meaningless to almost everybody else. Have you tried playing a record in the car lately? CDs have also bitten the dust. Personally, I wasn't that bothered to see them go. They just encouraged every band, including us, to try and find fifteen new tracks every time they made an album. It was more like making a double album would have felt like in the seventies.

All that said, I still enjoy making albums. I still think in terms of albums when I'm writing new songs. And our fans, I know, like the idea of having a new Quo album of some sort to look forward to. No, they don't sell in the numbers they used to. Nobody does, unless it's someone like Adele, or Ed Sheeran. But they are the exceptions to the rule. One-offs, unique. We used to sell more records in a day than the number 1 records of today sell in a month. But making records is what we've always done, and we've become really good at it again, even if I say so myself. Our 2011 album, *Quid Pro Quo,* went top 10 and was our biggest seller for years. Even the soundtrack album to our movie, *Bula Quo!,* in 2013, went top 10. Our first of two *Aquostic* albums, *Stripped Bare,* in 2014 went top 5 and gave us our first gold record in the UK since *Don't Stop* twenty years before. While the second *Aquostic* album in 2016, *That's a Fact,* was another big hit.

The idea behind those albums came from a TV commercial we did in Australia for Coles supermarkets. Me and Rick playing around going on about how prices were 'Down Down' while they played the backing track to 'Whatever You Want'. For some reason, these TV ads went down a storm in Australia, becoming the biggest for years. It was nuts. It was being talked about on TV and radio, being written about in newspapers. Simon looked into it and came back with the interesting fact that people really loved seeing me and Rick but actually really hated the ad. And that's the winning formula apparently. You don't want people to be indifferent to an ad, you want them to either love it or hate it. Or in the case of our Coles ad, both!

Anyway, while we were making the ads at Pinewood Studios, Rick and I were mucking about with an acoustic version of 'Down Down', just to keep time for the 'prices are down, down,' lines. But the response among the crew was so intense afterwards Simon had a light bulb moment and said, 'Hey, how about we do a whole album of acoustic versions of Quo songs?' I was like, 'No. That's too much like hard work.' While Rick was, 'Yeah! Great idea!', which was our usual response to most things. I'd start moaning about all the work that would be involved – then say yes and get down and do all that hard work. Rick would be super enthusiastic – then shy away when it came time to do the actual work.

Anyway, the fact is I really enjoyed making those records –reworking and stripping back songs like 'Caroline', 'Down Down', even 'Pictures of Matchstick Men' and 'Paper Plane'. Simon is very good at underplaying things. He just said, 'Look, give it a go at rehearsals and if you still don't think it will work we'll forget it and think of something else.' So we did and it sounded great. I still wasn't sure how it would go down with our fans but they loved it and turned up for the shows in droves.

That's the difference between now and where we found ourselves at the turn of the century. Simon knows the value of being able to offer the fans something more than just another Quo album. At the same time, he doesn't push for us to do cheesy covers albums. He's also a great strategist. The short tour we did with the *Aquostic* set in 2014 was sandwiched between lengthier tours of Britain and Europe with our full live show.

We did the same thing with the second *Aquostic* album a couple of years later. A short burst of acoustic shows between tours with the full electric show. It gave the band's profile a whole new perspective. Even my driver of sixteen years saw a new side to me. 'I didn't know you could play acoustic guitar,' he announced one day. 'That's proper music.' I've even had people stop me in the street to tell me they couldn't stand the band plugged in but that now they could hear the simple melodies of the songs they had become belated Quo fans.

At the same time Rhino has been able to get his own side band together, Rhino's Revenge, and take that out on the road and release a couple of albums, while his son Freddie accompanied us on guitar for the *Aquostic* tour dates. Andy Bown is the same. He's also made an album of his own in recent years.

The one that didn't go down that route, of course, was Rick. But Rick was busy having his own adventures. After a fallow period where he didn't write that much new stuff, he began working with different people like Wayne Morris and Simon Climie, and came up with a lot of great stuff over the last ten years of his life. Rick also toyed with various outside ventures like a board game he came up with called 'Rick Parfitt's Name Game'. Catchphrase: get the name win the game! They turned that into a book, film, DVD, you name it. (Ouch, sorry.)

Of course, not everything we've done in recent years has worked out as well as we'd have liked. For example, the great Quo movie that wasn't: *Bula Quo!* When we first agreed to it, it was actually quite a violent film. Then the script got watered down and I think we were imagining a sort of Quo-tastic version of *A Hard Day's Night* – which, looked at today, is actually not very good but all right for what it was at the time. Instead what we got was a ninety-minute cringe-fest. At least, it was for me watching it. Though I did enjoy a lot of what we got up to making it. Well, some of it anyway. The plot, such that it is, is this: the band goes to do a show on the island of Fiji where it stumbles upon a human-organ black market and finds itself embroiled in all kinds of whacky adventures.

The idea came from the director, Stuart St Paul, this larger-than-life character who has done everything: TV, film, stage, acting. We flew down to Fiji in 2012 just after the island's most devastating cyclone in its history. In terms of the acting, I realised after that what they should have done was leave it to Rick and me to see what happens, because we were both good at just going into something on the spur of the moment. We were naturals; there was always something funny to be said or done about things. Always. We would laugh at stuff together, get it wrong, then carry on anyway and it would become even funnier. But they didn't trust us enough as movie actors to do that. Instead, we had to stick to the script. And that didn't really work. It would have been nice if we'd done a second movie because we would have got better at it. The trouble is, like everything else these days, nobody has time any more for you to get better and lose money. It needed to make money. Just like the music business.

The good thing that came out of it, though, was the germ of the idea to put together a set of acoustic versions of our songs. We also got to meet and work with some amazing people, like Craig Fairbrass, probably best known for his past role as Dan Sullivan in the BBC soap opera *EastEnders*. A completely wild man who knew how to have a good time. Also Jon Lovitz, the American comedian, a veteran of *Saturday Night Live*, and Laura Aikman, a wonderfully talented young British actress who I really rate and who has been in countless hit TV shows and films.

And, of course, we've also kept up a steady stream of public appearances doing all manner of brilliant and sometimes not so brilliant things. When Rick and I appeared on a celebrity charity episode of *Who Wants to Be a Millionaire?*, I thought we'd never live it down. I got us out with the very first question, which was: 'How many knights on a chessboard?' I answered: 'Two.' Wrong! Doh! I knew the answer should have been four, two black, two white, but the heat of the moment just got the better of me. Fortunately, some kindly producer saved the day by scrapping the question and making us start again, because the question had been asked before. They said. I have no idea if that was true. But we got a second go at it and this time we did rather well. Rick and I ended up winning £50,000 for charity.

Then there was our stint on *Coronation Street*, the longest-running TV soap in history. Now this was weird. I'd grown up watching the original series back in the sixties, when fantastic characters like Ena Sharples and Annie Walker ruled the roost. Not to mention the curmudgeonly Uncle Albert Tatlock and the wonderfully workshy Stan Ogden. The idea of Quo suddenly being woven into the present-day storyline was not one I could easily imagine. I was like: oh no! It's going to be terrible! But it was a great few weeks, experiencing a completely different work environment. You had to be on set at 7 a.m. every day. Learning your lines. Getting your timing right. It was funny. Rick was being Rick. In one scene, going into the Rovers Return, all we had to say was, 'You got anything to eat, love?' And the barmaid has to go, 'Hotpot.' Then give us that look! I think Annie Walker passed it down through the years to Bet Lynch and Shelley Unwin, who was working behind the bar at the time we were on. Rick, who'd been brought up to show off, kept looking at the camera. He couldn't help it. It was just in his blood. They had to say to him, 'Rick, can you please stop looking at the camera when you're in shot?'

Then when the barmaid said, 'Hotpot,' it kept making me laugh. I said, sorry, I can't do this. Then there was the theme music, probably the most famous theme music now in British television. I absolutely hated it when I was a kid, trying to play it on trumpet. The neighbours would be like, 'Bloody kid with that trumpet!' Now I love it. It's so beautiful and melancholic and has such great chords. Not that I play it on trumpet. But on an acoustic guitar it sounds lovely.

We were in three episodes. The story was we were on our way to a show and the bus broke down – and so we ended up in the Rovers Return for about three days. When Les Battersby finds out he persuades us to play at his wedding to Cilla. I'm sorry if you're not a *Corrie* fan and none of this means anything to you but for me and Rick and Simon Porter getting to stand at the bar of the Rovers Return and have one of their coloured-water pints of ale was a bucket-list moment. It shaded into reality, too, as Bruce Jones, who played Les, really was a lifelong Quo fan and had been to quite a few gigs.

Before that, I had a certain view of soap actors, that they weren't 'real' actors, because that's how their business sells it to us. There are the 'proper' actors that do Shakespeare and big films, then the poor soap stars that are in a completely different category. But the actors on *Corrie* were brilliant. Really great at what they do, and very serious. They are not mucking about. Not only are they great actors but they need to have the whole thing done ready for the show to be put out six times a week over three nights or however many times they're on. They would be on set at seven in the morning, have one break for lunch, then be on set until seven at night, five or six days a week, every week. The viewers think they must be living the life of Riley. But you try it.

There were other things we did over the past ten years or so that I enjoyed but without really feeling strongly about. I no longer hated things we did. I accepted them because they were always coming from a good place. Simon was easily as good as David at concocting fabulous promotional ideas, but he is a much more agreeable man and would never make us do anything that felt really phoney. He actually did believe in us as a musical entity, not just a brand.

When I finally decided I was too old to carry off a ponytail, I had had it cut off – then auctioned it for charity. When we played at Glastonbury in 2009, we were treated like the coolest band in the world. It's become almost against the law not to like Quo these days. And I loved that. But I also saw it for what it was. The wheel had turned. What was out was now in, and vice versa. Whatever you thought of our music or us you couldn't deny we were authentic: the real deal. And authenticity is the true currency these days.

Like when we appeared back at Wembley for the 2007 Concert for Diana. A great day, huge Wembley crowd, we even opened with 'Rockin' All Over the World' again, but a totally different vibe to Live Aid. This was held at the newly opened rebuilt Wembley Stadium, and the crowd was seated. Ten years on from Diana's death, it took place on what would have been her forty-sixth birthday, hosted by Princes William and Harry with all proceeds going to Diana's charities, as well as to charities of which William and Harry are patrons. What's not to like?

But the truth is it was a huge publicity splash for all the acts involved. Does anyone really think they cared that much about Diana? I very much doubt it. Now I probably shouldn't say stuff like that but I daresay it's the truth. It was showbiz. Of course we wanted to do it. It's high profile. The thing I remember most, if you want the absolute truth, is that Rick's voice was in a bad way. On the recording we had to replace his voice with somebody else. It sounds like Rick. It's fine. But when confronted with that fact he said, 'Don't be so ridiculous.' I found that hard. It's one thing to seek a little help in the technical department, shall we say, on a recording. But to brush it off like it didn't happen? I found that frustrating. It was that whole denial thing that Rick had in the latter years.

Which brings me to what really became the defining strand in my own story over the past couple of decades with Status Quo: my up and down relationship with my oldest friend and closest workmate, Rick Parfitt. We used to joke and say we'd been together longer than any of our marriages, as if that spoke to the strength of our relationship. But it was a hollow joke really, as Rick and I had steadily drifted apart over the years. To the point where there were times I truly despaired of him.

Every Christmas after we'd finished our latest tour, Rick would come up to me and ask the same thing: 'We are going to be all right, aren't we, Frame?' I'd say: 'Yes, Ricky, of course. We're going to be fine.' And he would go off happy, satisfied that the band would be able to keep going for at least another year.

But the truth is, I always knew there would come a day when Rick wouldn't be around any longer to worry about that. And he did worry about things. For someone who had such a sunny public image, Rick became a real worrier. He was always either flying high or crashing down low.

His health had suffered a great deal. After that first massive heart attack in 1997, he suffered two more cardiac arrests. He came through both and came straight back to the band with the same attitude he'd had to the first. That it was simply a case of getting a bit of biological rewiring done, like putting a vintage Roller in for an overhaul. And he always emerged ready to carry on just as he always had before.

But of course, that wasn't the case. Simon and I used to openly wonder what we would do the day he didn't come back from another heart attack. Rick just kept smiling through it all. Kept drinking, kept smoking, kept having his 'big nights' whenever he felt the urge, which was most weekends from what I could gather. As he'd got older he also become dependent on different sorts of pills to get to sleep every night. For a long time he would use Rohypnol to help him relax and sleep. It was because of his refusal to go without his pills that he turned down the chance to go on *I'm a Celebrity . . . Get Me Out of Here!*, the biggest show on ITV. Think about it: Rick would have been the perfect campmate on that show. Funny, loveable, much more famous than most of them and completely game for any of the trials they threw at him. He'd have probably won it, knowing Rick. But he lost out because he simply wouldn't have been able to cope without his sleeping pills and his cigarettes. They said he could have a certain number of ciggies a day, five perhaps, but that was never going to keep Rick happy.

Then there was the horrible day a couple of years later, when the doctors suspected he might have throat cancer. He cried his fucking eyes out. I remember sitting in the production office at the Guildhall in Plymouth. He'd been to see this specialist in the morning. When he told me the doc thought he had throat cancer I just didn't believe it. But this fucking specialist had told him this so that was that. Of course, it scared the shit out of him. I'm sitting with him in the production office trying to console him. I'd very much become his dad by then, when it suited him. 'Can you do this for me? Can you do that for me?', which I was quite glad to do because I did love him. I said he should talk to Simon. But he said, 'No. You tell him.' He was sobbing his heart out. It was weird after all the heart attacks he'd had. I went to see him in the hospital after the last one, which was a very serious heart attack. He wasn't emotional at all. The throat cancer scare was the only time I saw him go to pieces like that. We weren't like that with each other. We would always joke about the worst things. Oh, leg fallen off, has it? Jog on then. But this was different.

As soon as the tests came back that the tumour was benign, though, he was back to being Rockin' Rick. The doctor told him he'd have to quit smoking and not to have more than a couple of drinks a day. Rick said to him: 'But if I don't drink at all in the week, does that mean I can have ten or twelve drinks on the weekend?' The doctor was like, 'No it does not!' so Rick did as he was told and cut down completely on the boozing and smokes – at least for a couple of weeks. It wasn't until his third heart attack in 2011 that he finally quit drinking and smoking. Well, for longer than a couple of weeks anyway. That was when he also lost a lot of weight. That was impressive. I was pleased for him.

It wasn't just Rick's health that got him into trouble though. It was his endlessly complicated love life. There were his exploits with various groupies, some of which landed him in the pages of the tabloids. Him and Ronnie Wood, I used to think, both great guitarists, both very similar sorts of devil-may-care personalities, loveable rogues, both old enough to know better, you would have thought. Rick, though, always had to take things one step further. As was the case when he married his third wife, Lyndsay Whitburn, in 2006.

Rick was back living with his second wife, Patty, when he first met Lyndsay, who was a fitness instructor. Then walked out on Patty after becoming secretly engaged to Lindsay, who he then married and went to live with in Spain. I thought, yet again, oh Ricky, what have you done? But he swore that this time it was true love. When he and Lyndsay had children two years later – beautiful boy-and-girl twins named Tommy and Lily – it was hard to argue with.

What was a lot harder to accept as the years flew by was my own relationship with Rick. Whether it was being on TV together, in films or onstage, Rick and I had long ago established ourselves as a kind of rock 'n' roll double act. Even when we received OBEs from the Queen for services to music and charity, in 2010, we were given them together.

They stand you in circles while you wait for the Queen to arrive. Rick and I are standing there at Buckingham Palace. It's kind of an audition before you get your gongs. I was talking to Sophie, Countess of Wessex, the one who married Prince Edward. She was very nice. Then up comes the Queen. I'm not a royalist by any stretch. But what their gig entails, they outwork any of us. They are really good for the country and that whole thing. I said, 'Nice to meet you again, ma'am.' She said, 'Do what?' Suddenly I could just imagine her and her sister Margaret, in the fifties, when 'Do what?' was a very hip saying. These days it doesn't sound right. But that's what the Queen said. 'Do what?' We made her smile.

We were quite good at that, except when people told us to do it. 'Can you do some of your funny stuff?' We'd both sit there going, um, ah . . . It was a very natural thing; it wasn't something we could just turn on. That was us just being us, when we were in the mood, until towards the end when it became a little bit forced.

I don't know who it was but during those last years together it was like there was someone or something digging at Rick. Whispering in his ear, telling him to not be that person. I think it would come up in what I call 'domestics', something in his personal life, some jibe that would be thrown at him. I don't know who it was but someone sowed that little seed of doubt with him. The thing is, you sow the seed of doubt and that's the fastest plant growing on the planet. It's the same with anyone. You mustn't do it to people yet we all do it all the time, if we're not careful. You should have heard what so-and-so said about you. Why, what did they say? Oh nothing . . . It's a killer.

With Rick, over the latter years of our career something was definitely digging at him inside. It was such a shame because it affected him and it didn't have to. Because when Rick was on form he was absolutely brilliant. Example: not too long ago we had to do a breakfast telly appearance. Rick had gone into his dressing room looking like a tramp – and came out looking like a million dollars. Like, 'Hey everybody! Let's get the show started!' Rick was really good at that and he was absolutely brilliant that morning.

In the end, though, it became too much for him. The guy I loved, and that thing that we had, was coming under so much pressure from people to be a particular way, it had a downhill effect. The whole 'not wanting to be number two' thing went back to the days after 'Rockin' All Over the World', when he would want to stand in the middle of the stage. I'd just shrug and carry on.

In those last years, though, more and more often his whole thing to me had become: 'I'm fed up being number two.' He'd come up to me doing that 'You, you, you...' thing. I mean, what was I supposed to do with that information? Go: 'All right then, I'll be the number two and you can be the number one'?

I mean, what would have changed? I'd still be the lead singer on most of the songs. That wasn't about ego, that was about just being the way we were. It would be like me suddenly going, oh, I want to be the drummer. Well, all right, but how will that actually work? Plus, I don't think anyone ever really saw things that way, that there was a pecking order between Rick and me. They just saw us together, as a double act. Equals.

Sometimes he'd be out of his head on the tour bus. He'd start going on and asking again why he was number two and I was number one. I'd say, 'I don't think so Rick. You're drunk so there's no point talking about it now anyway. You'll only forget everything the next day.'

Then he'd change and start crying. 'You let me in your group . . .' Oh, Christ! Then it would be, 'You cunt . . .' Whoa! It was this Jekyll and Hyde situation. Alcohol and insecurity and whatever other frustrations he was going through. It only came out like that though when he was drunk.

When we did the first *Aquostic* album, Rick wasn't on it. He wasn't on quite a few albums. For a while, that was fine. We'd say, that's OK, that's just Rick. We did the acoustic album at my home studio, which is where we had done all the recent Quo recordings, as we still do today, and he wasn't there at all. His twins had been born and he rightly wanted to spend as much time with them as possible. The only snag was he and Lyndsay and the kids were living in Spain. And yet, hard though it is to admit, I didn't miss not having him there. In fact, it was one of the best times I've had with the band in a studio for years. It was creative and enjoyable and we didn't want to stop. When we came to do a live performance and interview for the promotional video, Rick was in there first telling everyone how the album was made. Typical Rick! You had to laugh.

Then when we made the second acoustic album he phoned up the producer Mike Paxman and said, 'That's disgraceful what you've done with my vocal.' Mike told him, 'Rick, you were in such a state your voice was shot.' Rick was like: 'I was not. How dare you say that about me?' But it was true what Mike said. Rick had been drunk or hungover most of the time.

What was also true was that Rick really was a lovely bloke — when he was being a lovely bloke. He was a darling and I loved him. Except for those times, particularly in the latter years, when he wasn't and I didn't.

The psychologist and writer Jordan Peterson says that very successful people tend to be obsessive about what they do, or feel they have absolutely no choice in the matter: they have to do it. I look at my wife Eileen and I realise that if I had not married her I would never have been able to carry on with Quo in the late eighties. But because she was so important to me, I knew I just had to do whatever it took to keep the show on the road. No matter what, I had to make sure we kept going in the right direction. If that meant giving up drugs, I gave up drugs. If that meant giving up drink, I gave up drink. If that meant becoming the most unpopular guy in the band, then fine, that's who I would become too if that is what's needed. The leader is the one everyone else relies on to keep things together.

I hate discussing it, especially here. Written down it never comes across the right way. It doesn't read well. But I lament the fact that my and Rick's relationship didn't end well. I wish I never had to see him struggle with these things. In the end, it was the stuff other people were whispering in Rick's ear that ruined our personal relationship. I did my very best to take care of Ricky throughout our time together, when I wasn't up to my neck in my own problems. For some people now to suggest that I could have done more is very upsetting for me. It makes me angry. They don't know the real story and they never will know the full extent of it because even now I choose to try and protect his memory as much as I can.

It was such a shame. We had some great times together over the years, including a final hurrah together with the original band. Now this is something I didn't see happening at all – ever. Of course, I'd been asked countless times over the years: would we ever consider getting back together with Alan Lancaster and John Coghlan? And, well, you can guess what my answer always was.

Only this time it was different. Once again, Simon Porter was the *éminence grise* that put the chess pieces in the right order on the chessboard for it to happen. It all began with a phone call, which Simon arranged, between me and Alan while the band was in Sydney, when we were touring Australia, in 2010.

The clincher was when Alan said to me that Simon had proved that he was wrong. At last, I thought. At the time, when we went to court in the mid-eighties, Alan was telling people that we owed him £30 million. I was like, 'What the hell are you talking about, Al?' The numbers don't even come close. If he was really owed £30 million, on top of what he'd already earned, that meant we had earned at least £120 million between the four of us. And that would be after all the management commissions, repayment of record company advances, tour expenses, tax and everything else. I doubt the Rolling Stones earned as much as what Alan reckoned we did in the seventies. It was just not physically possible that Alan was owed £30 million in 1985.

When we talked things over in Sydney, Alan seemed like he'd finally come to his senses. So when Rick and I saw him and sat down together, we had to rub his nose in it a bit because, as far as he was concerned, he'd left us in the lurch. He really thought we'd never survive without him. When in fact we went from strength to strength.

Alan could be a laugh when he was in the right mood, particularly if he'd had a joint. When we met he would sometimes giggle and I felt like I did when I was twelve years old hanging out at his parents' house. Suddenly we were getting on great again. Just because of that brief visit, we started to think about things. You know, maybe we could do a few gigs. And from that everything escalated. It just seemed like such a good idea – on paper.

As Quo fans will now know, this resulted in what quickly became known as the Frantic Four tour. That is, the original seventies line-up of Quo – me, Rick, Alan and John – all touring together for the first time since the Never Too Late world tour of 1981. Rick was all for it. Alan and John practically bit our hands off. Even the current line-up seemed relaxed about it. We were only talking about nine dates around Britain in March 2013, then back on tour properly with the current band. Meanwhile, Quo fans of all ages began acting as though the Second Coming was on its way.

Unfortunately, it didn't quite work out that way. I knew as soon as we got to the first rehearsals and I could see the crew – they were pale. It was dreadful! It was obvious we would need some serious rehearsals to get the old band up to speed. But it was too late. I'd made that commitment. The announcement to the fans had been made so that was it, I was going through with it come what may.

Alan had recently been diagnosed with MS, I believe. I can't say for sure because at the time he was still denying anything was wrong with him. But he was clearly unsteady on his feet. The old fire was certainly still in his belly though. The tour itself, however, at least for me, was not a good one. Musically, I mean. I would walk offstage some nights and the crowd would be going crazy and I would think to myself: wow, there is something going on here that I just don't get. What they are hearing is so different to what I'm hearing. They seem to have been listening to a completely different band. For me, it was just a mess. Alan and John meanwhile loved every minute.

However, that's the same with me at most Quo shows. I'm never really satisfied, even when we've played a blinder. It's a good feeling when it's all over, either because it's been bad and you can't wait to get off, or because it's been really good and it's a great feeling to end a gig knowing it's been you at your best. I'm always about what's happening next. I can't help that. It's probably why I'm in showbiz.

I can't pretend I enjoyed the Frantic Four shows though. Alan made it tough for me on occasion. He thought he was back in 1977. A big star giving orders. But that isn't how we do things any more. One show, I saw Alan getting off the bus freaking out, screaming at people. 'What a two-bit outfit this arsehole crew is! Fucking shit catering!' Lyane Ngan, who's been our personal assistant for more years than Alan was in the group, was ready to kill him. She was trying to calm him down, find out what was wrong and he's screaming about how he hasn't slept on the bus, nothing's any good. So she goes, 'OK, that's it. You're off the bus. We'll get you a separate bus and you can travel on your own.'

That old-school way – you have a tantrum and everyone jumps – well, it's not like that any more. And the thing is, Lyane's really good at looking after people on tour. But if you mess with her you're in trouble. So when Alan then started slagging off various other crew members she put her foot down. 'You can't say that about my colleagues.' And she's the one who's going to win. Not you. Even Rick went for Alan. 'Will you fucking leave her alone? She looks after us.'

I went to him and said, 'You got a problem, Al?' He was like, 'I want my breakfast!' 'Then go and ask them to cook you breakfast.' But he was still chuntering away. I said, 'Look, you've had a bad sleep. I understand that. But you can't talk to people that work for us like that. Now go and apologise to her.' He's like, 'I am not apologising to anybody!' I said, 'Al, this won't go any further unless you address that now. We don't do that shit. Even Rick doesn't do that shit any more.'

But Alan had a lot of stuff he was carrying on his shoulders. He'd insisted on bringing his wife and family on tour with him. I think that made it harder for him, too. But he was insistent: 'They need to see me.' I said, 'Al, it's costing you extra money, you're not sleeping properly and you're ill.' Straight back at me: 'There's nothing wrong with me!' He nearly fell over a couple of times. Rick and I went to help him offstage one night when it looked like he was going to fall and he got all pissed off at us. We should have let him fall.

So even after all these years it was quickly back to where it was when we split up the first time. He would keep poking away at John, too. If I was the drummer and Alan was the bass player and he kept poking away at me like that I'd go mad. No wonder Coghlan used to fly off the handle all the time. Musically, onstage Rick was the only one holding it all together. We didn't have Andy with us so there were no keyboards to take up the slack, just me and Rick working overtime to keep the rhythm bubbling.

In the intervening years Rick and I had improved. We'd been touring together for nearly thirty years before the Frantic Four tour. And we'd gotten really good, as players, singers and as professionals. The others had been less active and the time apart showed, and not just musically. They tried to bring back that old culture but you can't. It's simply not there. They would get the hump with me because I didn't want to sit around with them drinking after the show. Well, I haven't been a drinker for decades now and I don't like being around drunk people. So obviously I'm not going to start doing that. Also, in the years that have gone by, I've developed my on-the-road routine. The things I need to do to survive long tours and still be able to put on a great show each night – and keep myself together physically and mentally.

John was the same as Alan: he had to bring his wife on the road with him. It cost him money and all it did as far as I can see was add to his stress levels. Gillie, his wife, wanted John to stay in the band forever, and thought we'd all be much better off that way, even though John hadn't had anything to do with the band for over thirty years. She said to me: 'Why aren't we going to Australia?' I said, 'What's the "we" shit?' The truth is the Australian promoters didn't want the Frantic Four anyway. She said, 'Surely *some* Australian promoter will take it?' I said, probably, and that's exactly why I'm not doing it. I don't want *some* Australian promoter. I only want the best for the band, which is what we have on all our other Australian tours.

Then Alan became convinced that if we made an album together we'd sell half a million copies in Britain. Based on what, Al? It was just figures plucked out of the air. Pipedreams. After a while it became tedious. Alan's wife, Dayle, was lovely. But Alan upset everybody. Like certain occasions when poor old John would walk in the room and Alan would start to goad him.

He was like that with everybody, one way or another. He probably didn't mean it to come off that way. At first it was great being back together. It was like being kids again. But when he asked if I would do any more I said no. I just told him on the phone: 'I can't do any more like that, Al.' At that point Alan said some very unpleasant things to me. I said, 'Don't start insulting me. We're not kids any more and I shall just cut the line of communication off.' But he wouldn't have it. I hung up the phone and haven't spoken to him since. I'm not eleven years old again where Alan can intimidate me.

I would think to myself: is that how it was with us all those years ago? Is that why Alan and John are like that? I would talk to Rick about it but it was hard for either of us to properly remember. So much time had gone by. So many wives, children, band members, albums, tours . . . Besides, it didn't matter what it had been like forty years before. We don't do coke, get drunk and eat spaghetti hoops any more either. Time had moved on. Status Quo had moved on. Alan and John hadn't. Or just didn't want to. Almost to try and prove a point, I think. Like, we're back now. We do things our way. Well, sorry, no, actually that's not how it's going to go. Even when it came to doing a soundcheck, Alan would want to use that time to just jam instead. I had to explain that we didn't work like that any more. That the band and the crew and everyone else working on the tour had a schedule they worked to. And that, yes, we really did need to do a soundcheck.

The important thing was that Quo fans enjoyed seeing the old band back together. I'm glad we did it for that reason. And also because now, with Rick gone, it can never be done again.

Even when things haven't always worked out in recent years, though, I've never regretted it. Not like I did in the nineties when it meant the gimmick hadn't panned out. Now I take pride in the fact that this is me giving myself heart and soul. My 2010 solo album, *One Step at a Time*, was not a big chart hit. But it gave me such pleasure to make that record. Some critics wondered why I needed to do it. The answer is: I didn't *need* to do it. I *wanted* to do it. For my own pleasure and satisfaction: for the good of my musical soul. The fact is I don't know if a ballad like 'One Step' would have been a good fit for a Quo album. I just know it was a song that really meant something to me and one I didn't want to worry about making 'fit' anything. It's nice also to be able to step out of my role as Status Quo frontman sometimes, as when I did a couple of solo shows around *One Step at a Time*. Or like when I did a string of Rock Meets Classic shows on my own in 2018. It's good to step out of your comfort zone occasionally – even if I say no to begin with. It's fun and it keeps you fresh for the next Quo adventure.

As I've been working on this book, I've been making another solo album, which I've called *We Talk Too Much*. It's actually a shared album with Hannah Rickard. I first met Hannah when we did the first acoustic Quo album. I said to Andy Brook, our engineer, 'I need a fiddle player.' He said, 'Well, luckily enough, I know one that's coming down on Friday from Newcastle.' I said, 'I don't care where he comes from, can he play?' He said, 'It's a woman.' I said, 'Oh, yeah, well, good.' I prefer working with women.

So we met Hannah Rickard. She came into my studio and played on the track 'Claudie' and did some other stuff on the fiddle that was fantastic. I thought, I like you! She's a proper Newcastle lass. Lovely person to be around, and what a singer and player. She also gets this look on her face sometimes like she's got a bad smell under her nose and I just like her. She's also very close to me in birthdays, very similar to me in a lot of ways. Kind of feisty.

When we were at the Hammersmith Apollo on the *Aquostic* tour I was chatting to her backstage. I said something about Connie Francis, whose songs I quite often play on my guitar in the morning to warm up to. Hannah said, 'So you still write songs?' I said, 'You cheeky cow, what do you mean?' I forget that when people look at me they're looking at an old bloke. I said, 'Yeah, I still write.' She was like, 'Oh . . .'

So I left and went back to get ready for the show, then I suddenly thought: wait, did I misunderstand her? Was she asking if I'd like to write some songs with her? So I texted her and asked. She texted straight back: 'Yes.'

I thought: well, you walked into that. She got me to say what she wanted me to say. But I really like Hannah. I get on so well with her. Then when I looked at her onstage I could see the old-school country music girl. She really is the real thing. Working with her in the studio I found out she can really sing too. She was in a band with a cousin of hers, Hannah Rickard and the Relatives, but it was all this rockabilly stuff. I said, 'Why do that and not country?' She said, 'Well, my band don't like my songs.'

I got annoyed then. I said, 'Wait a minute. You've got a band called Hannah Rickard and the Relatives – but they don't do your songs because your band don't like them? Which one of us is the fool here, you or me?'

So she stopped doing that band and we started to write together. The first time we tried to write she wanted to be very American and we came up with something that reminded me of the Everly Brothers. Well, that's me sold! So we carried on working and we have come up with a very nice album together that I'm very pleased and happy with, and that we want people to love. That's the thing I got from showbiz. I want people to love the songs and think I'm wonderful, of course I do. But there's some songs that I don't give a fuck what people say about them and 'Marguerita Time' is one of them. Same with a lovely acoustic ballad like 'Tongue Tied' or 'Rock 'n' Roll', with its whistling and lovely old-fashioned feeling.

That's where I'm coming from on the album. It's called *We Talk Too Much* after one of my favourite songs on it, which is 'I Know I Talk Too Much'. The track was inspired by the comedian-turned-actor Russell Brand. A lot of people don't like him because they just see him as a mouthy geezer who enjoys showing off. Who does that remind you of? I was watching him gabbing away at Jeremy Paxman on TV one night and I thought, you know what, he's got a point there. He actually reminded me of me. And the lines just came to me, 'I know I talk too much, about myself and such, I know a thing or two, but I'm no better than you.'

It's about that feeling you get, that nothing ever really changes. That is, things change all the time but everything stays the same.

Chapter Thirteen

Here We Are and Here We Go

Tuesday 14 June, 2016. We had just finished a show at the Expo Plaza in Antalya, Turkey. If Lyane hadn't gone into his bedroom to check on Rick when she did he would definitely have been gone beyond the point of no return. We wouldn't have known anything about it until the following morning. Instead, she found him lying on the bed, struggling. The venue was part of a hotel complex and as chance would have it an ambulance and its crew were nearby. The paramedics all rushed in the room and tried to revive him. As Rhino and I entered, one of them made that cut across the throat gesture and said one word: 'Dead.' Then they went back to work on him with their bits of equipment. It was ghastly.

Rick had more lives than a cat. Everyone knew that. When I saw him after that last heart attack, though, I knew what was going to happen. They pumped the fuck out of him. I saw what was going on and said, 'Leave him alone.' When I arrived in the room he was dead. That's what I was told. Then they started messing around with him on the floor. They dragged him off the bed and his head hit the floor – bang! Then they started the defibrillator. Oh God. I remember uncrossing his feet.

Then he was taken off to the hospital and we were sitting around talking about it. When he left the room he was dead on the trolley. Among all the shock and confusion, and concern for Rick's family, we were all like: what the fuck are we gonna do? On the flight back from Turkey, we decided to get in a temporary replacement. We couldn't afford to simply cancel all the shows we had booked. But when we landed at Heathrow, Lyane's phone went off; she had a message. She read it and said, 'Bloody hell! He's done it again!' I'm like, 'What?' She said, 'Rick's up having a cup of tea.' I said, 'He can't be! He was dead when we got on the plane!'

We were stunned and also saddened because we'd been told that on the very slim chance he did come round he'd be badly damaged physically and mentally. So we didn't know what to expect when we got the shock news that he'd regained consciousness. Later, when he was up on his feet again, talking about what had happened to him, he kept cutting down how long he'd technically been dead. Because he realised the longer he'd been 'dead', the bigger a chance there was that he'd suffered brain damage. The truth was he'd been out cold for quite a while and, in fact, he was brain damaged when he came round.

Anyway, we'd worked out what we were going to do without him and suddenly the bloke's alive again. Typical Rick. Always upsetting plans. All joking aside, though, we were all very relieved indeed. We paid for him to be flown back privately to England. That was another palaver. He was still somewhere else mentally and he kept getting up from the bed wanting to pilot the plane. When he got to the hospital in the UK, he phoned Lyane to tell her he'd had another heart attack. She said, 'I know, Rick, I was there!'

When Simon, Lyane and I went to visit him, Rick asked if it would be all right if he bought the new Rolls-Royce that had just come out. Simon asked how much it cost and Rick said something like ten grand. Simon was puzzled. Had Rick seen an old model going cheap? Rick said no, it was brand new. Eventually Simon figured it out. Rick was still so befuddled he thought it was 1973.

Then he told me the nurse was up to no good. Now I was really confused. Until I realised that what he said the nurse had said and done, she actually hadn't. Again, he was just confused, lost somewhere in the past. Then he told me about this new band he was forming. He said, 'Because you and me, we're no more, are we?' By now I realised what was going on so I just humoured him. Then he told me all about this new motor he was getting. Presumably the Rolls-Royce he'd just spoken to Simon about. That was always Rick's thing. 'I'm getting a new motor.'

These were the 'cognitive impairments' we'd been told to expect in the wake of his near-death. Rick was told he had every chance of recovering from them and he definitely seemed more like his old self as time went by, though still physically weak.

A month after Rick's heart attack, we were back on tour. Rhino's son, Freddie Edwards, joined us temporarily. Then the young guy we got in to replace Rick took over. His name was Richie Malone and he had been the frontman in his own band Raid, based in Dublin. We already knew Richie through his father, who first took Richie to see us live when he was just thirteen. Since then he'd become one of those regular fans that come back afterwards and say hi. He was a big fan of Rick's playing, to the point where he'd had a replica of Rick's trademark white 1965 Telecaster made. He even grew his own curly blond hair long, though he cut it shorter when he joined Quo in order to not look so much like a young Rick.

We still didn't know for sure if Rick would recover enough in time to come back to us, so Richie and Freddie had done a fantastic job filling in until we could figure out what the long-term plan was. It became clear pretty soon that Rick would not be well enough to re-join us and that's when we came to the mutual decision that he should leave the band. When I say 'mutual', we left the final decision up to Rick. The fact is he was very unwell for a long time after getting out of hospital.

It was hard to get a true perspective on it at the time. Much like when John and then Alan left the band, at first many fans thought that we wouldn't be able to carry on without Rick. If anything, this only spurred us on to prove them wrong. The main concern was that Rick should be all right. Once we set off again on tour without him, though, I would be dishonest if I didn't admit to feeling a certain sense of rejuvenation about the band on a musical level and on a personal level. We were out to prove ourselves again and that is always a spur for any creative person, however sad the circumstances behind that feeling.

Whether he would have come back and worked with us on any future albums was something we left open. We didn't actually have any plans to make more albums at the time. We had quietly been discussing packing it in, in fact. That's partly why the tour was called 'The Last Night of the Electrics'. Though of course we'd had those discussions many times before. 'We'll be all right, won't we, Frame?' 'Yes, Ricky, we'll be all right.' He'd been working on a solo album, *Over and Out*, and was planning on writing his own autobiography. He was even discussing making some new recordings with Alan and John. They asked me to be involved too but I wasn't really interested. I showed interest mainly to cheer Rick up but it was never really going to pan out – not with me involved anyway.

Instead, we had gone ahead and recruited Richie Malone into the band full-time. We couldn't have foreseen what a boost of energy he would give us. As a guitarist he's just propelled the band into a new high gear. It's his youth but mostly just his sheer exuberance onstage and off. He very quickly went from being 'Rick's replacement' to his own distinct personality. Rick was also very happy with our choice to replace him. He sent Richie a note wishing him luck, saying, 'You're the one!'

On tour with Richie, Lyane and I were going to meet Andy at this place for something to eat. Richie and John were going to come too. Richie said, 'We'll take a cab, it's only about twenty shitters.' I should explain: 'shitters' is what all bands call foreign currency, going back to the days when if you toured Europe you were constantly having to change currencies. To avoid confusion over what money you had, you just called them shitters. Don't ask me why. It probably goes all the way back to the Beatles. So anyway, Richie said, 'Let's take a cab, it's only twenty shitters.' John, who was wearing a backpack, said, 'No. If we take the bus it's only four shitters.' Richie: 'There's got to be a certain amount of the rock star when we turn up somewhere, surely?'

And Richie was right. You've got to find the balance between being a star and being a pillock. Having found it, don't let the fans down. Give them a little bit of the star when you're out in public. That way it's fun for everybody; just don't turn into Elvis and have traffic stop for you. Don't get carried away with yourself. Rick would get carried away. Rhino goes the other way and can't figure out why it should be any different. But it comes with the gig. You have to have a certain amount of aloofness but don't you dare shit on people. Balance. It's everything. No one likes an arrogant arsehole. But you don't pay to see someone onstage *not* put on a show.

So that's where we were up to our final show of 2016, at the Echo Arena in Liverpool, with Richie settling into the band and bringing his own personality. I remember waking up in my own bed the following morning for the first time in weeks. It was Christmas Eve, one of my favourite times of the year. Not because I'm a big fan of Christmas. I just love that whole winter vibe. I love the idea that the world isn't allowed to intrude on you for a few days. I love the cold and the dark early evenings, sitting by the fire, doing the crossword in the paper.

Not this day, though. It's funny how you can sometimes 'read' the ring of a phone. As soon as my phone sounded I sensed it would not be good news. It was Simon, telling me Rick had just died at a hospital in Spain. From sepsis, a horrible infection that causes multiple organ failure and death if not caught in time.

At first, I couldn't process this information. Rick had already died once that year. He'd also been in and out of hospital with various life-threatening things for years. Now I was being told he was dead. Really? Were they sure?

Yes, they were. He'd been complaining about his arm, being in constant pain apparently, so decided to check in at the local hospital, where he died forty-eight hours later.

Do what?

Do fucking what?

I was numb. The news had been coming for such a long time that when it finally arrived it was hardly a big surprise. It was a shock though, mentally, physically. We used to joke, Rick and I, that he'd be found dead in a Mandrax factory. We used to joke about it all the time. It was always going to be that or dead in a car crash, or just from another heart attack. But not like this. Bad arm. Hospital. Infection. Dead.

I didn't cry when Rick died, something that was made a big deal of when it came out in the press. It doesn't mean I didn't care. It was the same when my mother died. I went over to where my mother's body lay in bed and I touched her face. I went, 'Oh, Annie.' She was gone. It wasn't her lying there. That was a good lesson for me. It's like there's a list of things people 'should do' – at funerals, at weddings, when a baby is being born. All these different things that people look at you as though you're weird if you don't do. But to me it's all rubbish. I'm sorry but I'm just not having it. People said, 'Oh, I'm so sorry your mother died.' I would say, 'Why are you sorry? You never knew the woman. In fact, she could be nasty when she went really religious at one point and you wouldn't have liked her. So why are you telling me at her funeral that you're sorry I've lost my mother? I haven't. She's in that box.'

People think that's me being cold but it's not. It's me being me. I'm the same with birthdays. I don't even give my own kids birthday presents. We might have a little celebration but presents – no. Why? Because every day is like a birthday for my kids: whenever someone in the family really wants something, they get it. There's no waiting for the big day. Same with death. Once they're gone, they're gone. I don't cry. I don't mourn. I get up and go about my day. Same as always.

It was the same for me when Rick died. We dealt with it. We knew it was coming. Had been for years. If I really didn't care, as some people have insinuated, then nothing would matter to me. But I'm not going to walk around wailing and moaning, tears running down my face. It's all showbiz bollocks. Doesn't mean anything to me. It's not real. What was real was the lifetime I spent working with Rick and knowing him better than I will ever know anyone else in my life – and him knowing me.

It's why I keep dreaming about him as though he's not dead. He almost died so many times, then came back, it still feels like he could walk through the door again at any moment – at least it does in my dreams. In my dreams I never remember that he was cremated. I always believe he must have been buried, otherwise how could he come back? Yet there he is. Big smile on his face! In the dreams I say to him, 'I thought you were dead!' He goes, 'Yeah, well, you know.' And I think, yep, that's Rick. Turning up even though he's dead. Typical.

I don't want to dwell on some of the negative things Rick's family had to say about me after his death. They were grieving for their father or husband – or ex-husband. They didn't know him like I did. They weren't there whenever I would cover for him in the studio or there on the bus at night on the road while he moaned at me or got angry or started crying. And they weren't there when the two of us were experiencing the best times of our lives together. From the perils of sharing a musty bed at Butlin's to the impossible highs of playing to millions of people for so many years, selling millions of records, writing songs that are now beloved as some of the finest rock anthems ever.

The people I really feel for, after Rick's family, are the Quo fans. Many of them still don't understand why I kept the band going. What was I supposed to do – just vanish? Go away forever? I don't understand that mentality. Other than a misconception on the part of some Quo fans about how the relationship between Rick and me actually worked. And how that relationship fitted in with the rest of the band. Don't forget, Rhino has been a full-on member of Status Quo now for over thirty years. Andy Bown has been with us even longer. Were we all supposed to just throw the towel in and retire when Rick died?

If anything, Rick's passing has left me hungrier than ever to carry on. Particularly after all the snide comments about how we would never be so good again. It's just made us more determined to dig in. You never know how much time any of us has left. You would be a fool not to make the most of it. I also still have a family to watch over. Eileen and I had a couple more kids in the nineties: Kiera Tallulah, born in 1994, and Fursey, born in 1996. They are all grown up now but that doesn't stop me worrying over them, sticking my nose in if I think I need to. I also reconciled with my daughter Bernadette. We didn't see each other for years but we eventually got back in touch, and I was so proud to be a guest at her wedding in 2018. I want to stay alive and kicking for all these wonderful people.

And for the band. And for myself.

I'd be lying if I didn't admit I have thought about retiring once or twice over the last couple of years, particularly with Rick going. I decided I'd definitely had enough at one point. Not just because Rick was gone – he'd already left the group months before he died. But then things changed again after Richie joined the band. Everything is different again now. Everybody had to pull their socks up when Richie joined. Suddenly it feels more like it did when we were younger. It feels like it's us against the world again. Having to prove ourselves: like there's something really at stake again.

All that said, you can't get to my age and not think about your own mortality. I was lying in bed last night thinking: 'I'm nearly seventy. This is a joke. What am I doing at nearly seventy?' Sitting here now, though, writing this, the following morning, I don't *feel* seventy. But then when I get up to leave and pass a mirror I'll look into it and think: 'Jesus, is that who's been sitting here all this time? But he's old!'

A friend of mine who's older than me told me that when you hit sixty, it's fine, because you begin to coast. He said when he hit seventy, things started to change, he started to slow down a lot more. After that, all bets are off . . .

You can't torture yourself like that, though, or you'll go mad. Or at the very least make all the wrong decisions. I know people much younger than me that have retired and seem perfectly happy. They ask me sometimes when I'm thinking about retiring. I think: never! Not me! But then I recognise that I am getting older and, yes, I do get more tired. But that doesn't mean I don't want to still be in the game. I still have a ton of energy. I still exercise like a demon every day. I don't drink. I don't smoke dope any more. And the band feels like it's got a new lease of life. So why should I worry about giving it all up to sit in a comfy chair by the fire?

It's all about having that balance in your life, between going for the things that really make you feel alive, and not knackering yourself so that you can't enjoy yourself any more.

Take Bob Young. Bob is four years older than me. We have been working together recently writing songs. The first time he came round I looked at him and thought: what happened? I don't know if it's something in him or something in me but whenever he comes round he starts talking about the past – and I'm not interested. I just do not want to talk about the past like some old man reminiscing from his rocking chair in front of the fire. I want to talk about the songs we're doing together now, not what we did years ago. He says, 'Yeah, but it's our past.' I say, 'I'm still making my past!' It's like Bob has drawn a line under the past and he keeps getting further and further away from it. Like, there it is! The past! Isn't it marvellous?

Well, yes, some of it. But that's not the end of the story, surely. Not for me it isn't anyway. Even when I do talk about the past with him, he gets his days wrong. I say: 'You want to talk about the past but you don't even remember it.' Silly sod. I suppose it is just getting old. That's why I work out every day exercising. Why I eat properly and don't drink. I want to keep going without always hankering for the past like an old man. Bob will start telling me about the next holiday he's going on. I'm like, 'I'm not interested in your bloody holidays! Why are you so fascinated with going on holiday the whole time?'

Jordan Peterson, the psychologist, makes the point that the heads of all these corporations and such – men, particularly – are so driven they can be vicious. Not because they aren't nice. But because they are so single-minded in one thing, so obsessed by it, they have to score. I saw him talking about it on TV and I thought, oh dear, that's me. I realise I was lucky that Eileen let me be so single-minded. I got away with it with my first wife because those were very different days. But Eileen obviously had a choice and her choice was to let me pursue my obsession.

Keeping working may not necessarily keep you young but it keeps you alert. Alert is good. It frightens me to think of retiring if it means all you think about is putting your feet up and watching telly. I swim fifty or sixty lengths in the pool every morning. I push it as hard as I can. I have periods where I won't eat bread but I'm on and off with it. I was saying to Eileen just the other day, I love white bread. There's something about it that is an addiction for me. I'll have white bread and butter with all my meals sometimes – or I won't have any bread at all.

I saw Keith Moon a few days before he died and he was really bloated. There was about an inch of blubber all around him. In Keith's case it was almost certainly for reasons other than eating white bread. But the lesson was there: you can't pretend to be a rock star and be a lump of lard. Even though I haven't eaten any white bread for a few weeks, as I write this, and even though I exercise every day, I still have about an inch extra all over my body. I do not like it.

New ideas. New projects. It's exciting. It's what keeps me going. Something to look forward to doing tomorrow, not dwelling on the things I did yesterday.

I'm going back to work on new material. Will it be for a new Status Quo album? Let's just say you ain't seen nothing yet. I'm really enjoying the whole process again, making records again and playing concerts. I get tired at the end of the day. But I still practise every night on the guitar even when I'm feeling done in. I don't intend to ever start dressing as an old man either. When I go out, I like to wear a well-made suit. Or I like to go out with a shirt and tie and I like my collar done up. No jeans or trainers. That sense of standing out without making it too big a deal came to me from knowing Rod Stewart. We both started out as mods before we were rockers in bands. Which means when I wear a tie it has to be with a Windsor knot. I like looking smart, even when I'm sitting around at home.

I wasn't going to do a new Quo album. I didn't want to be in a position where I'm trying to prove that this band can function without Rick and blah, blah, blah – overthinking everything. On the other hand, I'm definitely not comfortable with simply allowing the idea to develop that Quo are just no good without Rick, because that's not true. The way the band is playing so well live with Richie proves that. Then I look at friends like

Brian May, who goes out on these big tours with Queen – without Freddie – doing great shows, enjoying himself, and that inspires me too. Adam Lambert sings the first song, then tells the audience: 'I know what you're thinking: I'm not as good as Freddie. But that's OK because I'm not trying to be Freddie.' Everyone goes, well that's a relief, and moves on and enjoys the show.

It's not like it was in the 1970s or 1980s when having a new member of the band was such a big deal. Here in the twenty-first century nobody is hung up on that any more. As I have said, look at the Stones, look at Guns N' Roses, look at AC/DC. In Quo, there's only me left now from the original Frantic Four, but three of the line-up have been together for over thirty years. Rick would still be in the band too if he hadn't become ill and then died. He wasn't sacked. He left of his own free will because he wasn't well enough to tour any more. So why shouldn't we keep going? We have as much right as any other band.

It just takes that one little spark to be creative and I'm determined to keep that good feeling going while I'm working on the album. I'm spending this morning working on this book. Then I'll be working on the new Quo album in my studio this afternoon. I will finish at 5 p.m., then spend an hour working out. Then I shall eat. Then I shall sit with my wife for half an hour. Then I shall go to a room and play the guitar for an hour or so. Then tomorrow I shall do the same thing over again.

One of the new songs Bob and I have come up with is called 'Waiting for a Woman' and right now, sitting here having just listened to it again in the studio, I love it. Sitting down with Bob, lyrically, we've been writing so well again, and with Andrew too. I hope this doesn't upset Andy, but with Bob he and I know each other so well we can do things in our heads without having to discuss it first. With Bob and me, we've got rhymes and things that work automatically. Like me, he also enjoys making the words to the choruses different each time. Which is not supposed to be how it's done and which you can shoot yourself in the foot doing sometimes. But when it works it's marvellous. My aim is to make something that pleases the long-time Quo fans. But to also have a bit of who-gives-a-fuck? in there. You need that bit of daring to make what you've got truly exciting, not just painting-by-numbers.

Everyone keeps saying they miss John, or they miss Rick or Alan or whoever. But I'm still here and I don't wish to fuck off. I still write tunes. I still sing and play tunes and I still enjoy what I'm doing in Status Quo. Why shouldn't I? I know Rick would have done the same if things were reversed and he was the one left alone.

People say I'm the lucky one. And they're right. I have been incredibly lucky. I've also worked incredibly hard and planned incredibly hard and over-analysed everything incredibly hard to get to where I am today. Things have not always worked out for me. Right now, though, I'd say I'm as happy as I could possibly be – and I can be a grumpy sod when I want to be, as you will no doubt have noticed by now.

I finally sold The Glade, the house I'd bought for a song in the seventies when Quo was first taking off. This was about ten years ago. I bought Eileen and me a brand new place instead. Literally brand new as in newly built.

Truthfully, I liked The Glade more. Unfortunately, houses built between the wars didn't have the best materials, the building regulations weren't there, and so there were a lot of things wrong with the old place and parts of it needed rebuilding. But it had so much charm and character I loved it. Fortunately

Eileen didn't mind living there so we did for years. Never a word about any of the previous women that had lived there. No complaining about how old the place was. But all our children were born there. My mother died there. I was very sad to leave.

The house we live in now is very similar to the house I grew up in with my family. Lovely grey stone. Seven bedrooms. I spotted it when I was walking the dogs one day. I took Eileen down to look at it and we squeezed in through the gates and had a good look around. We didn't like the driveway. There were no gardens at the front. But we went around the back and it was really nice. Spacious garden but still cosy somehow. There were no lawns or plants or proper landscaping but we fixed all that after we bought the place.

This all happened in 2007. Looking back, I see that we had to make our own home. Everything in the garden has been put there or planted by us. Everything in the house has been put there by Eileen. I wanted a home for her that really was her own. And no one has ever lived here before us. It really is all ours. I now refer to Eileen as Lady Greystone. We've been here for over ten years now and we have never been so happy.

When I bought The Glade all those years before, I remember thinking: how much money would you actually need to live on if the Quo thing suddenly ended overnight? Well, you'd need your house bought and paid for. You'd want your car paid for. I was always thinking: if we can just keep things going for another year or two . . .

I still am.

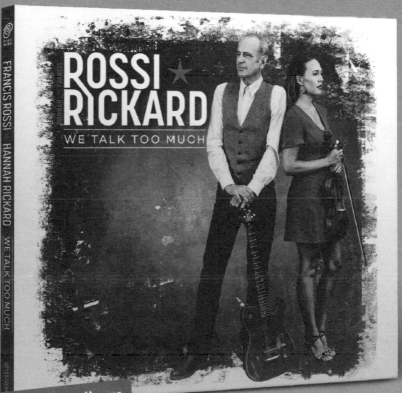